LIVING
M

LIVING

MUSEUMS

Iain Gale and Richard Bryant

A Bulfinch Press Book
Little, Brown and Company
Boston • Toronto • London

Library of Congress Cataloging-in-Publication Data
Gale, Iain.
    Living museums / by Iain Gale: photography by
    Richard Bryant.—1st U.S. ed.
    p.   cm.
    "A Bulfinch Press book."
    Includes index.
    ISBN: 0-8212-1963-4
    1. Historic buildings—Guidebooks. 2.
    Dwellings—Guidebooks. 3. Architecture,
    Domestic—Guidebooks. I. Bryant, Richard. II.
    Title.
    NA7123.G35 1993
    910' .2'02—dc20   93-6780

Bulfinch Press is an imprint and trademark of
Little, Brown and Company (Inc.)
Published simultaneously in Canada by
Little, Brown & Company (Canada) Limited

PRINTED IN HONG KONG

Contents

F o r e w o r d

The house is often described as an extension of its owner's character. To visit any house is to step inside a private universe. Every house is effectively a "living museum" of the life and times of its inhabitants. By looking at the interior and what it contains we can begin to gain an understanding of a style of decoration, a way of life and ultimately a personal history. All of the houses presented in this book are carefully preserved pieces of living history. Some were designed by renowned architects and some by the owners themselves. In other cases, their inhabitants merely chose the furnishings. However, whatever the origins of the building, in each one the visitor is able to experience an individual taste or sample the way of life of a bygone age.

Every house in this book has a story to tell. In Ruggles Sylvester Morse's Victoria Mansion, Theodore Mander's Wightwick Manor, David Gamble's home and Colonel George Hampton Young's Waverley plantation, we can see the house used as an expression of the status of the self-made man. Others, such as Charleston Farmhouse and Carl Larsson's home are the focus of family life or artistic community. However, fine design and good taste are no guarantee of a happy ending. Homewood's magnificent exterior hides a tale of financial and personal ruin and Paris's Nissim de Camondo is a monument to a father's grief, while Jim Thompson's House on the Klong is haunted by the mystery of the businessman's unsolved disappearance. Some dwellings are influenced by religious or philosophical considerations – from the Hancock Shaker Village to a 15th-century house in Seville, whose plan echoes the stations of the cross, and the 16th-century Humanism of Andrea Palladio's villa at Maser.

But there is more to *Living Museums* than a mere lesson in social history. This is a book which invites comparison. Throughout, key names in the history of design recur, encouraging the reader to make connections and to establish a line of stylistic inheritance. In effect, *Living Museums* provides a history of architecture and interior design, from the austerity of 14th-century Italy to 20th-century Australian modernism.

Looking at Palladio's villa in the Veneto, we can trace the architect's legacy in the neoclassical revival of 18th- and 19th-century Europe with Robert Adam in Scotland and Sir John Soane in England. The influence of Adam then follows on in a German palace designed by Karl Friedrich Schinkel and an American townhouse built by Charles Carroll Junior. It is a fascinating and addictive process which repays close examination. The influence of William Morris, whose style is exemplified at Wightwick Manor, surfaces at Charleston Farmhouse and across the Atlantic in The Gamble House. With a convincing subtlety, the history of design becomes clear.

This book provides a unique opportunity to understand the responses of architects and designers to specific problems. Theories put into practice in real situations survive today as a testimony to their creator's success and failure. We can examine in particular the houses which architects built for themselves. Each one tells us much about the architect's concept of the idea – from Sir John Soane's neoclassical home to the medieval nostalgia of Eliel Saarinen's Hvitträsk, from the Art-Nouveau extravagances of Victor Horta's town house to the airy modernism offered by Harry Seidler's parents' home.

The owners may not always be illustrious – there is often as much to fascinate in a Glasgow tenement as in George Washington's country house. Fame, though, can add an extra dimension to the appeal of these monuments. Here are the houses of artists and writers – the visionary Gustave Moreau, Johann Wolfgang von Goethe the poet and the painter Carl Larsson. Here too are houses that inspired, from the country idyll of Bloomsbury artist Vanessa Bell's Charleston to the claustrophobic shadow of the house of Marcel Proust's aunt. Within their architectural shells, seen in the environments for which they were originally intended, objects and artefacts take on a lively meaning and their true function and style become immediately understandable. Gone are the days when a museum implied anonymous corridors filled with collections in cabinets or glass cases. Welcome to the "living museum".

The Americas

Above: It may astonish the visitor, when looking at Homewood House from the outside, to realize that it was not designed by a professional architect. With its splendid columned portico, Homewood gives the appearance of a perfectly planned country mansion of the Federal style, betraying no evidence of either the trouble which dogged its construction or the sad history of its young owner, Charles Carroll Junior.

Right: In the dining room, the chairs are fitted with loose gingham seat covers typical of the period. The covers were designed to preserve the fine silks underneath and would only have been removed when the dining table was set for a formal dinner. The table is adorned with Birmingham silverware and an elaborate candelabra, as well as a variety of wine glasses which point to the source of the owner's downfall.

Charles Carroll Junior had always been a spoilt child. Whatever he asked for his wealthy parents had given him and when he was married in July 1800, to the daughter of the Chief Justice of Philadelphia, Benjamin Chew, it did not strike anyone who knew the Carroll family to be in the least bit odd that Charles Carroll Senior should give Charles Carroll Junior a house. Well, it was not a house exactly, but the wherewithal for Charles to build and furnish a house for himself and his bride on a generous plot of land close to the leafy town of Baltimore. Charles Carroll Junior had been educated in Europe and the plans which he drew up for his new mansion reflected the urbane tastes which he had developed while he was away on his grand tour of a continent which was then undergoing the early years of the great neoclassical revival. Charles's new house was to have an elegant pillared and pedimented entrance portico with a grand staircase sweeping down to the formal lawns at its front. Every detail of the building was to demonstrate his good taste and erudition – from the proportion of the windows to the references to the antique made in the design of the plasterwork mouldings. The house, which Charles Carroll Junior named Homewood, took six years to complete and stands today as one of the most impressive and important Federal buildings in the United States. Sadly, though, it is also a living testimony to a father's misguided love for his son and a reminder of the expensive consequences of that folly.

In retrospect, Charles Carroll Senior should have realized the potential expense at the outset of the project. Although he had already returned his son's original plans for the design of the house with the firm, if diffident advice that they should be "reduced so as to make it comfortable", nothing more was said at this stage. However, it was as the house began to take shape that things began to go awry. Charles Carroll Junior's first mistake had been his decision not to engage an architect. Such was the arrogance of the young man that, not content with his conviction that he knew exactly what he wanted from the house, he had decided that he was capable of both designing and

Homewood House

Far left: The hall encapsulates all the aspirations to elegance that Carroll developed on his European Grand Tour. The entrance to the house is guarded by two busts by Giuseppe Caracchi and Alexander Hamilton and the Adamesque glazing bars of the inner door echo the decoration of the portico. The hall is lined with a suite of chairs by the English cabinetmaker Kirkman and is hung with engravings of Philadelphia by W.R. Birch. The floor, which appears to be tiled, is in fact covered with a trompe l'oeil *painted floorcloth.*

Left: Looking along the passageway which connects the major rooms at ground level, you catch sight of the drawing room, which is dominated by a harp. It is easy to imagine the candlelit soirées that would have taken place in these surroundings in the early years of Carroll's marriage.

building it himself. But Charles Carroll Junior had one basic problem. He just couldn't decide what was to go where. In the course of the house's construction, which spanned a total of four years, the rooms were moved and enlarged, the exterior rethought and the detailing redesigned and refined. It should not surprise us that the army of craftsmen employed on the project found the whole thing utterly miserable and frustrating. The consequence was the momentous account for building work which faced Charles Carroll Senior. His generous wedding present seemed to be fast turning into an endless money pit which even he, the richest man in the state, could ill afford.

In May 1802, two years after the initial purchase of the land and a mere 12 months after the start of building work, a worried Carroll wrote to his son: "I cannot support these heavy and frequent changes . . . I therefore shall not advance any more money for improvements on your farm." However, his son was used to such protestations. He knew that now, as in the past, he would get his way. The changes continued to be made and as the house rose, it became quite clear that Charles was no architect. Within the first year of work the roof had begun to leak and had to be replaced, at no little cost, with a completely new one. By the following year his father was again putting pen to paper, vowing that his son would get "not another shilling". The bill so far stood at

For a house which took so long to build, the ground plan of Homewood is pleasingly simple, with the major rooms being easily accessible off the long central corridor which also gives the entire ground floor its wonderful sensation of light.

However, as you make your way around the house, the decline of Carroll becomes apparent. The drawing room seems to sum up the early days of Charles's marriage and it is not difficult to imagine his wife, Harriet Chew, seated at the magnificent single-action pedal harp in the corner, made in London by Sebastian and Jean Baptiste Everard in 1805. Images come to mind of candlelit assemblies held here in an atmosphere of restrained elegance, amidst panelled walls painted in a cool dove gray and highlighted in pale cream. The

Far left: The harp in the drawing room was made in London by Sebastian and Jean-Baptiste Everard in 1805.

Left: Every corner of Homewood House bears some evidence of Charles Carroll Junior's passionate enthusiasm for the neoclassical style.

Below: In one of the recessed windows, the light picks out the intricate moulding around the decorative fielded panels.

some $40,000 – a small fortune for the early 19th century. Charles Carroll Junior realized that this time he might have gone too far. It was possible that his father's protestations might be in earnest and so he finally decided that it was time to complete his home. By the spring of 1806 it was done.

It has to be said that there is no evidence today of this apparent final haste in the finished building. Homewood seems to the visitor quite what its builder intended: a grand mansion based on the neoclassical ideals of Europe's finest architects, which reflects the refined taste of a cultured designer. The restrained use of red brick and the high-columned portico, with its Adamesque "Etruscan" festoons, give it a flavour of antiquity which is continued within.

Here, in the entrance hall, the Adam theme is reiterated in the thin glazing bars of the fanlight. The room is lined with a set of English sidechairs, and also features a pianoforte by Kirkman of London and a collection of William Russell Birch's classically inspired views of Philadelphia. The dark-green paint of the walls is almost too dark for the Adam style which Carroll seems to have favoured throughout the house, being more characteristic of the later Empire style, a fact which seems to identify the Federal style as a link between the lightness of the Adamesque and the grandiosity of the Empire. Here also stands a marble bust of Alexander Hamilton after Giuseppe Ceracchi. It is interesting to note that the floor is not, as it at first appears, made from squares of marble but covered by a floorcloth, cleverly hand-painted in black and white checks.

Opposite: The intricate "Etruscan" style carving of the glazing bars is evidence of the influence that the neoclassical architect Robert Adam had over Charles Carroll Junior's design.

Far right: The civilized drawing room was the domain of Mrs Carroll and here, as you might expect, the table is set for tea. Over the fireplace hangs a portrait of the first President, George Washington, possibly by Gilbert Stuart.

Right: In the study, an open ledger on the bureau is written evidence of Charles Carroll Junior's indulgence in an extravagant lifestyle that he could ill afford, and of his eventual alcoholism.

English mahogany table belonged to Peggy Chew Howard, Carroll's sister-in-law, and dates from 1800, while the fancy painted chairs that surround it were made in New York at about the same time. Among the relatively few ornaments which adorn the room are a bronze gilt clock made by Dubuc of Paris in 1805 and two classic Argand lamps, which had been replacing the ubiquitous candle since the 1790s. A portrait of George Washington, a friend of Charles Carroll Senior, probably by Gilbert Stuart, surveys the room.

Having achieved his goal of constructing the house of his own devising, Charles Carroll Junior became gradually more and more dissolute. Not only did he fail to live up to his father's expect-ations of him as the able manager of the family estate of Doughoregan Manor, near Baltimore, but he seemed to be increasingly hapless, listless and generally lethargic. The open ledger on the closed bureau in the parlour at the rear of the house seems to sum it all up.

Charles Carroll Senior could only rant at his son in despair. But Charles Carroll Junior found diversions in pursuits of a more worldly nature. In the four-poster bed which dominates the main bedroom of Homewood, his wife Harriet bore him five children. For a while, it would appear, the family must have been fairly happy. Evidence of the young man's final route to downfall is to be found in the dining room. Here, on the cloth-

covered table, alongside the Birmingham silverware, sit an impressive assortment of wine glasses. Charles had discovered his love of fine wines and spirits at an early age and when the pressure began to tell it was here that he found solace. As early as 1809 his father wrote to him beseeching him to go carefully with "wine and heating liquers". Such advice was of no use. By 1814 it was his custom to drink two bottles of wine every morning before breakfast. In a letter to Charles's parents, his nephew wrote of him: "What will be the end of this it is impossible to say – we can't get him to shoot himself, so must bear with his degradation still longer". It is hardly surprising that two years later Harriet could bear him no longer and moved out of Homewood, taking the children with her and leaving her sot of a husband to his own self-destruction. However, it was another nine sad years before, in 1825, the son who had been his father's greatest hope, was found dead in his room in the enormous and by now empty mansion which had once been the embodiment of his youthful dreams.

HOMEWOOD HOUSE,
BALTIMORE, MARYLAND
ARCHITECT: CHARLES CARROLL JUNIOR
CONSTRUCTION: 1802-1806
SEE ALSO GAZETTEER, PAGE 185

$\mathcal{W}$averley

Colonel George Hampton Young was a devoted fan of the work of Sir Walter Scott and therefore when, in 1836, he purchased his huge 40,000-acre estate on land taken by the government from the Choctaw Native Americans in Columbus, Mississippi, he named it after Scott's most famous novel, *Waverley*. Young was a lawyer by profession who, having been educated in New York, travelled south in search of his fortune. His first move was to build a house on his land. It was a simple two-storey log cabin for himself, his wife Lucy and their young child. This house was intended to be a temporary structure which would suffice while Young constructed the cotton plantation with which he intended to make his fortune. He determined that once this was done he would build the house his status deserved. However, it was to be another 16 years before Young considered the time was right for such a venture. In 1852, he finally demolished the log house and began to build anew. Sadly his wife did not live to see their mansion completed but she had borne Colonel Young ten children and throughout the years that these offspring lived at Waverley it was always a bustling family house. The building which Young commissioned was to be a worthy symbol of all the good old Southern virtues for which he stood. It would also embody the Romanticism suggested by its literary name.

Today Waverley, which has been painstakingly restored over a period of 25 years since it was purchased by its present occupiers in 1962, stands for just that. It is an extraordinary building. Young deliberately employed an architect of Italian extraction, Charles I. Pond, to create a neoclassical palace and the house's main feature, the enormous octagonal rotunda of the roof, which strikes you at first sight, clearly reflects its designer's country of origin. Pond's house for Colonel Young was built in the "winged pavilion style" that was popular at the time. The entrance to the house lies under the old Southern Cross of the Confederate flag, through a typically Southern plantation-style two-storey portico, articulated by two elegant Ionic columns and doors surrounded by red- and blue-coloured glass.

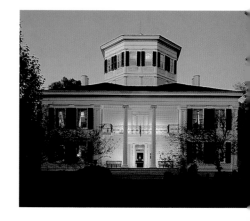

Above: The most striking exterior feature of Waverley mansion in Mississippi, built for Colonel George Hampton Young in 1852, is its roof which features an octagonal tower. It is possible that the architect, Charles Pond, sought to evoke Italy, his ancestral home, in creating this extraordinary tour de force. The lofty cupola also serves the practical purpose of keeping the inside of the house several degrees cooler than the humid summer climate outside.

Left: Upstairs, the furniture of the Egyptian bedroom includes a magnificent four-poster bed in carved rosewood that was made in France in the 1820s. In the middle of the room stands a marble-topped table and, beside it, a green-painted dowry chest from Tennessee. The eagle-crowned overmantel is also French and was made in the popular Second-Empire style of the 1850s.

Right and Far right: Crossing the threshold of Waverley house you enter the hall, which also doubles as a ballroom and is lit by the sunshine that enters through the windows at the top of the cupola. A grand double staircase sweeps up to the upper storeys. It is easy to imagine the impact that many a Southern belle would have made as she walked down these stairs during the early days of the house's occupancy.

The flag is touchingly significant. It was only nine years after the house was built that the Southern states found themselves drawn into conflict with the north in the calamitous and bloody Civil War. Throughout those dreadful years Waverley was a loyal seat of Confederate sympathizers. The six sons of Colonel and Mrs Young went off to fight in the war as Confederate officers. As we know now, their cause was not to prevail. Five returned home. One of them, Captain Billy, was the last of his family to inhabit the old mansion and until his last days in 1913 he lived the life of a Southern gentleman, content to indulge in cockfights, midnight poker games and sipping whisky. After his death, the Southern soul of the old house seemed to have disappeared forever. In fact, before its present owners, Robert and Donna Snow, moved in during the early 1960s, the house had stood vacant for nearly 50 years. However, the restoration of the house has been a labour of love and, entering Waverley today, the imaginative visitor can recreate a little of that Southern grandeur which was wounded, but not destroyed, after the surrender of 1865.

Inside the main door, in the cavernous entrance hall, or Rotunda, which also doubled as a ballroom, you find yourself met by a vast sweeping double staircase. One of Young's neighbours described his new home as "a centre of refined and extended hospitality" and today you can almost imagine the young Southern belles in their taffeta gowns and their beaux in Confederate gray uniforms as they waltz, gavotte and polka in a scene reminiscent of *Gone with the Wind*. Looking up, you see the three floors of the house, cantilevered balconies, built inside the cupola around a gallery. It is interesting to note that apart from its aesthetic purpose, the octagon was also of practical use, acting as a giant air vent which in the hot southern summers would keep the room below ten degrees cooler than the humid climate outside. From the ceiling hangs a magnificent French chandelier, dating from the 1850s, which is suspended from a 65-foot (19.5-metre) chain. It is tempting to climb the stairs and investigate, but for the moment remain in the 1860s and follow the guests as they proceed from the dance floor to the dining room. In this room, the sophistication

Above: The parlour is filled with the imported French and English furniture of the 18th century which would have appealed to the taste of a Southern household of the 1850s. A Boule table, inlaid with red tortoiseshell, bronze and ormolu, supporting an Imali temple vase, stands before a fine English George II secretaire dating from 1750. The Louis-XVI fauteuil is part of a magnificent French suite covered with gold leaf.

Top right: The small sitting room contains French-made furniture, notably a lacquer cabinet and other Louis-XVI pieces.

Opposite: The splendour of the Youngs' lifestyle becomes particularly evident in the dining room. The table is English and dates from the 1850s, some hundred years after the chairs were designed by that doyen of English cabinetmakers, Thomas Chippendale.

Bottom right: Although the house was principally lit by gaslight, candles housed in elegant holders, such as this delicate French porcelain candelabra, provided a secondary means of lighting.

of Young's taste is on show with the elegant English 1850s dining table, its French porcelain centrepiece and a set of fine Chippendale chairs imported from England. Next door, the parlour and drawing room continue the graceful Southern style as they feature Louis-XVI and lacquerwork furniture and heavily valanced windows.

From a balcony off the hall a small English boxwood garden can be seen. Laid out by Mrs Young some 150 years ago, it stretches out toward the farmland of the estate. In its heyday, Waverley was a highly efficient working plantation for corn, oats, cotton and livestock, which was farmed by 1,000 slaves.

Upstairs an air of softness and decadence pervades the bedrooms, which open out onto outside galleries. The Egyptian bedroom is dominated by an intricately carved rosewood bed, a French piece of the 1820s. Beside it, in keeping with the *Gone with the Wind* theme, stands a green-painted dowry chest made in Tennessee in 1866. Beside the heavy, marble-topped table is a classic Belter side chair. Along the corridor, in the Green Bedroom you will find another rosewood bed and a suite of carved armoire and dressing table on which stand a pair of French porcelain candelabra.

However, the most impressive of the bedrooms is the master bedroom, with its half-tester bed whose posts when raised are designed to hold a mosquito net. Here, on a still Mississippi evening, as the light from the gas lamp flickers and fades, those of you about to leave the old house can be forgiven for imagining that you can hear the sound of feet padding up the stairs to bed and perhaps, as the bedroom door swings open, a soft Southern voice uttering the immortal words: "Tomorrow is another day".

WAVERLEY, COLUMBUS, MISSISSIPPI
ARCHITECT: CHARLES I POND
CONSTRUCTION: 1852
SEE ALSO GAZETTEER, PAGE 186

V i c t o r i a M a n s i o n

When Ruggles Sylvester Morse returned to his home town of Portland, Maine, in 1858 he was determined to make a point. Over the years in which he had been away, Morse had worked hard to make a considerable fortune in the luxury hotel trade and the holiday house which he determined to build for himself and his wife on the corner of Danforth and Park Streets in Portland was to be more than just a place to spend the summer. It was to be a deliberate statement of Morse's wealth and social position as one of the country's most prestigious hoteliers and it is testimony to the thoroughness with which he tackled his task that it still stands today, as the plaque outside proudly proclaims: "the finest and least altered example of a brownstone Italian villa town house in the United States". The house, which took a total of four years to construct and cost nearly $400,000, was the creation of the architect Henry Austin.

Morse had made his money in the luxury hotel business and it seems likely that he had the architect's reputation for opulent detail in mind when he commissioned Austin to construct his own private luxury hotel, where he and his family might relax during the summer months.

From the outside the house hints at the rich variety of design and decoration that lies within its walls. For their basic design Morse and Austin looked to the design of a typical North Italian villa, of precisely the same type that Queen Victoria's architect had envisaged when he constructed Osborne House on England's Isle of Wight in 1845. Here in Portland we find the same wide eaves, colonnaded portico and *oeil de boeuf* and Venetian windows as at Osborne House and, dominating all, the same high belvedere above a fanciful *campanile* (bell-tower).

From the moment that you enter the house, the tone of the decoration is set with the imposing hall. Lined with neoclassical statuary and painted with *cartouches* depicting Italian peasant girls, the style reiterates the Italianate exterior. The steep staircase is flanked by a pair of fine Viennese baroque *torchères* in the form of scantily draped classical figures who raise their round gas lamps

Above: In the hall, a neoclassical statue sets the tone for the decoration throughout the house.

Left: The elegant Louis-XIV-style interior of the music room at the Victoria Mansion in Portland, Maine, displays the aim of its owner and builder, Ruggles Sylvester Morse, who wanted his house to demonstrate his own good taste. The walls are decorated with trompe l'oeil *panels depicting allegorical figures painted by the Italian-American artist Giuseppe Guidicini. The marble of the fireplace, with its supporting figures modelled on Canova sculptures, harmonizes with the ultramarine and gold of the walls and carpet.*

Above top: The doorway of the drawing room is decorated with twisted carved wood surrounds topped with putti and a scallop shell which point to the trompe l'oeil *painting within.*

Above bottom: The ceiling of the music room is the most elaborate in the house. A combination of real and painted stuccowork, it gives a complex impression of contrasting shape and depth.

Above right: In the music room, the face of Bacchus, god of wine, apparently revealed by a trompe l'oeil *drape, smiles down from one of the wall paintings.*

Far right: Although less fanciful than the music room, the drawing room presents an intriguing combination of trompe l'oeil *and plasterwork decoration. The table and chairs make up an unusual suite of furniture – the legs resemble cloven hooves and the supports for the arms and tabletop take the form of putti and harpies.*

up to the lofty, *trompe l'oeil* painted ceiling. To the right a doorway leads to the music room. This, the most elaborate room in the house, is decorated with a profusion of painted detail, the creation of the master-decorator Giuseppe Guidicini (a New York Italian) and his team of expert painters who had been engaged by Austin in a number of his previous commissions. Every available inch of the wall and ceiling space appears to have been painted in the Rococo revival manner that was popular in both Europe and the United States during the 1850s. The walls carry huge painted panels decorated with colourful Florentine plant forms and central *vignettes* depicting allegorical figures on the theme of music. The room is conceived as an exercise in colour harmony, mixing the gray of the skirting boards or base boards with ultramarine, blue and gold, all of which are picked up in the expensive carpet with its French-inspired pattern. The fireplace, one of seven in the house, is hand-carved from Carrara marble with supporting figures on either side which derive from the sculptures of Antonio Canova. The

eclectic combination of Italian and French styles is completed with a suite of Louis-XIV-style furniture, deeply upholstered in a pale-blue silk damask and made, like the majority of the furniture in the house, by the New York cabinet-maker Alexander Roux.

Opposite the music room, through the barley-twist surround of the high doors, the decoration of the drawing room presents a rather more sober contrast. Here, the colour scheme is of a restrained pale gray and beige with fine gold detailing. Once again, the walls are painted with *trompe l'oeil* panels, although in this instance the allegorical figures are seen in appropriate attitudes of repose. As in the music room the combination of genuine plaster moulding and *trompe l'oeil* detail, here concentrating on the characteristic scallop shell of the Rococo, produces an undeniable opulence. While the original upholstery was sand-coloured, this has been replaced over the years with dark-brown satin. Nevertheless, something of the intended effect of an elegant Louis-XIV interior in regal white and gold can still be felt.

The dining room continues the French "Louis" theme, although here it looks to an earlier reign and becomes rather darker, almost Renaissance in appearance, chiefly on account of the heavy use of dark woods. The *boiserie* is carved in great detail with motifs appropriate to the function of the room – from fruit and vegetables to fish and game birds – which would have been mirrored in the very real contents of the gilded porcelain dining service set before the guests at the lavish banquets that the Morses hosted during their summer vacation.

Off the dining room, the library transports you into a yet darker and more intimate world. With its arched recesses, articulated with pierced tracery, *quatrefoils* and a panelled frieze, the room is a triumph of neo-Gothic romanticism. Warlike equestrian bronzes create the atmosphere for what would undoubtedly have been "serious" after-dinner rituals of port and cigars.

While these four rooms constitute the principal reception area of this idiosyncratic house, the other floors contain a profusion of bedrooms, bathrooms and dressing rooms and an informal family sitting room, all of which exhibit a similarly exuberant, if perhaps not quite so ornate, *trompe l'oeil* painted decoration. However, one room merits particular mention. The tiny Turkish room is an unexpected gem of unrestrained eastern exoticism, easily missed behind the stained-glass doors which lead from the upper

floor gallery. With its richly coloured carpets and painted walls, the room reflects the fashion during the late 19th century, throughout Europe and the United States, for "Orientalism" engendered by the colonial expansionism of the great powers. In a *tour de force* Guidicini's painters bring to the Portland mansion a flavour of eastern mystery with their flowing arabesques, tendrils and spirals in bright primary colours of red, blue, green and gold. More than any other room in the house the Turkish room seems to sum up Ruggles Sylvester Morse's intention on building his mansion. Victoria Mansion was to be his own private hotel – a place of retreat, to which he could escape with his family and where he might sample the taste of the eras and countries which he most admired. Variously, Gothic, Renaissance and Rococo; French, Italian and Oriental; this house is a private palace, designed purely for pleasure with a room intended to suit the every mood of a man who had very clearly "made it".

Above and Below left: In contrast to the pale elegance of the two reception rooms, the dining room (top) and library (left) are dark and intimate. With their carved boiserie, gothic tracery and bronze equestrian statuary they have an air of romanticism that makes them a welcome refuge from the outside world.

Far left: Upstairs, in one of the many bedrooms, an intricately carved table hints at the exotic details that can be found in every room of the house.

VICTORIA MANSION, PORTLAND, MAINE
ARCHITECT: HENRY AUSTIN
CONSTRUCTION: 1858
SEE ALSO GAZETTEER, PAGE 188

Hancock Shaker

When Ann Lee stepped ashore at New York in August 1774, from the ship which had carried her from Liverpool, England, she can have had no idea that the religious movement which she brought with her to America, that of the Shakers, a breakaway sect of the Quakers, would one day be known across the world. What might astonish her further, were she to return today, would be that the spread of this knowledge has been achieved not through religious ministry, as "Mother" Ann had envisaged, but through art.

With their simple line, subtle colour and emphasis on fine craftsmanship and ecological considerations, the art and design of the Shakers seems perfectly suited to the late 20th century. Nevertheless, aesthetics aside, if today's many devotees of Shaker furniture and design were to examine the principles behind their prized pieces, they would soon discover just how closely art and belief are interlinked. This relationship is exemplified at the historic Shaker settlement, perfectly preserved for posterity at Pittsfield, Massachusetts, where the 20 buildings of the Hancock Shaker Village include dwelling houses, meeting house, schoolhouse, dairy, workshops and a magnificent round stone barn.

It was to the site on which the Trustees' House at Hancock now stands that Mother Ann Lee came in August 1783 to preach her gospel of the oneness of religion and life, celibacy, sexual equality and segregation and, above all, peace. However, it was not until some seven years later that work began on the construction of the village. The first building was, appropriately for this devout religious movement, the Meeting House. Although the present Meeting House at Hancock was moved here from Shirley in Massachusetts in 1962, it is identical to the original one that was raised in 1790. Gradually other buildings followed and by the 1850s the Hancock Shaker Village was a thriving community of some 250 brethren and sisters. However, the popularity of Shakerism was relatively short-lived, and from the late 19th century the movement gradually began to go into decline. The last community of Shakers left Hancock in 1960. Thankfully, though, their

Above: The great brick dwelling house to the right of the picture was built by William Deming in 1830 and provided living accommodation on six storeys for almost half of the 250-strong population of Hancock Shaker Village.
The red-painted laundry and machine shop in the foreground was provided with power by an overshot water wheel.

Left: Inside the house, the most comfortable of the sleeping dormitories is the infirmary. In this starkly furnished interior, patients would lie in oversize rocking cradles which they believed to help the healing process by returning the sick to the comforting environment of their childhood. A classic feature in any Shaker room is the painted pegboard, on which they hung anything – from a mirror to a piece of clothing.

Village

Right: The position of the stove in a Shaker household gives an indication of the importance that the brethren placed on social harmony and equality. It was always located in the middle of the room so that its heat would diffuse to as many people as possible. Such formulaic clarity in the arrangement of the furniture was a characteristic of Shaker style. Cupboards were plentiful to make sure that there would never be any clutter in the rooms and, consequently, few objects adorn them. This, together with the simple lines which characterized all Shaker design, resulted in an atmosphere of calculated restraint and austerity. In this downstairs room of the dwelling house such qualities have the effect of focusing attention on the fine craftsmanship of each individual item – from the plain lines of the black-leaded stove and the typical acorn-topped chair to the simple table and the bent-wood box, which, uncharacteristically, are left without the usual painted finish.

buildings have been carefully restored and preserved as a memorial to this extraordinary phenomenon.

Throughout the village, you are confronted with the perfection and symmetry which lay at the heart of Shaker belief. The exteriors of the square-built buildings, with their subtle shades of specially mixed paint in red, blue, green, ochre and mulberry – thought to be the colours that are found in heaven – lead us into the equally calm and calculatedly harmonious interiors. These were based upon a uniform pattern since restraint, simplicity and lack of decoration were considered conducive to spiritual well-being.

The Dwelling House was built in 1830 to designs by the Shaker Elder, William Deming. It consists of six storeys, with a huge attic, living quarters and kitchens. Two storeys are devoted to sleeping areas, which could accommodate up to 100 people. Since an important part of the Shaker doctrine was the segregation of the sexes, the dormitory-like arrangements were essential.

The kitchens are situated in the semi-basement. The simple, scrubbed wooden floor and oak furniture are typical of the Shaker work environment. The preparation of food was central to Shaker thought. While the brethren toiled in the fields, the sisters would cook. The simplicity in design and material of utensils – such as baskets, bowls and pots – was symptomatic of the ethic which believed that it was possible to make something that would be at the same time functional, unadorned and aesthetically pleasing. Everything had a strict order in Shaker life and mealtimes were no exception. Breakfast was taken every morning at half past six, with dinner at midday and supper at six in the evening. After supper, time was set aside for devotional study and the bureaux and chairs that abound in Shaker houses testify to the observance of this practice.

The ladder-back chair, with neat, turned acorn finials on its backposts, is probably the most distinctive piece of Shaker furniture. Always with three slats at the back and a rush seat, wider at the front than at the back, these chairs were designed to aid study rather than relaxation. The only concession to comfort in Shaker seating is made in the appearance of the occasional rocking chair. Shaker chairs, along with the bureaux and most of the larger pieces of furniture, were made from local woods, mostly maple, birch and walnut.

Above left: Many features of the Shaker interior come together in the Elder's room – a chair hangs out of the way on the painted pegboard which runs the length of the room and, beneath it, a thin single bed offers little comfort in the way of sleeping accommodation. In the middle of the room, once again, the stove becomes the focus of attention.

Above right: One of the most enduring qualities of Shaker lifestyle was their obsession with neatness. It is revealed here in the ingenious manner of hanging both towels and mirror from the pegboard, thus saving space on the floor and on top of the washstand.

Far right: This corner of the Manager's room embodies the Shaker lifestyle. All the paraphernalia of everyday life has been securely tidied away in the many drawers and cupboards which line the wall, leaving only a desk and chair ready for daily tasks and contemplative worship.

Their simple style was always austere, with a natural uniformity of pattern and serenity of line.

Cupboards abound in the Shaker house, tidiness being yet another Shaker pre-requisite. This obsession with order and neatness is best seen in the widespread use of pegboards which run around the walls of each room. Anything might be stored on these – from a walking stick or a mirror to a clock and, most often, a chair. The continuous line of the pegboard gives all Shaker rooms a sense of proportion within which every piece of furniture can take its appointed place. Even the simple, black-leaded stove is positioned in keeping with this spirit of spatial harmony since it was felt that in a large egalitarian community, fireplaces, with their natural focal attraction, were inappropriate.

While downstairs, in the meeting rooms, the colours of the wainscotting and pegboard are restricted to the natural hue of the wood, upstairs, on the retiring storeys, these features have been picked out in a distinctive shade of blue-green paint which was considered to be conducive to rest. These were, after all, the colours of Paradise.

Apart from its dyed wood, the Shaker bedroom differs little from the other rooms. Of course there are beds here – long, thin bunks made with the same careful craftsmanship that was applied to all Shaker cabinet-making. But their sparse mattresses could scarcely be called "inviting". Only in times of illness did the famous Shaker severity relent, and the Infirmary at Hancock contains several of the rocking beds that were considered conducive to recovery. The theory was that to return the patient to a state of childhood in these giant cradles was the best aid to spiritual healing.

If the Dwelling House seems a triumph of craftsmanship and ingenuity, then the round stone barn is a revelation. The Shakers were essentially a farming community and this remarkable building is evidence of their ability to apply their talents to everyday requirements. The barn was built in 1826 to a plan conceived by the Shaker engineer Daniel Goodrich. It was designed to contain up to 50 cattle and a considerable amount of hay during the winter. Its three floors could also be used to accommodate hay wagons, ten of which could be unloaded at any one time.

However, today there are no haywains unloading in the barn. Although Hancock is run as a thriving activity village where you can learn about the Shakers, the genuine religious community is gone. Nevertheless, in empty Schoolroom and Dwelling House alike, the Shaker tradition lives on and as you enter the Meeting House you might even fancy that you hear a snatch of a long-forgotten hymn floating on the air:

"My work on earth is holy, holy and pure
That work which will ever, forever endure".

HANCOCK SHAKER VILLAGE,
PITTSFIELD, MASSACHUSETTS
ARCHITECTS: VARIOUS
CONSTRUCTION: 1790-c.1850
SEE ALSO GAZETTEER, PAGE 188

Above: The exterior of Loren Pope's house at Falls Church, Virginia, instantly communicates to the visitor the essential love of nature of its architect, the modernist virtuoso Frank Lloyd Wright. Despite its angularity, the house almost seems to rise from the ground as a part of the natural landscape.

Right: The master bedroom looks out onto the surrounding woodland through full-length plate-glass windows. Against one wall stands a simple bureau, designed by Wright and illuminated, with typical lack of clutter, by a single angle-poise lamp. The armchair is upholstered in Wright's "Imperial Crystals" fabric.

"There are certain things a man wants during life", declared the American journalist Loren Pope in 1939: "Material things and things of the spirit". Pope believed that he had found the answer to both. What he wanted was a house. But his was to be no ordinary dwelling. Pope's would be the perfect house, created by the perfect architect. In Pope's eyes that architect was Frank Lloyd Wright. Pope's words had in fact been addressed to Wright in a letter. "The writer has one fervent wish", he wrote. "It is for a house created by you". Pope sent the letter and for what seemed like an eternity he and his wife Charlotte held their breath. Within two weeks, Wright had replied: "My dear Loren", he wrote. "Of course I am ready to give you a house". The couple were overjoyed: "My heart pounded", wrote Pope.

What was it though that made Wright so special in Pope's eyes? The son of an immigrant Welsh farming family, Frank Lloyd Wright had studied at the University of Wisconsin and then under the celebrated architect Louis Henry Sullivan in Chicago. Having left this apprentice-ship shortly before the outbreak of the First World War, he made his name designing public buildings – The Midway Gardens in Chicago (1913) and the Imperial Hotel in Tokyo (1916-1920) – that brought to international recognition his individual and angular brand of design. Under the influence of Sullivan he concocted a personal style whose tenets he later partly defined in his prolific writings: "Simplicity and repose . . . nature with a capital N . . . integrity". Above all, though, Wright's style was governed by what he considered to be appropriate for the individual purpose of each of his buildings. It was equally important to him that they should reflect something of the character of whoever it was that commissioned them. While it is true to say that, in this way, everything he designed was unique, perhaps that sense of individuality is best summed up in his domestic architecture.

The house which Wright designed for Loren and Charlotte Pope at Falls Church, Virginia, between 1939 and 1941 is a fine example of his answer to the challenge of the smaller dwelling.

Pope-Leighey House

Above: The corner of the bureau in the master bedroom shows the attention which Wright paid to detail in all his work, although on account of its simplicity this is not always immediately apparent.

Right: The stairs lead from the entrance to the living area, which was designed to be adjustable according to use. Above a dining table and chairs in Wright's "Liberty" weave fabric, lights have been sunk into the ceiling to create a soft, restful atmosphere.

Far right: The dining table is typical of Wright's furniture, which was designed for aesthetic appeal as well as practicality. The chairs are styled to angle down toward the back and thus provide support for the diner, at the same time as being eminently comfortable.

Around 1936 he had invented a term – "Usonian" – which he used to describe those of his buildings that were designed for the requirements of living in America. While there is no sure description of the Usonian house, its basic feature was the use of a simple geometric living module, which was repeated over and over again throughout the building. The Popes' house was built in just such a way, using the ground plan of an "L" shape. But this simplicity of conception does not imply the necessity of a lack of decorative interest or any cold, analytical approach. Ornament was an integral part of Wright's design philosophy. Although a concentration on abstraction and geometry in Wright's use of the sphere, the cube and the pyramid was essential to its being, his art was not created from mere mathematical precision and an obsession with proportion and scale. The true basis of Wright's architecture lies in his use of organic form. He himself wrote: "Study nature, love nature, stay close to nature. It will never fail you".

From the moment you catch sight of the Popes' house, you are made aware of the importance which Wright attached to nature. The building itself appears to rise from the ground as a part of the wood, despite the fact that it no longer occupies its original site. The house was in fact transported ten miles from Falls Church and rebuilt at Mount Vernon in 1964 when the Popes' successors as owners, Robert and Marjorie Leighey, made the discovery that a proposed interstate highway would warrant its destruction and gave it to the National Trust for Historical Preservation, together with $31,500 which helped pay for the cost of moving it to a safe site.

Entering the house through the Japanese-inspired *porte-cochère*, you find yourself at once cocooned in a warm and welcoming environment made from natural wood and brick in Wright's "Cherokee" red, which for him was the archetypal colour of America.

The house is constructed from brick, glass, concrete and plywood clad with fine-grained cypress wood. On the right of the entrance area is a small "sanctum" set aside for study, and descending the small flight of red brick steps you find yourself in the dining and living area which Wright designed to be adjustable to suit the needs of the owners. For example, the impressive dining

table is made up from three modular tables which have been clamped together. Like all the furniture in the house that Wright designed the table is not at all obtrusive and the four chairs around it, with their angular-patterned cushions in Wright's "Liberty" weave of 1926, might just as easily be used in the living area. The geometric patterns cut into the legs of the table draw the eye curiously to the walls and ceiling, where they are cleverly echoed in the similar designs of cut-outs, inspired by organic and animal forms, which constitute the panels of the clerestory windows.

The house is designed to be filled with light and Wright employs all the means at his disposal to encourage this effect. Light was all important for Wright, who deliberately chose the sites of his buildings to exploit its fugitive qualities to the fullest extent. His use of electric light was likewise always calculated to harmonize with the natural illumination which entered from outdoors. In this house he placed electric bulbs high in the coffers of the ceiling to reflect the changed tones of dawn and dusk in the most subtle way imaginable. The main windows of the house have all been made as tall as possible – both in the living area, along the glass-fronted corridor and in the house's two bedrooms. In the master bedroom a simple late Wright-style dressing-table is illuminated by a single, understated metal angle-poise lamp. The room demands nothing more. The majority of the light in the bedroom floods in through the tall windows, filtered through the birch trees in the woods beyond – that natural world with which Wright was so in harmony and whose teachings he used to give this extraordinary home its sense of genuine humanity; what Loren Pope called its "great and quiet soul".

It comes as no surprise to learn that on the day that the removal men finally arrived to move Loren Pope and his family out of their home of only five years, the journalist should have sat down on his hearth and wept. He had suddenly realized, all too late, that he was leaving behind him not just a home; he was leaving a friend.

Above and Left: Throughout the living area, clever cut-out shapes in the woodwork admit small pockets of light and stimulate the eye. The shapes themselves, inspired by animal forms, provide yet another link between the architect and the wild natural landscape which surrounds the house.

POPE-LEIGHEY HOUSE,
MOUNT VERNON, VIRGINIA
ARCHITECT: FRANK LLOYD WRIGHT
CONSTRUCTION: 1939-1941
SEE ALSO GAZETTEER, PAGE 187

The Gamble House

Contrary to the wayward image suggested by their surname, David Gamble and his wife Mary were the embodiment of that spirit of righteousness which affected the American middle-class at the turn of the 20th century. Hard work, cleanliness and godliness were central to their philosophy of life. In particular, though, they believed in cleanliness – it only stood to reason when you belonged to a family which had made its fortune from selling soap. David B. Gamble was one of ten children of the founder of soap manufacturers Proctor and Gamble and he spent all his life in the family business. It was typical of the enterprising nature of the family that having spent 50 years in his home town of Cincinnati, David looked toward the West. Those were the years of the great California settlement and David took his family to the growing city of Pasadena. Here in 1907, at the age of 59, he decided to build his ideal home.

Despite his comfortable middle-class background, David did not head for the obvious location of South Orange Boulevard (Millionaires' Row), but instead bought a plot of land in a small private street called Westmoreland Place. He was attracted by its view across the Aroyo Seco, a river bed that remained dry for most of the year and was scattered with meadows and oak trees.

Gamble commissioned a firm of architects, Greene and Greene, to build his house. The brothers, Charles and Henry Greene, who had already built two houses in the locality, were designers in the tradition of William Morris's English Arts and Crafts movement. They had attended Washington University and studied under Calvin Woodward, a devotee of Morris, and his mentor John Ruskin. Having first experimented with neo-Georgian and Queen-Anne styles, the Greenes had by the early 1900s settled on a style of their own. Their guiding principles were a restrained use of decoration and a devotion to natural materials. Such ideals of purity and restraint greatly appealed to Gamble, who commissioned them in February 1908 to build his house. The building was finished one year later and today it is carefully preserved as one

Above: The architects Greene and Greene were fascinated by traditional Japanese architecture and this influence is demonstrated in their design for The Gamble House, Pasadena, where exposed joints and open balconies are placed alongside deep, overhanging eaves.

Left: The ground floor of the house is an early example of the open-plan principle whereby various living areas are separated merely by partitions. Here the entrance hall opens onto the spacious living room, with its large inglenook fireplace. The treatment of the doors, which open out onto the garden terrace, is another feature suggestive of Japanese influence.

a natural feature. The house clearly has something of a Japanese flavour and this influence undoubtedly has its roots in the Greenes' visit to the Japanese Ho-o-den pavilion at the Chicago Worlds Columbian Exposition of 1893. The sense of purity of natural form and material expounded by Japanese architects was evident in the buildings that the Greenes saw there. In 1909, the English craftsman and historian Charles Robert Ashbee wrote of Charles Greene, "the spell of Japan is on him, he feels the beauty and makes magic out of the horizontal line".

One of the special features of The Gamble House is its large, exposed joints which resemble those found in traditional Japanese architecture. Such a resemblance is also apparent in the addition of an outdoor porch and balcony rooms which the architects built to take advantage of the temperate climate that first attracted the Gamble family to California.

Today, you approach the house up steps from one of the three terraces which link the building to its gardens. Beyond the teak and Tiffany glass doors, the hall opens up as a welcoming natural environment. The light is dim but warm, reflected off the untarnished natural wood of the walls. The eye and mind are engaged by the use of a variety of different motifs which, despite their apparent contrast, manage to work here in perfect harmony – a leaded ceiling light, reminiscent of Ashbee and Mackintosh, and a screen decorated with the ancient Chinese "cloud lift" design.

The interior was conceived as an interlocking series of three separate areas: the southern rectangle of the dining and kitchen area, the

Above: The dining table is made from Honduras mahogany and is lit from above by a huge clouded-glass lantern.

Right: The exposed joints on the exterior of the house are also in evidence inside, especially on the staircase.

Far right: The living room was designed so that it could be rearranged according to the season. In the summer, the occupants' attention would have been focused on the huge plate-glass window, while during the winter months the furniture was grouped, as here, around the fireplace. The deep inglenook fireplace is a feature that William Morris also employed extensively.

of the finest examples of their work. The Greenes were given a free hand to design everything for the house – from the building itself to its furniture, light fixtures, windows and accessories. Every detail was conceived to harmonize with the whole under the overall guiding tenet of truth to nature. Even the hardware for the doors and the electrics were plated to the desired patina so that they blended with the soft curves of the hand-carved and hand-polished wood.

The house was intended to blend in with the surrounding landscape and today you can immediately appreciate the subtle means by which the architects succeeded in this task: the building appears to rise from the surrounding gardens like

work areas of the house had been neglected. It was a notion which concurred perfectly with the Gambles' attitude of benevolent philanthropism. The kitchen provided the servants with an elegant dining room and the cook and butler with efficient working areas. Even in this room we see encapsulated Henry Greene's influential dictum which applies throughout the house: "Make the whole as direct and simple as possible, but always with the beautiful in mind as the final goal".

Far left and Left: The Greenes' style is characterized by their attention to the tiniest detail – from the finish of a piece of wood to the tailored shape of a screw or bolt. The mahogany lantern that is suspended from the living room contains Tiffany glass.

Bottom: The sprawling oak-tree stained-glass design on the triple-entrance doors was designed by Charles Greene and executed at the Tiffany Studios.

THE GAMBLE HOUSE, PASADENA, CALIFORNIA
ARCHITECTS: CHARLES AND HENRY GREENE
CONSTRUCTION: 1908-1909
SEE ALSO GAZETTEER, PAGE 188

central hall and staircase and, to the north, the cruciform shape of the living room and "den" which served as Gamble's office. The hall gives on to an arch which opens out into the living room, lit from above by a clouded-glass lantern. Its main feature is the large, cosy version of an inglenook fireplace. Opposite, a floor-to-ceiling window fills the room with light during the summer months. Thus the focus of attention can be changed from hearth to landscape with the seasons, and the furniture, specially designed by the Greenes for this room, can be moved accordingly.

Crossing the hall, you enter the dining room, the heart of hospitality in the house. The room seems lighter than the living area, principally because its panelling and furniture are made from Honduras mahogany rather than teak. Above the table hangs a huge obscured-glass lantern which provides subdued lighting. It is not difficult to imagine the feeling of contentment experienced by the Gambles' guests when, retiring from this table and climbing the stairs, they were faced with the inviting guest bedroom, with its soothing colour scheme of natural brown and comfortable, reassuringly solid furnishings. This was truly a house designed for living a life of comfort and culture and this was precisely what the Gambles required their architects to produce.

Even downstairs, in the seclusion of the kitchen, the Greenes' attention to craftsmanship is in evidence: "The whole construction was carefully thought out, and there was a reason for every detail". For too long, they believed, the

Above: The house which George Washington built for himself and his family at Mount Vernon in Virginia sits squarely in the landscape, overlooking the Potomac river. Mount Vernon house is the embodiment of all the good, solid virtues which the first President of the United States himself espoused.

Right: The family dining room is furnished and decorated on a far more intimate scale than the large formal banqueting hall at the opposite end of the building. The table is laid in a typical setting of the 1790s, with glasses for wines, including the obligatory port and Madeira, and nuts and fruit. On the sideboard are two open knife boxes and beside the window a stand is set with servings of desserts in glasses.

George Washington was at heart a natural commander. For five years as Commander-in-Chief he led the American forces in the fight to liberate the colonies from British Rule. The war was bloody and bitter but in 1783 the struggle for liberty was finally realized and the last of his weary soldiers began to make their way home, as free men. Their general too surrendered his commission and returned to his mansion at Mount Vernon in Virginia. It was time to make the final improvements to his country house which had been taking place gradually over the past ten years. Washington took on himself the role of master architect. As a soldier, Washington had never been able to command his forces from the rear and as a builder, he was no different. Indeed, one of his house guests noted: "He directs everything in the building way, condescending even to measure the things himself, that all may be perfectly uniform". The house which stands today as a national monument to the first President of the United States is, perhaps more than any other, the creation of its owner.

Mount Vernon stands in a commanding position above the Potomac river on a plot of land which had been purchased by Washington's great-grandfather in 1674. The mansion itself was built according to Washington's design from the 1760s, on the site of a smaller dwelling constructed by his father. Mount Vernon had been continually enlarged in the years before 1787 when the last feature, a weather-vane in the shape of a dove of peace, was added. The house takes the ordered form you might expect from so military-minded a designer, with a central block of three floors and two flanking pavilions joined by colonnades. On its east front an impressive columned piazza, Washington's architectural masterpiece, overlooks the river.

You enter the house via a small entrance hall on the west side where, among other curios, hangs the key to the Bastille which was presented to Washington by General Lafayette in 1790. To the left, lies the part of the house reserved for formal entertaining while to the right of the hall, are the Washington family's living quarters. Turning left

Mount Vernon

first, you find yourself in the Little Parlour which is where the family and their guests used to gather in the evening. Music was an important part of life at Mount Vernon and the room is dominated by a fine English 18th-century harpsichord. Next door in the West Parlour, a table is set for tea with a splendid silver urn and a Chinese export porcelain tea service. This, the more formal of the two sitting rooms, is dominated by the Washington crest, sculpted into the plasterwork above the fireplace. Its walls are hung with family portraits, including a fine painting of the President himself by Charles Willson Peale. The walls of the room, painted in a light Prussian blue, give it an air of refined elegance. In Washington's own words, it was "The best place in my house".

The parlour leads to a tall, two-storey banqueting hall, quite the most stately room in the house, which contains two principal features. One, the impressive Palladian window, was copied by Washington from one of the European pattern books which he studied with such relish when designing his house. The other, directly opposite, is an imposing marble fireplace which was given to Washington by a liberally minded Englishman. The room, which is totally symmetrical in appearance, is Adamesque in decoration, with its verdigris-green walls and "Etruscan" plaster detailing.

Left: The little parlour was the focal point of family life at Mount Vernon. Its centrepiece is a harpsichord made in England in the mid-18th century. Here the family would have gathered with their guests before and after dinner.

Above: Perhaps the most fascinating room at Mount Vernon is George Washington's study which contains, among other things, a classic pedal-operated fan chair, a printing press and a wide-ranging collection of books.

For family dinners, the Washingtons used the small dining room across the passage. Its walls are also painted green, but this is a dark, glazed green reminiscent of the early 18th century rather than the pale elegance of the 1780s. The fine mahogany table is laid out to appear as it would have been in the late 1790s, just before Washington's death, with port and Madeira, nuts and fruit. The Washingtons were a close family. Apart from the President and his wife Martha, there were Martha's two children John and Martha and also John's two children. It was in this room that they all came together. From the engraving above the fireplace members of the Washington family look down on the table around which they would have gathered when they were alone. However, such occasions were all too rare. Washington himself wrote: "Scarcely any strangers who are going from north to south or from south to north, do not spend a day or two". But quite apart from its role as a place of entertainment, Mount Vernon was a working home.

In between surrendering his military commission in 1783 and becoming President in 1789, George Washington continued to work here at his house for the good of the nation which he had helped to create. Immediately after rising every morning, he came to his study, next door to the dining room, by way of a private staircase and

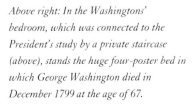

Above right: In the Washingtons' bedroom, which was connected to the President's study by a private staircase (above), stands the huge four-poster bed in which George Washington died in December 1799 at the age of 67.

The room was decorated by the President's wife, Martha, and her good taste and unpretentious style is demonstrated in the subtle harmonizing of the white drapery of the bed with the soft blue-painted detailing of the walls.

Above: In the formal west parlour a table is set for tea with a fine Chinese export porcelain tea service of the 18th century and a silver tea urn. Above the sofa hangs a rare painting of Washington by the artist Charles Willson Peale.

Right: Walking through the small entrance hall of Mount Vernon, the visitor is met by tantalizing glimpses of the living rooms where George and Martha Washington once entertained their guests.

often remained there until he retired to bed. Washington's study is a modest room devoid of the bright colours of the rest of the house and furnished with a few items of personal interest. These include a globe, a pedal-operated fan chair and a portrait of Washington's father. Washington was a voracious reader and the room is filled with his extensive collection of books which range from the poetry of Robert Burns to Batty Langley's famous 1720s treatise, *Principles of Gardening*.

Washington's interest in the agricultural side of his property is well recorded and is testified by the many outhouses, servants' and slaves' quarters which surround the mansion itself. To manage this estate, which he himself referred to as "a little empire", was a huge task and it was here in his study that, when not attending to affairs of state, Washington would put his household in order.

After a weary day at his desk, he would ascend the stairs to his bedchamber, which is in fact a suite of three rooms in which the President and his wife could be completely alone. Here Martha had her bureau – a French piece dating from 1791, which stands beneath portraits of two of her grandchildren. We know that she was responsible for the decoration of this room and chose the pale blue of the detailing to harmonize with the white hangings of the bed. It was the Washingtons' custom during their later years to retire to this four-poster bed at nine o'clock and sleep undisturbed until morning. However, on the night of 13th December 1799, George rose in the night because he felt unwell. Typically, he "would not allow Mrs Washington to get up or the servants to be waked". He was no better by the morning and the doctors were called for. However, their ministries were to no avail and on the evening of Saturday 14th December George Washington died at the age of 67. He passed away just as he had anticipated the previous September, when he had written: "When the summons comes I will endeavour to obey it with a good grace". Today, that spirit of graceful obedience, service and order is still preserved in the house which he loved so dearly.

MOUNT VERNON, MOUNT VERNON, VIRGINIA
ARCHITECT: GEORGE WASHINGTON
CONSTRUCTION: c.1760-1787
SEE ALSO GAZETTEER, PAGE 187

*E*urope

Above: The exterior of Sir John Soane's house in London, with its protruding facade populated with draped antique figures, at once betrays its owner's obsession with the architecture of the ancient civilizations of Greece, Rome and Egypt. Built by the Regency architect himself between 1792 and 1824, the house falls neatly into two parts – the professional on the right and below, and the domestic to the left and above.

Right: Here in the south drawing room, overlooking Lincoln's Inn Fields, it is possible to experience something of the family atmosphere of the domestic side of Number 13 Lincoln's Inn Fields, which Soane originally planned as a home for his wife and his two sons. In this room, light from the high, full-length windows falls through alcoves filled with books and hung with swag-and-tail drapes onto the comfortable upholstered settee and polished floorboards.

Tucked incongruously among the legal offices of London's Lincoln's Inn Fields lies the former town house of the great neoclassical architect Sir John Soane, designer of the Bank of England. To visit the house is to journey through Soane's imagination. The building, which is in fact three houses constructed by Soane over 32 years between 1792 and 1824, was for him an encapsulation of his theories of design and sources of inspiration, as much as a display of his wide-ranging taste. The son of an Essex bricklayer, Soane grew into something of a polymath, a Renaissance man who was forever investigating new aspects of art and antiquity.

In 1792, at the height of his popularity, Soane built number 12 Lincoln's Inn Fields, the farthest left of the three houses, as a family home for himself, his wife and his two sons George and John. However, as his collection of artefacts and works of art grew, Soane evolved the idea that it should be put on display, both for the common good and in order to educate his two boys whom he intended to be the inheritors and progenitors of a dynasty of super-architects. With this in mind, he built a country house, Pitzhanger Manor in Ealing, near London. However, in 1810, following a feud with his younger son George which shattered his dynastic aspirations (the elder, John, had long since given up the study of architecture), Soane abandoned this grandiose project, sold the country manor and moved his collection of fine art and artefacts to London, rebuilding number 13 Lincoln's Inn Fields to accommodate it. Thus this huge house was created, becoming at the same time a residence and a museum.

On entering today, it is the domestic side of the house that you will first encounter, although the neo-Egyptian facade outside leaves little doubt as to the profession of its former occupant. Inside, the entrance hall, its walls painted to resemble porphyry, continues the neoclassical tone with a dome that is based on that of the temple of Mars Ultor in Rome. There is little light here and it comes as something of a surprise to emerge from this Stygian gloom into the combined library and dining room.

Sir John

Soane's Museum

depicts a sacrifice to Zeus, and, flanking it, four vases dating from the 18th century – two Italian and two Chinese. Despite the opulence of its decoration, this room was designed principally for everyday use and the other furnishings are mostly contemporary. For instance, the chairs were made in 1828 to a similar design to those by Soane for the Governor of the Bank of England.

The quasi-domestic function of the house is carried through to the upper floors. Here, Soane himself chose a bright yellow for the walls, exploiting to the full the light from the windows overlooking Lincoln's Inn Fields. In the North Drawing Room an air of informality is tempered by the siting of a large cabinet, flanked with drawings by Giovanni Paolo Pannini and Soane himself and containing a fine collection of drawings by Soane's master, George Dance. It is surmounted with a model, made by Jean Fouquet, of a temple at Palmyra, one of no less than 20 bought by Soane in 1834. From the top of the curved bookcase which lines the west wall, Soane's mentor, Andrea Palladio, looks down. The adjoining South Drawing Room has an altogether softer atmosphere, its yellow swag and tail drapes, upholstered settees and sofa tables offering a suggestion of what everyday life might have been like in this otherwise austere household. The painting to the right of the fireplace is of Sir John Soane, at the age of 51, by William Owen.

The transition between family house and museum takes place back at street level. The Breakfast Parlour is Soane's greatest triumph of domestic

Divided by a triple arch, these two areas glow in their Pompeiian red, articulated with green detailing on the woodwork and by the slim, unadorned metal pillars which appear to support the dividing span with a tenuous grace. Set in the ceiling, between yet more green finials, are paintings by Henry Howard, the neoclassical artist-friend of Soane, which depict Phoebus, Aurora and a fanciful assembly of Greek gods. Mirrors set in the walls complete the decorative richness and a discreet sign on each wall indicates one of the points of the compass. The late classical vases sited on either side of the arch are echoed in a magnificent display in the window. The window display consists of the Cawdor vase, a rare 4th-century-BC Apulian crater bought by Soane from the collection of Lord Cawdor in 1800, which

Above: The entrance hall, with walls painted to resemble porphyry, contains neoclassical sculpture which forewarns the visitor of the atmosphere of academe and antiquity which pervades the entire house.

Right: Against one wall of the library sits one of Soane's most prized possessions. It is an Apulian amphora, dating from the late 4th century BC. To the right, a bust of Napoleon presides over another of the poet William Dodd who was executed in 1777.

Far right: In the breakfast parlour Soane created a false ceiling into which he inserted oeil de boeuf *mirrors. The overall effect was designed to control the light which enters the room, channelling it to the sides and down the central lantern.*

architecture, perfectly uniting form and function. It presents something of an optical illusion, as its domed ceiling gives a rounded appearance to what is in reality a perfect square. However, what is perhaps most remarkable about this room is its light. The effect is achieved by Soane's skilful insertion of the central canopy which rises from four arches and is further articulated with *oeil de boeuf* mirrors. In the middle, light descends from an octagonal lantern, decorated with stained glass, while additional skylights to the north and south allow shafts of light to illuminate the walls. Soane himself was sufficiently pleased with the effect to consider it a near-perfect example of what he referred to as "the poetry of architecture".

A peaceful place in which to have breakfast, the parlour also contains a variety of fascinating artefacts. Above the bookcases, before a drawing of the Soane family tomb and engravings by Angelo Campanella, stands a bronze of Victory, found in Rome by the sculptor John Flaxman and installed here by Soane a mere ten days before his death in January 1837. On the south wall, Flaxman's own work is on view: plaster busts of William Hayley, Henry Howard and the sculptor's own father stand on the black marble fireplace. Beneath a painting of Oberon and Titania by Henry Howard hangs a terracotta model by John Michael Rysbrack for the tomb of the Duke of Marlborough, and below this are a collection of Napoleonic memorabilia and a clock by Benjamin Lewis Vulliamy.

Importantly, alongside two portraits of Napoleon hang two plaster casts – one taken from the Donatello *Madonna and Child*, now in London's Victoria and Albert Museum, the other from a 5th-century-BC Greek bronze – which between them set the tone for the museum proper, of which we are afforded a tantalizing glimpse through the windows of the north wall.

Walking through from the breakfast room, you will find the Dome, originally part of Soane's office, which was built on the site of the old stables and is the oldest part of the museum. The dome itself is in fact a large skylight, below which are assembled a few of the many pieces of sculpture which seem to fill every corner of the house. Most striking is the full-length cast of the Apollo Belvedere, so beloved of many 18th-century artists, opposite which sits a bust of Soane himself, made in 1830 by Sir Francis Chantrey, of which

the sculptor confessed: "I have never produced a better". Other sculptures on show are by John Flaxman and Robert William Sievier, while classical pieces include sarcophagus panels, statuary from Hadrian's villa and a bust of a Roman noblewoman dating from the 1st century AD. Opposite sits a Roman copy of a bust by Polycleitus, supposed to be "Augustus Caesar when a boy". Directly below and open to view lies the basement and its "sepulchral chamber", containing the massive stone sarcophagus of Seti I, excavated at Thebes in 1815. One of Soane's most valued prizes, he bought the sarcophagus in 1824 after the British Museum had failed to find funds to do so.

A sculpture-lined corridor, which bears witness to Soane's magpie-like passion for collecting, leads from the Dome to the picture room. This canopied chamber, typical of the architect's later style, is an

Left: The library is painted a distinctive shade of red which was inspired by the colour of the walls in the Villa of the Mysteries, unearthed at Pompeii. It is complemented by dark-green detailing which lines the triple arch that connects this room to the dining room at the front of the house. Inscriptions give the room's position within the points of the compass.

Above: Soane devised an ingenious system by which to display his picture collection in the small gallery that he built specifically for that purpose. On the north side of this room, his own architectural watercolours are hung behind William Hogarth's Election series. These open onto a recess containing neoclassical sculpture and detailed models of some of Soane's most ambitious building projects.

ingeniously designed gallery, purpose-built to display his magnificent collection of paintings. The walls are in effect a series of cleverly hinged panels, hung with works of art on both sides, thus doubling the available wall space. On one side hang works by Richard Cosway, Giovanni Battista Piranesi, J.M.W. Turner and Soane himself. On the other, William Hogarth's important series of eight pictures, *A Rake's Progress,* and his four hilarious paintings of the *Election* series, are on view. Other artists that are represented include Francis Danby, Francesco Zuccarelli, Giovanni Battista Piranesi and Jean-Antoine Watteau, while swinging back the two sets of panels on the south wall reveals a stunning array of scale models of Soane's unbuilt projects, bathed in the eerie blue light from a stained-glass window.

The charm of Soane's architecture lies in its subtlety as much as its monumentality, and it is typical of his style that for all its splendours it should be an often-missed corner of his museum which has the final word. Descending a narrow staircase you arrive in the basement, a maze of cellars filled with sculptural fragments. However, one room seems strangely out of keeping. The Monk's Parlour brings you closer to the human side of Soane than any of the treasures on the floors above. Known by its creator as the "Parloir of Padre Giovanni", it was intended as a satirical jibe at the rarified fashion for Gothic melancholy engendered by the Romantic movement and anathema to Soane's restrained classicism. Tongue firmly in his cheek, Soane recreated a corner of a ruined abbey, complete with tombs, medieval carvings and an inscription which provides an insight into the true character of this fascinating and complex man: "It may perhaps be asked, before leaving this part of the museum, at what period the Monk existed whose memory is here preserved, and whether he is to be identified with any of those whose deeds have enshrined their names. The answer to this question is provided by Horace: Dulce est despere in loco". (It is good to be nonsensical in the right place.)

Left: Upstairs, at the rear of the living accommodation, lies a cabinet of architectural fragments. Among them are a model of a building at Palmyra, one of 20 purchased by Soane in 1834, and a model of the State Post Office, Soane's last major public work, built between 1829 and 1833.

Above: A deep well, lined with fragments of ancient sculpture, forms the heart of the museum. Particularly prominent here are a cast of the Apollo Belvedere and, opposite, a bust of Soane himself by his sculptor-friend Sir Francis Chantrey.

SIR JOHN SOANE'S MUSEUM, LONDON
ARCHITECT: SIR JOHN SOANE
CONSTRUCTION: 1792-1810
SEE ALSO GAZETTEER, PAGE 182

Above: The exterior of Edinburgh's Georgian House forms one of the central elements in the neoclassical facade of the north side of Charlotte Square. Built by Robert Adam in 1791, the building was designed to resemble the facade of a classic country mansion.

Right: In the dining room, the table is laid for dinner. Alongside the original Regency dinner service, in Wedgwood's popular "Absalom's Pillar" design, are wine glasses with their rinsing bowls, linen napkins and an impressive collection of silver tureens which would have contained an elaborate assortment of dishes.

In 1752 a pamphlet was circulated among the people of Edinburgh, Scotland, bearing the title: "Proposals for carrying on certain Public Works in the City of Edinburgh". The final lines concluded: "the leading men of a country ought to exert their power and influence and what greater subject can be presented to their view, than that of enlarging, beautifying and improving the capital of their native country?" Scotland's leading men were not slow to take up this challenge and in their response to the proposal over the following 80 years they created one of the most beautiful cities in the world.

The New Town of Edinburgh stands to the north of the old medieval capital, the Royal Mile, on a long hill with imposing views over the Firth of Forth to the ancient Kingdom of Fife. In its elegant neoclassical squares and crescents, the town embodies the sensibilities of the Enlightenment – the age of the philosphers Jean-Jacques Rousseau and David Hume. Nowhere is this architectural perfection more clearly evident than in Charlotte Square, a classic 18th-century square, laid out in 1791 by the great Scottish neoclassicist Robert Adam.

In his plan for the square, Adam introduced something quite new to Edinburgh. Known as the "unified frontage", in which a street of individual houses was made to resemble the facade of a large, Palladian-style country house, Adam's work stood out from the simple, understated style that had come to characterize Edinburgh architecture over the previous 40 years. In the middle of the row was a pedimented villa, with four Corinthian pillars, joined by two wings to what appeared to be pavilions at either side. Throughout, the facade was adorned with stone balustrades and decorations in Adam's distinctive "Etruscan" style. The ten houses were each three stories in height, with an attic and a basement. Charlotte Square had two such facades, one to the north and one to the south, linked on the east side by a smaller row of houses opening to a wide street and on the west by the domed edifice of St George's Church. In the middle of the square, a garden completed the semi-rural atmosphere.

The Georgian House

have preserved its main rooms as they would have appeared at the time of the house's first owner. The two upper floors provide the official residence of the Moderator of the General Assembly of the Church of Scotland. The house offers a fascinating reflection of the taste and lifestyle of a late Georgian household of the "Athens of the North" at its height.

The visitor should approach the house from the main square, up the two carriage-mounting steps from the street, and enter past the spiked iron railings, passing over the well into the light, stone-flagged hall. Walk past the sedan chair and, as the 18th-century visitor would have done, ascend the staircase which is lit from above by a classic Adam domed fanlight.

To enter the drawing room is to travel back in time to the zenith of 18th-century Britain. The room is arranged formally, with the chairs pushed back against the walls in the manner which had been typical in the houses of the aristocracy and gentry since the 17th century, but was soon to change in the more relaxed social atmosphere of the early 19th century. The drawing room was the focus of formal entertaining in the house and is designed for show. Light pours into the room through the high sash windows which overlook the crocus-filled lawn of the square. The pale-green paint of the walls, a colour that is used repeatedly throughout the house, was a hue that Adam particularly favoured. His hallmark can also be seen in the elaborate freize in the "Etruscan" style. The carved and painted suite of furniture, dating from between 1785 and 1790, is upholstered in a striped satin fabric of the kind that remained popular throughout the period. Typically, the suite includes one of the newer, more comfortable sofas with squab cushions, which had become fashionable during the latter half of the 18th century. On the relatively simple chimneypiece are two Chinese *famille rose* vases of the Chi'en Lung dynasty, dating from the mid-18th century, and an early Worcester bowl. Among the pictures, which reflect the eclectic taste of the Regency gentry, are two fine Scottish landscapes in the style of Alexander Nasmyth, a white cockatoo by the Dutch painter Melchior de Hondecoeter, two earthy genre pictures by David Teniers, a pair of Italian views and some rustic English scenes by George Morland. Against one wall a neat square piano, dating from 1805, by the

Above: The household was provided with food by a team of servants who laboured in the cavernous kitchen in the basement. Everything was prepared on the open fire to the left, with accompanying bread oven, until the large close-fire range, furnished with a "batterie" of numerous copper pots and pans, was introduced in 1802. On a draped table in the middle of the room, silver salvers of steaming food await delivery to the diners upstairs.

Below right: That the house was divided into two areas – above and below stairs – is seen nowhere better than here in the scullery at the solid-stone sink which is filled with water from the single hand-pump to its left.

Far right: A corner of the dining room captures the gentle pace of life in an upper-middle-class household of the late 18th century. Here, beside a wide-seated side chair, is some of the paraphernalia of everyday life: a Regency veilleuse *(food warmer), a wine strainer and a punchbowl. It was a leisurely life for those lucky enough to be born to it, as is testified by the noble and contented countenance of Janet Grant, Countess of Hyndford, whose portrait, copied by the Regency artist Sir Henry Raeburn from an original by Allan Ramsay, surveys the scene.*

Building began on the north side of the square in 1792 and it is perhaps hard to imagine today, when you are faced with its breathtakingly simple elegance, that when John Lamont of Lamont, 18th chief of the clan Lamont, took out his "feu of purchase" for the building of number 7 in 1796, only one other house had already been built. Lamont paid £1,800 to purchase the house, although by the time he and his family came to leave the house some 20 years later in 1815, Lamont had made a handsome profit of £1,200. Since its construction, the house has passed through only four family ownerships. Today it is owned by the National Trust for Scotland, who

Above: Contrary to modern conventions, the master bedroom of the house is situated not on one of the upper floors, but at street level. This was quite normal for a house of the late 18th century. The room is decorated in soft tones of yellow and cream which complement the original 18th-century moreen bed-hangings. The pastel portrait that hangs between the windows is of Lucy de Lutherbourg by François Xavier Vispre.

Edinburgh piano-maker Richard Horsburgh, stirs the imagination to thoughts of formal musical evenings like those which fill the pages of Jane Austen's social comedies.

Off this formal reception room is the smaller parlour, which would have been the true heart of the house and the Lamont family's everyday sitting room. Here they would have gathered in the afternoon and evening, seated on furniture arranged informally in close proximity to the open fire, which would have been the sole means of keeping warm. In keeping with the intimate, understated nature of the room, much of the furniture is of Scottish manufacture, although a nod to fashion is given in the smart black horse-hair upholstery of the chairs. The two globes were

bought from Messrs. Whyte & Company of Edinburgh and the barrel organ, which is contained in a mahogany case and dates from 1800, plays a selection of Scottish tunes that were popular at the time and far removed from the refinement of the drawing-room piano. Above the fireplace hangs a portrait of *Jane Ross of Shandwick* by Alexander Nasmyth, while on either side hang paste medallions made by the late 18th-century Scottish artist James Tassie. Between the 1760s and 1790s, Tassie executed an extensive series of these miniature portraits in a vitreous paste of his own formulation. Among his sitters were Bonnie Prince Charlie, the philosopher David Hume and Robert Adam, architect of the house, whose image is seen here.

Descending from the upper floors, follow the route of the Georgian visitor from drawing room to dining room. It seemed logical at that time to position the dining room at street level. It was unnecessary, after all, to have a good view from this room where the business in hand was strictly culinary. Consequently the windows are no taller than those of the drawing room. They are framed with wooden panelling grained with paint to resemble expensive mahogany, as was the fashion of the period. The dining room was designed for formal entertainment and the table is laid for a full dinner with a Regency Wedgwood service in the *Absalom's Pillar* design that was introduced in 1812. Dining was the supreme ritual in the house-hold and the elaborate table furniture includes covered tureens and ashets (meat plates) in silver plate and fine porcelain. Symmetry was of the essence – from the neatly folded rectangular linen napkins to the wine glasses, each with its own wine cooler whose purpose was to rinse the glass before a different wine was served. Although the knives and their matching two-pronged forks have green ivory handles, for the most formal occasions the family and their guests would undoubtedly have used the heavy, old-fashioned pistol-handled silver cutlery contained in the handsome inlaid mahogany canteen that stands on the sideboard. From the walls, portraits of past generations gaze down at the diners, including a portrait by Allan Ramsay, which hangs above one of the English Chippendale chairs, and a portrait of Lady Margaret Macdonald, possibly by Joseph Highmore.

While it might seem strange to the modern mind that the master bedroom should also be situated at street level, next to the dining room, such an arrangement seems to have been the norm in late 18th-century Edinburgh. Visitors might like to imagine themselves in the persona of one of the inhabitants of the house, retiring to their room for a good night's rest after the departure of the guests from the dinner table. On the way into the bedroom, take a look at the wooden box that is concealed between the two rooms. This is a portable water closet; by Regency standards an ingenious and advanced form of sanitation, conveniently situated for the use of the family and guests, who earlier in the century would have been accustomed to using a chamber pot behind a screen in the corner of the dining room.

The focal point of the bedchamber is the magnificent carved and painted four-poster bedstead, draped with moreen needlework hangings that were made in the last quarter of the 18th century. Above each pillow is a small em-broidered pocket into which the sleepers would have placed their pocket-watches. Beside the fire sits a Scottish 18th-century "lug" chair with a loose cover, which contrasts with the three carved Sheraton chairs. Among the other pieces of furniture in this room are a Scottish serpentine-fronted chest of drawers and a medicine chest from Messrs. James Robertson of Edinburgh which contains its original labelled bottles for such exotic medicines as laudanum, chloroform and camphorated hartshorn. Between the windows hangs a portrait of Lucy de Lutherbourg by the French artist François Xavier Vispre.

If, on leaving the bedroom, you find yourself lost in a reverie of gracious Regency living, you might like to pause for a moment and consider the day-to-day life of the house. While doing this, your attention might be drawn to the plain stone steps on your right. These lead to a hidden world. Downstairs, in the basement, we find the domain of the servants. Just as the upper floors were a place of leisure and entertainment, the basement was a place of hard work. In this dimly lit under-world a row of bells hang on the wall, each one designed to summon a servant to a particular room in the house. The kitchen is a perfect period re-creation. You will find the open range, the spit and the hot plate, ready to receive the food for a grand dinner. Nearby are the china closet, filled with the same Wedgwood service that can be seen in the dining room, a fine 1803 silver cruet set by Paul Storr and an enviably well-stocked wine cellar hung with copper jugs. However, although it is fascinating, the basement could hardly be called inviting and a glimpse of the primitive stone basin and hand pump would be enough to drive even the most romantically minded visitor back upstairs to the comfortable elegance of Regency Edinburgh.

Above: The informal parlour or back drawing room was the heart of family life and it was here that the Lamont family gathered to take afternoon tea. The set of tea cups which stand on the breakfast table in the middle of the room are Minton and date from 1810, while the silver tea and coffee pots were manufactured in Newcastle in 1788.

THE GEORGIAN HOUSE,
EDINBURGH, MIDLOTHIAN
ARCHITECT: ROBERT ADAM
CONSTRUCTION: 1796
SEE ALSO GAZETTEER, PAGE 184

Above: With its plain brown stone, alleviated only by a simple sculpted door pediment and bay windows, The Tenement House in Glasgow's Buccleuch Street is a typical example of the intensive housing-development projects that took place in late 19th-century Britain to accommodate the ever-expanding workforce.

Right: Inside the tenement there was only one living room – the parlour. Although this room was used only for special occasions, we see that Mrs Toward has left her needlework here, together with the sewing machine on which she is busily finishing for a client the smart suit which hangs on the tailor's dummy beside it. Typically, a pair of Staffordshire dogs, known colloquially as "wally dugs", adorn the mantelpiece. Beside them is the clock that kept the household to its strict routine. The box bed in the corner would have provided additional sleeping accommodation before beds of its sort were banned in 1900.

Glasgow is a city born of the British industrial revolution. From the mid-19th century it was continually expanding and by the 1920s, Glasgow contained one-fifth of the entire population of Scotland. It was, literally, a city of the people. Here they lived, packed into the famous "tenement" apartments. Sometimes there was only one room to accommodate an entire family. Others were more fortunate. One of the lucky ones was Agnes Toward, who in 1911 moved with her mother into a tenement at 145 Buccleuch Street. This was no slum tenement but a relatively luxurious "house" which reflected the comparative gentility of its occupants.

Agnes Toward was the daughter of a commercial traveller, William Toward, who, like so many of his contemporaries, was determined that his family should have the best of everything. The Towards were local people. Agnes was born in 1886 in nearby Renfrew Street and attended the school in Buccleuch Street itself. They were a happy family until Agnes's father died in 1889. Her mother was left to bring up the three-year-old girl as best she might. Agnes's mother was a seamstress and dressmaker by trade and managed to eke out a precarious living by making clothes for the wealthy Glasgow middle-classes and taking in lodgers. When she reached her late teens, Agnes too went out to work, first as a typist and later as a clerk. The move to Buccleuch Street represented the very best that the two women could have hoped for.

The large four-storey block of 56 tenement apartments extends along Buccleuch Street on a plot of land which was bought by a local property developer, James Ferguson, in 1892. The building was conceived in a neo-Jacobean style, although this was later refined to reduce costs. Number 145 was one of the first apartments to be completed in September 1892 but it wasn't until 1911 that Agnes and her mother moved in. Following the death of her mother in 1939 Agnes did not change a thing in the apartment and continued to live there right up until the day that she left to go into a nursing home in 1965. As you walk around the Towards' home today you will experience what it

*T*he

Tenement House

was like to live in Glasgow, or for that matter any British industrial city, in the early to middle years of this century.

Just as Agnes did for 50 years, make your way up the plain stone "stair" which leads to the front door and enter the small hall. The atmosphere is so strikingly Edwardian that it is hard to believe that the apartment was occupied by Agnes until comparatively recently. In the hall, pride of place is given to the Scottish grandfather clock dating from the 1790s. All of the rooms in the apartment – parlour, bedroom, bathroom and kitchen – are accessible from the hall.

In the Towards' small household, accommodation was at a premium. There were two beds, one in the bedroom and one in the kitchen. While her mother was alive, we can be sure that it fell to Agnes to occupy the kitchen. The bedroom is furnished as it would have been in the 1920s. Beside the bedstead of iron and brass is a marble washstand with a ewer and basin which was filled from the bathroom every morning. A collection of souvenir ornaments decorates the elaborate late-Edwardian wooden overmantel above the tiled fireplace.

Next door in the parlour we find evidence of Mrs Towards' profession. A tailor's dummy in the corner wears a half-finished skirt and jacket and beside it an American 1860s sewing machine lays

idle. It seems as if we have stumbled into the parlour just at the time when the Towards are expecting a visitor. The fire is lit and the table, mahogany like all the furniture in this room, is covered with a lace tablecloth and laid up with an impressive array of cakes and scones, ready for afternoon tea. After tea it seems possible that we might be entertained with a recital on the small Victorian piano which was the Towards' only means of entertainment.

Above left: The bathroom is notable both for its cleanliness and the spartan simplicity of its decoration.

Above: Despite the intense nature of employment that was carried out by both members of the household during the daytime, the tenement was always kept neat and tidy and there was always a good "spread" on the mahogany tea table if visitors were expected.

A similar collection of containers can be found in the small kitchen which is the real heart of the house. The refined display of the parlour was in effect only to impress the Towards' visitors. Their everyday life was spent in the kitchen, huddled around the large black-leaded range. There were no labour-saving devices here; washing was done by hand and wrung dry through a mangle. Floors were scrubbed and swept and surfaces polished clean. Irons were heated on the range and the women even made their own jam. The evidence of the drudgery of household chores is all around us. Despite its relatively small size, there were still many jobs to be done and it is easy to imagine Agnes, tired after another day in the office where she worked as a clerk for 45 years, coming home to more work before being able to climb into her tiny bed, hidden behind a curtain or drape at one end of the kitchen. To our modern minds it seems a thankless existence. But Agnes had never known anything different and was happy to live this way almost until the end of her days. As the words above her mother's bed read: "There's no place like home".

THE TENEMENT HOUSE, GLASGOW,
STRATHCLYDE
ARCHITECT: JAMES FERGUSON
CONSTRUCTION: 1892
SEE ALSO GAZETTEER, PAGE 184

Right: In a corner of the kitchen, a small alcove containing Agnes Toward's bed is concealed by a simple curtain. The bed, which Agnes occupied for 30 years until her mother's death in 1939, was heated by a single earthenware hot-water bottle. The cramped nature of the apartment is well conveyed in this dual-purpose room, which was where Agnes prepared her food, ate her meals, washed and ironed her clothes and slept.

The formal gentility of the parlour and bedroom is echoed in the bathroom, itself a luxury in an apartment of this period. Here everything has been left just as it would have been during Agnes's lifetime. Soap and brushes are laid out on the marble-effect washbasin, while beneath the window is an intriguing range of original pill boxes and patent medical preparations – from cartons of liquorice powder and bottles of iodine solution to boxes of boracic acid and jars of glycerine.

Wightwick

In 1887 the Victorian businessman Theodore Mander bought two things. One was a plot of land, the other a book. In uniting the two Mander created one of the most impressive of Victorian country houses, Wightwick Manor, near Wolverhampton in the West Midlands, England, which today exists as a perfectly preserved time-capsule of the Arts and Crafts style that was popularized by William Morris in the latter half of the 19th century.

It comes as no great surprise that Mander, a successful paint and varnish manufacturer from Wolverhampton, should have chosen to buy the land on which to build his house three miles away from his home town. What might seem more of a riddle is why such an industrialist should have chosen for its design and decoration a style which is generally associated with infant socialism and free-thinking liberalism.

The answer is provided by Mander's second purchase. The book, John Ruskin's *The Seven Lamps of Architecture*, first published in 1849, was a bestseller among the Victorian middle classes, as its advocacy of the virtue of honest toil appealed to their own conviction that riches were the reward of hard work. In aesthetic terms its essential dictum that architecture was a mere servant to the two true arts of painting and sculpture laid the way for an entire school of design, and it was to this that Mander was drawn.

With worthy singlemindedness he set out to create his ideal. To design the house he employed Edward Ould, who had made his name in the design of comfortable country houses in the mock-Elizabethan half-timbered style that had become popular in the 1870s. However, for the interior Mander looked to the Arts and Crafts style typified by the work of William Morris.

From the outside, Edward Ould's masterpiece works in perfect harmony with its surroundings and the positioning and scale of every element in its construction is calculated to satisfy Ruskinian theory, from its curvilinear timbering to its barley-twist chimneystacks. Despite the fact that the house was built in two parts, the first in 1887 and the second in 1893, no distinction is evident

Above: To all outside appearances, Wightwick Manor in the West Midlands might be mistaken for a genuine Elizabethan manor house of the 16th century. It has all the characteristic features of the period – from the barley-twist chimneys to the classic black and white half-timbered walls and small leaded windows. However, on closer examination, it becomes evident that the house dates from some 300 years later.

Left: The dining room was the focus of formal entertainment in the house and its wood panelling, Delft tiles and table laid with all the attention to detail of the late Victorian era reflect its function. Compared to the colourful romanticism of the William Morris decoration that is used throughout the rest of the house, this room has a feeling of austerity relieved only by the flamboyant Italianate swirls of the plasterwork on the frieze and ceiling.

M a n o r

Right: Light is admitted to the entrance hall by means of a bay window in a small alcove. The decoration on the stained-glass windows depicts images of six women in medieval dress by C. E. Kempe, each of whom depicts an aspect of peace.

Bottom right: In one of the smaller bedrooms of the house, "Honeysuckle" fabric by William Morris forms the background for a black-painted fireplace and a wicker-seated chair, also by Morris, above which hangs a watercolour by Frederick Sandys.

Far right: The great hall is the heart of the house and was devised by Mander and his architect Edward Ould as a recreation of what they perceived as the essence of the medieval manor house.
Wightwick Manor was bequeathed to the National Trust in 1937, and since that time it has been restored to its original appearance. In a continuing effort to achieve this aim more fully, the furniture in this room has been moved in position since this photograph was taken.

between the two wings, which have a convincing air of authentic craftsmanship. Inside, John Ruskin's words from the *The Seven Lamps of Beauty* come readily to mind, in particular his plea to the designer to work by hand so that the decoration will demonstrate "the sense of human labour and care spent upon it". Human labour is well in evidence here in the great profusion of carved wooden panelling throughout the house and it is this which immediately strikes you from the moment you enter the long hall.

Mander declares his intention to follow Ruskin's dictums from the start. The hall gives way to a stepped recess in which, against a mullioned stained-glass window, a chair, writing table and winged armchair are grouped around that ubiquitous feature of the Arts and Crafts style, an inglenook fireplace.

It is worth noting that although over the years Mander and his descendants completed the decoration sympathetically with designs by Morris, it was not to the Kelmscott master that Mander himself turned in the first instance, but to one of his lesser-known followers. C.E. Kempe had a reputation as a skilled stained-glass craftsman and also appears to have dabbled in interior decoration. For the hall recess at Wightwick he was commissioned by Mander to design a stained-glass window depicting six women in imagined medieval dress, each one representing a different aspect of peace. To judge from the richness with which Kempe executed these windows, it would seem likely that Mander went to him not to cut costs but in an attempt to

be somewhat different to those of his contemporaries who chose William Morris's rather more restrained approach.

Nevertheless, in the adjoining drawing room, Mander did allow Kempe to pay homage to Morris in further window panels. These take as their subject matter Morris's popular poem *The Earthly Paradise*, published in 1868. A Chaucerian epic, it tells of the discovery of a forgotten ancient land by a company of Norsemen, and provides a basis for the uniting of Norse and Celtic myth.

Apart from Kempe's glass, the great hall contains many of the key elements of Morris's style and it is hard to know quite how much of the decorative scheme was conceived by Kempe and how much by Mander himself. The Italian Renaissance-style fireplace is hung with a decorative tapestry cloth and embellished with wonderfully animated tiles, decorated with images of animals and birds, derived from Persian Iznik ware of the 15th century and made by the influential ceramicist and friend of Morris, William de Morgan. The carved panels over the mantelpiece, the Japanese vases around the walls and the lavishly decorated Queen Anne marquetry cabinet all combine to create that comfortable sense of eclecticism sought by William Morris and his followers, any undue extravagances of exotic pattern being kept in check by the soft tonalities of the wallpaper and textiles. The one concession to richness in the scheme is in the treatment of

the ceiling, which is a riot of extravagant plaster-work in a convincing 17th-century style. Although the same detailed stucco work is encountered in the dining room, this, with its plain panelling, built-in sideboard, stone fireplace and Delft tiles depicting marine scenes is a much more formal environment.

In all of these rooms Mander declares his taste without reservation. He intended his new house to be a definitive statement of both style and fortune and for this reason he devised its showpiece, the Great Parlour. This is the heart of the house and here, taking as their model the medieval great hall, Mander's designers created a *tour de force* of Victorian revivalism.

Below a minstrels' gallery a large inglenook, half-papered in a Morris design, is decorated with carved roses and black and gold stripes. Striped too is the high, vaulted ceiling, beneath which runs a painted frieze by Kempe depicting the story of Orpheus and Eurydice. Around the walls a collection of blue and white porcelain is arranged and in the window bay a writing desk and curved chair covered in Morris's "Tulip and Rose" fabric bear witness to the curious mixture of pomp and informality which was the intended atmosphere of the Victorian Great Hall.

However, it is at the far end of the room that the artistic taste of the period is most effectively summed up. Here hangs Edward Burne-Jones's magnificent painting *Love Among the Ruins*, which depicts on canvas everything Theodore Mander attempted to express in the design and decoration of his house. Placing his medieval figures in a classical frame, Burne-Jones set out to harmonize northern romanticism with the ancient world, just as Morris had tried to do in his poem *The Earthly Paradise*. But more significantly, the picture stands in Wightwick Manor as a symbol of Mander's vision. In creating his dream house Mander was aiming to recapture a vanished world of Olde Englande which had never really existed anywhere other than in the mind of William Morris, one of England's greatest designers.

Above: One of the finest paintings in Wightwick Manor is Sir Edward Burne-Jones's magnificent medieval allegory Love Among the Ruins. *In its unrestrained romanticism, this piece seems to encapsulate all the nostalgia for a bygone age which affected Mander and his architects during the construction and decoration of the house.*

Left: A feature of Wightwick is its large number of fireplaces. Here in the entrance hall we are met by a magnificent beaten-copper fireplace hung with fire irons and pieces of brassware. The length of the hall serves to accentuate the medieval character of the house, whose plan is in fact a clever exercise in deliberate chaos.

WIGHTWICK MANOR, WOLVERHAMPTON,
WEST MIDLANDS
ARCHITECT: EDWARD OULD
CONSTRUCTION: 1887-1893
SEE ALSO GAZETTEER, PAGE 183

Above: The exterior of the old farmhouse at Charleston in Sussex does not give the visitor any clues to the sparkling wit and artistic talent to which it played host over the 60 years during which it was the home of Duncan Grant and Vanessa Bell, the leading lights of the bohemian Bloomsbury Group.

Right: It was in the garden room, an intimate little room filled with an odd collection of furniture and a home-made log-burning fire constructed by Roger Fry, that the family and their friends and guests would congregate after dinner to tell stories, read or play chess. The overmantel, with its mirror held between two semi-nude women, is typical of the painted decoration that gives the house its quirky character.

On 24th September 1916, the novelist Virginia Woolf wrote in a letter to her sister, the painter Vanessa Bell: "I think the country there is superb to live in – I always want to come back again, and one never feels it dull. . . I'm sure, if you get Charleston, you'll end up by buying it forever. If you lived there, you could make it absolutely divine".

The Charleston to which she referred was a farmhouse, near Lewes in Sussex, England. Vanessa and her husband Clive Bell, the art critic, were keen to rent the house and in October 1916 they moved in. Fulfilling Virginia's prediction, they bought it "forever" and today the house is preserved by the charitable trust that was set up by their son Quentin in 1979. It stands as a living testimony to their achievement and a unique surviving example of the Bloomsbury style of domestic decoration.

What we today refer to as the "Bloomsbury" style was the creation of a small group of artists headed by the critic Roger Fry, Vanessa Bell and Duncan Grant. The works of art and design which they produced in London and afterward at Charleston were inextricably intertwined with the school of literature and thought that centred around the writers Lytton Strachey and Clive Bell, who had been students at Cambridge in 1899. Together, this influential circle of friends became known as the Bloomsbury Group, after their headquarters in that area of London. The group evolved a philosophy, in life as much as design, which emphasized the importance of the individual and thrived on a mixture of friendship, creativity, experiment and, notoriously, free love. Bloomsbury reached the height of its influence in the 1920s, before being reinterpreted by a later generation during the 1960s. However, in its first impetus, the Bloomsbury style was largely inspired by the work of the painter and craftsman William Morris. In 1913, the group spawned the Omega Workshops where, in the production of decorated furniture and *objets d'art*, the Bloomsbury artists expressed their reaction against the clutter of the Victorian interior and the stylized exoticism of Art Nouveau.

Charleston

However, the back streets of Bloomsbury proved too claustrophobic for its avant-garde artists. In the city all was bustle and business. They needed room to think and Charleston provided the necessary space and tranquil setting.

From the start, it was clear that Vanessa Bell saw the house itself as a potential work of art. When she and her young family arrived, the walls were whitewashed, both inside and out, presenting a very different vision to the house which greets the present-day visitor. It was a blank canvas waiting for an artist. Quickly at first, and then more gradually and thoughtfully over the years, decorations began to appear. One of the first rooms to be transformed was Clive Bell's study on the right of the main entrance. Vanessa Bell painted the decorative panels in the window overlooking the pond as early as 1916, and the following year Duncan Grant executed the bold still life on the door.

Emerging from this room, avoid the temptation to cross immediately into the dining room; instead turn right and climb the stairs to the upper floor and the library. Here too is an early scheme, with panels painted by Duncan Grant in 1917. The walls are painted in different colours – a classic Bloomsbury trait. On them hang a copy of Raphael's *Colonna Madonna* by Vanessa Bell and a painting of the *Entry into Jerusalem* by Frederick Etchells. The small bathroom next door was installed in 1939 when Clive Bell moved permanently into the house. The bath, which was painted with panels of reclining nudes by art-historian Richard Shone in 1969, serves as a reminder that for more than 60 years the house remained a living assembly of artistic activity.

Adjoining the bathroom, Clive Bell's bedroom offers a good example of the Bloomsbury style at its best. Despite an overall feeling of decorative interest, there is no thoughtless covering of every surface with pattern. The walls have been left quite plain in their *eau de nil* colours – a single central panel of painted trelliswork provides the necessary variety. Instead, Vanessa Bell chose to focus her attention on the 18th-century French bed head, painting the board with a vibrant still life that is reminiscent of those by Henri Matisse. Along the corridor lie two further bedrooms.

Charleston was not only a home to the Bell family and to Duncan Grant; over the years the house became a haven for a stream of visitors and it is not surprising to find alongside Duncan Grant's bedroom one reserved for the economist John Maynard Keynes. Within Duncan Grant's room, through an extravagantly painted door, lies the painter's dressing room, with, under the window, a table painted by him that depicts the figure of Arion riding a dolphin. The curtains or drapes are rare Omega originals in the "Maud" print, dating from 1913.

The spare guest bedroom, its walls hung with paintings by Walter Sickert, Vanessa Bell, Duncan Grant, Nina Hamnett and others, appears comparatively austere. Perhaps the artists felt inclined not to inflict quite so exuberant a decorative scheme as that which they themselves enjoyed upon guests who at any one time might include the writers E.M. Forster and T.S. Eliot, the dancer Frederick Ashton, the composer Benjamin Britten and the singer Peter Pears, the actress Peggy Ashcroft, the art historians Kenneth Clark, Herbert Read and Anthony Blunt and painters too numerous to mention.

Leaving Duncan Grant's rooms and returning downstairs you can almost imagine the ghosts of past guests following you into the dining room and seating themselves in the great red-lacquer Omega chairs, set around the circular painted table, to enjoy one of Vanessa's typical lunches of cold ham, baked potatoes and walnuts, washed down with stout.

Above: The principal feature in the library is a huge bookcase painted by Duncan Grant in 1917.

Left: It is in the studio that the spirit of the artists seems to linger most evidently. Here an unfinished canvas by Duncan Grant rests on the easel. The mantelpiece is crammed with personal memorabilia.

Below: The spare bedroom looks onto the garden and links the natural world to the interior painted by Vanessa.

Leaving the dining room, the passage comes as a surprise, for you notice for the first time the lack of colour in the corridors – a deliberate device, used to emphasize the richness of the rooms themselves. Such richness is perhaps epitomized in the garden room, located along the passage past Clive Bell's study. It was in this room that family and friends would gather after dinner to read books or play chess before what Clive Bell later described as "a curious fire-place, devised and constructed by Roger Fry to heat with logs a particularly chilly room". Above this fireplace, in place of a mirror, stands a painted overmantel of flowers held by two nudes, reminiscent of Jean Auguste Dominique Ingres, executed by Duncan Grant.

While the garden room was kept strictly for formal occasions, the everyday hub of the house was the studio, which is reached by way of the corridor that leads past Vanessa Bell's bedroom. The studio was where, among others, Angelica Garnett, daughter of Vanessa Bell and Duncan Grant, found her spiritual home, later recalling "after breakfast. . .Vanessa and Duncan retired to this area of peace and calm. . .". Music always filled the room – Beethoven, Mozart or Debussy –

crackling out from the gramophone contained within the cupboard painted by Angelica in 1936. It is here, more than anywhere else in the house, that you can sense the presence of the artists. Such an illusion is encouraged by the unfinished bottles of whisky and vodka on the 18th-century chest of drawers and by the contents of the mantelpiece, which is crammed with mementoes. The studio's furniture is typically eclectic – from the 1937 chair made by Heal's of London to the Regency walnut cabinet which once belonged to the novelist W.M. Thackeray but is now filled with a collection of Omega pottery.

It seems natural to walk from the studio into the garden, where the mass of colour found in the house is continued in the spectacular flowerbeds. A small statue of Venus stands on the shelf in a corner of the garden. This seems to embody Charleston, which was described by Roger Fry as "the most peaceful domestic existence conceivable . . . a model of what family life should be", yet, at the same time, it was for over half a century one of the seedbeds of British intellect and a melting pot of ideas. However, at Charleston, Venus, the classical goddess of high art, seems somehow different: from the top of her gracefully modelled torso there blooms a spray of bright wild flowers.

CHARLESTON, LEWES, EAST SUSSEX
ARCHITECTURAL STYLE: VERNACULAR
CONSTRUCTION: 18TH CENTURY
SEE ALSO GAZETTEER, PAGE 181

Left: Around the house, objects are gathered in seemingly indiscriminate groupings which together make curious companions. This mantelpiece in the garden room is a typical example, with its porcelain lion, vase of flowers and hand-painted egg-cup.

Below left: The upstairs bathroom was installed by Clive Bell in 1939. The ever-changing nature of the decoration of the house is well demonstrated by the fact that it was some 30 years later, in 1969, that Richard Shone painted the bath panels with a reclining nude.

Right: Clive Bell's bedroom is a fine example of the Bloomsbury style. The walls have been left undecorated save for a thin section of trelliswork. Instead, the main interest is provided by the painted bedstead, which was decorated by Clive Bell's wife, Vanessa.

Above: Entering the high marble hall of Nissim de Camondo, you are met by the graceful sweep of the main staircase which curves around to the upper storeys. At the foot of the stairs, Venus and Cupid set the style for the 18th-century decorations and furnishings which the mansion was constructed to house in 1914.

Right: The Grand Bureau is the most sumptuously decorated room in the house. Above the glazed doors two nymphs playing musical instruments look down from their grisaille panel onto a collection of Louis-XVI furniture and artefacts. Perhaps the greatest treasure here is the set of Aubusson tapestries which line the walls, telling stories from the fables of La Fontaine.

In a small street of the quiet 17th *arrondissement* of Paris, France, well off the tourist track, a discreet iron gate in a yellow stone wall guards the entrance to what appears to be an 18th-century town house. It is an illusion. Certainly the house is real enough, but rather than dating from the 18th century it was built in the early 20th. However, few passers-by would guess that behind this facade is housed one of the world's greatest single collections of genuine 18th-century antiques. This is the Nissim de Camondo Museum. Its curious name and spectacular contents are permanent reminders of the twin passions of one man, the Count of Camondo; his love for his only son and his obsession with the elegance of a vanished age.

The Camondos, a Spanish family, had fled to Italy under the Inquisition. In the early 19th century they moved to Constantinople where they founded the bank of the same name which established the family fortune. Ennobled in 1867 by Victor Emmanuel II for their part in the unification of Italy, the Camondos subsequently settled in Paris under Napoleon III and bought two *hôtels* on the Parc Monceau. In the refined atmosphere of Second Empire Paris the two young scions of the family, Isaac and Moise, developed into considerable connoisseurs. While Isaac was passionate about the Far East and also chose to patronize the controversial contemporary art of the Impressionists, his cousin Moise exercised a rather more conservative taste. He assembled a collection of 18th-century French *objets d'art*, redolent of the grandeur of the ancien régime which had vanished with the Revolution.

In 1911, on the death of his parents, Moise inherited one of the Parc Monceau houses and immediately set about rebuilding it as a showcase for the treasures which he had accumulated over the past 40 years. Taking for his inspiration Richard Mique's *Petit Trianon* at the Palace of Versailles, his architect, René Sergent, set out to construct an edifice of sufficient grandeur to house Camondo's remarkable collection. By 1914 it was ready: a miniature château in town, enclosed by leafy gardens and set back from the everyday world by a high-walled courtyard.

Nissim

de *Camondo* *M*useum

However, no wall was high enough to shut out the real world and even in this secluded palace the Camondos were struck by the fateful events of 1914. Moise's only son, Nissim, volunteered for the cavalry and subsequently the air force. Three years later he was dead, shot down in the skies over Flanders. Heartbroken, his father shut himself off from the world and on his own death in 1935 he bequeathed his magnificent house and its contents to the French nation, on the condition that it should bear the name of his son, Nissim, and that everything in the house should be left just as it had been during his lifetime.

His wishes were respected and today the house still retains an eerie air of habitation. In the vestibule a gilded bronze clock sets the tone for this most regal of French museums. Beneath it stands one of a pair of ornate consoles, an embodiment of the Rococo style of the 1740s, while on either side classical urns, supported on tall granite columns, provide a note of sobriety. The hall is lit from the well of the grand staircase, to the foot of which the eye is drawn by a sinuous white marble sculpture group of Venus and Cupid. On the landing a pair of lacquered and gilded corner cabinets support two perfume burners dating from 1775, below a gilded lantern of the same era. As you climb the stairs you begin to feel as if you are being drawn back in time to the age of Marie-Antoinette.

Instead of stopping at the upper level, it is perhaps better first to proceed further up the stairs to the topmost floor, where it is possible to capture an aspect of the more intimate side of the house. Here the visitor can explore the family bedrooms and pause for a moment in the relative austerity of the room which still contains the personal effects of the ill-fated Nissim. Also on this floor, at the domestic heart of the house, is the library, which demonstrates Camondo's own scholarship of 18th-century art. Although the decoration is admirably restrained, the carved panelling dating from 1775, the understated Aubusson carpet and the elegant bronze-gilt tripod lamp all carry the unmistakable hallmark of Camondo's good taste.

On descending the stairs, you find yourself once again in the formal part of the house. In the *Petit Bureau*, against red silk walls, hang reminders of a lost world. Above the Turkish marble fireplace, between two fine paintings of Venice by Francesco Guardi, hangs a portrait painted in 1781 by Jean Duplessis of Jacques Necker, the French financier who played an instrumental role in the mismanagement of the Royal economy during the last days of the French monarchy. Around him, almost accusingly, are gathered 17 terracotta reliefs by J. B. Nini which portray key figures of the ancien régime – including Maria Theresa of Austria, Catherine the Great and, ironically, Louis XVI and Marie Antoinette. On a fine Aubusson carpet, dating from 1790, decorated with garlands, flowers and oak leaves, stand two inlaid rosewood display cabinets by Roger Vandercruse, known as Lacroix. Alongside is a suite of furniture in carved and painted wood upholstered in lampas, that fabric so characteristic of the late 18th century. The green watered silk, decorated with white putti and garlands, echoes the twining foliage of the carved wood frieze.

The corridor which leads from the *Petit Bureau* to the *Grand Bureau* is lined with fine porcelain in glass cases, which, in its carefully assembled completeness, bears testimony to Camondo's commitment to the creation of his period piece. The Buffon dinner service which is displayed here is in fact made up from two services. Both dating from the 1780s and made in Sèvres from soft- and hard-paste porcelain, they are decorated with exquisite images of birds in the style of François Boucher and *oeils de perdrix* in green and gold. Alongside sits a Meissen tea and coffee service

painted with birds and flowers and dating from the 1740s, the factory's greatest years and the height of the Rococo.

Camondo's collection is so rich that it is wise to leave his greatest treasure to last. The *Grand Bureau* is where Camondo achieved perhaps the most complete realization of his dream. It is a magical room, a sumptuous, glittering floral gem of the Louis-XVI style which succeeded the Rococo in the 1750s. Lit by 15 candles from a 1780s chandelier, from the collection of the Prince d'Arenberg, the room is dominated by a gilded chimneypiece set above the white marble fireplace which was bought by Camondo from a house in Bordeaux. The chimneypiece, along with the rest of the panelling, is made from carved oak and dates from 1775. Over the doors hang two *grisaille* panels by Piat-Joseph Sauvage which depict children at play and nymphs. These are recalled in the pair of *baccante* candelabra after Claude Michel Clodion which stand on the mantelpiece. This is flanked on either side by two rosewood sideboards with violet inlay which support a pair of rare blue-lacquer vases of the type designed in the 1750s to imitate Chinese porcelain. On two Aubusson carpets, decorated with baskets of flowers, the furniture is arranged in the style of the period. Before the fire stand two *prie-dieux* made in August 1789 by Jean-Baptiste Sene, beside these a pair of *bergères* and around the

room a set of eight chairs by Nicolas-Quinibert Foliot, upholstered in Aubusson tapestry. These are complemented by two screens, one of which, purchased by him from the Wallace collection, demonstrates Camondo's search for precisely the right pieces, as does the bronze bust of Madame la Comte by Guillaume Coustou which came from a Russian collection. However, it is not one single piece in the *Grand Bureau* which impresses, but rather the room's overall effect, to understand which you must look at the walls. These are hung not with pictures, but with a breathtaking set of six Aubusson tapestries, decorated with images from the fables of La Fontaine. One of these tales depicts an old man telling three youths about the value of planting trees for the enjoyment of future generations. "Would you prevent a man of sense from taking pains to please posterity?" he asks, continuing: "It may be I shall see the light of more than one dawn after you are dead". His words seem to ring with a poignant irony since their personal relevance cannot have escaped the creator of this 18th-century treasure house.

NISSIM DE CAMONDO MUSEUM, PARIS
ARCHITECT: RENÉ SERGENT
CONSTRUCTION: 1911-1914
SEE ALSO GAZETTEER, PAGE 170

Far left: The Petit Bureau*, hung with portraits in terracotta of personalities of the ancien régime by J. B. Nini, provides a poignant reminder of the fate of the aristocracy that originally commissioned and owned the furniture and works of art that are housed here. These coveted pieces, which were assembled by Count Camondo during his lifetime, provided the* raison d'être *for his magnificent Paris house. On the overmantel hangs a portrait of the financier Jacques Necker by Jean Duplessis.*

Left: The mantelpiece of the Grand Bureau *is a triumph of gilt and marble.*

Below left: The chairs in the Petit Bureau *are upholstered in green watered silk, decorated with putti and garlands.*

Above: The relatively plain, unassuming exterior of 14 rue de la Rochefoucauld does not hint at the wonders that lie within, in the suite of apartments which were once the home of the highly individual French symbolist painter Gustave Moreau.

Right: Moreau's living accommodation is relatively modest compared to the space given over to his paintings. In this small study-bedroom are gathered personal artefacts and mementoes which had a personal significance for the artist, together with a collection of books, a chess set and, draped across a chair, the ornate ceremonial-dress costume of a Chevalier *of the* Légion d'Honneur, *to which station Moreau was elevated in 1875.*

In 1852, Louis Moreau, an affluent Parisian architect, purchased from the Marquis of Padua a smart town apartment at 14 rue de la Rochefoucauld which he presented to his son Gustave. It was also in this year that Gustave first exhibited one of his paintings at the coveted Salon des Beaux Arts. It was the first step on the ladder to artistic success for the 26-year-old, but young Gustave was a visionary with greater ambitions than to show merely at the Salon. He wanted to paint great pictures – pictures that would take the viewer to the heights and depths of emotion – and it was Gustave's greatest wish that they would be shown to the public together in one place. In 1862, at the age of 36, drawn to the contemplation of his own mortality by the death of his father, he made a note at the bottom of a sketch: "I think of my death and of the fate of all these works and compositions I have taken such trouble to collect. Separately they will perish, but taken as a whole they give an idea of what kind of an artist I was and in what kind of surroundings I chose to live my dreams."

Throughout the following 30 years Moreau achieved great critical success. In 1895 he enlarged his house, building over the small front garden and adding two new picture galleries at the top of the building. He connected these to the rest of the building with a spiral staircase. On his death in 1898, Moreau's wish to display his work to the people was realized. He bequeathed to the nation the house which his father had bought in 1852, and all of the pictures it contained, as a museum of his art. In 1903, the house was finally opened to the public as the Musée National Gustave Moreau, and today it stands just as it was during his lifetime, a monument to this remarkable artist.

From the outside, the Moreau house seems an unremarkable Parisian building of the Second Empire; a solid-stone edifice whose only character is provided by the columns which flank its windows. However, once inside you are transported into another world. In an age when the artistic avant-garde was generally concerned with the depiction of landscape and reality, Moreau's paintings were uniquely cerebral; the visual

Gustave

Moreau Museum

Above: The ormolu clock on the mantelpiece dates from the period of the French Empire of Napoleon, while the small, white figures in biscuit porcelain are from the Sèvres factory.

Below right: In the inlaid cabinet and around the walls are hung a collection of paintings, drawings and photographs which held a personal significance for Gustave Moreau.

Opposite: Moreau lived a simple life in this small room, which in places seems almost shrine-like and gives only the subtlest of hints as to what the visitor is to expect from the two storeys of galleries above which contain the artist's paintings.

antithesis of Impressionism. They sparkle like jewels against the red, silk-covered walls of his cavernous gallery.

Although at first sight the museum appears to be simply an art gallery of his work, Moreau's apartment at 14 rue de la Rochefoucauld looks today exactly as it did in his lifetime. Moreau lived from day to day in a house designed for the contemplation of his life's work. The gallery area of the house contains over 800 paintings and 13,000 drawings and watercolours by the artist. However, before investigating this collection in detail it is best to equip yourself with an under-standing of the character and history of the artist himself. In order to do this we must first visit Moreau's living rooms.

Climbing a few stairs you find yourself in Moreau's inner sanctum. It seems extraordinary that the artist should have lived in so small an area of his huge house. Moreau occupied a modest study-bedroom. It is an intimate little room whose air of seclusion is made all the more visceral by the sombre green of its late 19th-century wallpaper. The room is hung from floor to ceiling with small paintings and drawings, each of which had a particular personal significance for the painter. Renaissance works hang side by side with portraits of family, admired poets, writers and fellow artists. Angels and figures from classical mythology dominate the imagery just as they do Moreau's own work. This classical influence is carried through to the furniture and in particular to the Empire-style bed with its two neo-Grecian heads and acanthus leaves on the headboard. The artist's considerable intellect is also evinced here in the rows of books which line the wall and in the wooden chess set, apparently abandoned in mid-game. However, it is clear from the collection of fine *objets d'art* gathered here that Moreau's theorizing did not preclude an appreciation of the decorative. Moreau demonstrates his discernment and connoisseurship in the ormolu Empire clock and the pair of French enamelled urns on the mantelpiece and the small group of Sèvres biscuit-porcelain figures.

But the real world of 19th-century France and the path of the artist to professional success is not entirely forgotten. Here we see it in the splendid full-dress uniform of the *Chevaliers* of the *Légion d'Honneur*, to which honourable body Moreau was appointed in 1875.

In effect, the artist lived a double life. Although by day he might have been regarded as something of a mystery by the majority of patrons of art of his age, Moreau was by night a denizen of the Parisian society of the *belle époque*. Throughout his life, he attended the theatre and opera regularly and in his youth he was quite a dandy. By contemporary accounts he was of diminutive stature with a fiery temper. Although his speaking voice was described as "metallic sounding" he was particularly renowned for his own fine singing voice. Many a fashionable Parisian soirée was not considered complete without the sound of Monsieur Moreau's accomplished tenor. Perhaps the modest size of the artist's apartments can be partly explained by the fact that he was hardly ever at home. Moreau was constantly seen at the smartest Paris salons. The Comtesse Greffulhe (who inspired Marcel Proust's *Duchesse de Guermantes*) and the Comte de Montesquiou vied for his attendance at their glittering parties and he was consistently lauded by such luminaries of aestheticism as the writers Marcel Proust, Oscar Wilde and J. K. Huysmans and the composer Claude Debussy.

With the physical evidence of the painter's character fresh in your mind, you are ready to enter the gallery, the main salon of which was previously the apartment occupied by his parents in later life. Here you can meet Moreau face to face in a small self-portrait, painted in 1850. The

Opposite: The walls of Moreau's galleries are hung with paintings. The central focus is the terrifying tableau of Jupiter and Semele. Painted in 1895, the subject concerns the Greek myth of the girl Semele who, obsessed with the god Jupiter, dared to ask to visit him in heaven. Her wish was granted, but in the course of their embrace, which resulted in the creation of Bacchus, Semele died in a fit of divine ecstasy. The picture is a complex tapestry of characters and events. Most tellingly, Cupid flies out of the canvas, hiding his face in sorrow at the prospect of this suicidal love. Jupiter himself, bolt upright on his bejewelled throne, is a figure of unrelenting terror whose Gorgon stare freezes the viewer with penetrating blankness.

Left: The two storeys of galleries are reached by an elegant spiral staircase of wrought iron.

young artist gazes out with a somewhat quizzical expression and at the same time welcomes us into his home and invites us to explore his gallery. Moreau was a great friend of Edgar Degas and a teacher at the École des Beaux Arts of, among others, Henri Matisse and Georges Rouault and you can almost imagine the witty and influential conversations which must have taken place in the shadow of these paintings.

This strange house was above all a place of contemplation and a haven for the painter from the very different social life which he lived outside its walls. Perhaps the words which best describe both house and owner are those uttered by the hero of Huysmans' infamously scandalous novel *Against Nature*, published in 1884: "Gustave Moreau. . . The painter seemed to have wished to assert his intention of remaining outside the bounds of time . . . this great artist, this mystical pagan, this illuminee who could shut out the modern world so completely as to behold, in the heart of present-day Paris, the awful visions and magical apotheoses of other ages."

GUSTAVE MOREAU MUSEUM, PARIS
ARCHITECT: UNKNOWN
CONSTRUCTION: c.1850-1895
SEE ALSO GAZETTEER, PAGE 170

Above: Although the exterior walls of the house of Marcel Proust's "Tante Léonie" at Illiers-Combray in Normandy are not exactly as they would have appeared during his lifetime, the house still exudes that air of friendship which filled the young author with anticipation whenever he returned to it during his weekend visits as a child.

Right: The dining room is given its sepulchral atmosphere by the mahogany panelling which lines its traditional Norman earth-and-straw walls. The central table, with its lace tablecloth and Henri II-style chairs, is quintessentially French in appearance.

"I raised to my lips a spoonful of the tea in which I had soaked a morsel of the cake. No sooner had the warm liquid mixed with the crumbs touched my palate than a shudder ran through me and I stopped, intent upon the extraordinary thing that was happening to me." With these words, among the best known in the history of French literature, Marcel Proust launches the reader upon a voyage of exploration into his memory of the past. In the course of his epic work, *A la Recherche du Temps Perdu (Remembrance of Things Past)*, Proust explores in minute detail the sensations and perceptions of a single life, from childhood to maturity. Among other things, the work is a recollection of place. As the narrator continues: "Suddenly the memory revealed itself. The taste was that of the little piece of madeleine which on Sunday mornings at Combray . . . my aunt Léonie used to give me . . . Immediately the old gray house upon the street, where her room was, rose up like a stage set . . ."

It might surprise the reader of Proust's fiction to discover that the house of Tante Léonie actually does exist. Here, in the little Norman town of Illiers-Combray, truth meets fiction.

Proust's "old gray house" at 4 rue du Saint-Esprit actually belonged to his uncle, Jules Amiot, the local draper. Amiot dealt in wine from the recently established French colony in Algeria and lived at Combray with Proust's aunt Elizabeth with the fortune he had made from his businesses.

Proust spent many happy weekends at Illiers in his early childhood until the age of nine and a half. Then, in 1881, he began to suffer from asthma and was advised by his doctor to holiday at the seaside rather than in the country. He was to visit the house only once more in his lifetime, to attend the funeral of his aunt in June 1886. In the course of that day, Proust caught sight of an old lady who was living in a small bedroom overlooking the market-place. She was in fact his grandmother, who herself died only three years later. The Tante Léonie of *A la Recherche du Temps Perdu* is in effect a compound of these two indomitable women, Proust's aunt and his grandmother, but the memories evoked by that

M a r c e l

Proust Museum

brief return visit remained with the writer for many years to come and it was these thoughts which lay at the back of his mind when, prompted by the madeleine, he began to write his masterpiece.

After the death of Proust's uncle Jules in 1912, the house changed ownership three times, before being bought in 1947 by the Amiot's grand-daughter, who subsequently gave it to the Proust society in 1976. On account of the vicissitudes of the various owners the exterior of the house is not, sadly, as it would have appeared in Proust's day, having been given a picturesque Norman half-timbered appearance which disguises its famous "grayness". However, inside the interiors which so moved Proust's youthful imagination have been painstakingly recreated.

Proust himself admitted that the little town was "a trifle depressing" and it is fortunate that today the visitor enters the house from the garden, which still resembles the typical late 19th-century pleasure garden that was laid out by the novelist's uncle Jules.

The downstairs rooms lie off a gloomy passage-way, filled with what Proust himself describes as "religious darkness", which runs between the garden and the front doors. Given the importance which Proust attaches to food in his works, it seems only fitting that you should enter the kitchen first. Situated on the righthand side of the passageway, this is the kingdom of the fictional maid Françoise, a confection of the Prousts' own cook Félice and that of the author's grandmother, Ernestine. In the writer's imagination, Françoise wore a bonnet "as stiff and fragile as if it had been

Left: From a corner of the drawing room, a portrait of Proust himself looks out with an expression that is at once both effete and incredulous. Beside him, a painting from the 19th-century French Orientalist school is a reminder of the livelihood of Proust's uncle, the wine-importing Jules Amiot who inspired the Uncle Adolphe of A la Recherche du Temps Perdu.

Above: The room closest in appearance to Proust's narrative is surely the kitchen, where the red-tiled floor would gleam "like porphyry". "The back kitchen seemed not so much the cave of Françoise as a little temple of Venus. It would be overflowing with the offerings of the dairyman, the fruiterer, the greengrocer, come sometimes from distant villages to

made of spun sugar" and here we find it, hanging on the back of the kitchen door.

It was here in the kitchen that Françoise created the delicacies savoured by the narrator's epicurean aunt Léonie and today the room is just as he describes it: "its red-tiled floor gleaming like porphyry". At one end stands the black-leaded cooking range on which rests a loaf of bread, whose sweet baking smell Proust so vividly recalls. It is easy to imagine Françoise, "a colonel with all the forces of nature for her subalterns . . . stirring the coals, putting the potatoes to steam and, at the right moment, finishing over the fire those culinary masterpieces which had been first got ready in some of the great array of vessels . . . tubs and boilers and cauldrons and fish kettles . . . moulds for pastry . . . an entire collection of pots and pans of every shape and size." Here they all are before you and on the table are all the ingredients, or as Proust saw them "exquisite creatures who had been pleased to assume vegetable form".

Along the passageway from the kitchen is the dining room, a dark sanctuary, typical of the houses of Illiers, in which the traditional walls of earth and straw have been covered with mahogany panelling. On a table, surrounded with late 19th-century bourgeois chairs in the Henri II style and covered with a lace tablecloth, sits a bowl of the exquisite madeleines, the taste of which provoked in Proust's narrator an immediate sensation of re-living the past.

On leaving the dining room, turn a corner and ascend the winding staircase to the bedrooms. Upstairs you will find the rooms of Tante Léonie,

dedicate to the goddess the first fruits of the fields."

On display here are the huge cast-iron cooking range and the "great array of vessels" in every shape and size that Françoise, Proust's fictional cook, employed in her creation of the mouth-watering dishes that the author described so vividly in his works.

Top right: The aquamarine painted door from the little informal drawing room opens out onto the Amiots' back garden, which Proust's uncle Jules laid out with such care and devotion. In the summer, the room is filled with the vivid scent of the plants, flowers and fruit trees beyond, which Proust describes with such imagination in his works.

including her sitting room, with its antimacassars and stamped velvet *prie-dieu*, and next door her bedroom whose smell so enraptured Proust that he returned there "with an unconfessed gluttony to wallow in the central, glutinous, insipid, indigestible and fruity smell of the flowered bedspread". It was in this room that Tante Léonie lay perpetually, overlooking the street in which she would survey "like the Persian princes of old, the daily but immemorial chronicles of Combray, which she would discuss in detail later with Françoise."

On the opposite side of the corridor was Proust's own bedroom, where he often lay on the bed reading. Despite its cool red tiles, it seemed to him that the room "quivered with the effort to defend its frail, transparent coolness against the afternoon sun behind its almost closed shutters". It is a simple room, with a box bed framed by lace drapes, and, as Proust himself pointed out, is "filled with things of no use".

Returning downstairs you finally enter the little drawing room of the house. This is the imaginary room of the narrator's uncle Adolphe which, even with its windows open to let in the sun, "would

never fail to emit that oddly cool odour, suggestive at once of woodlands and the ancien régime. . ." The pair of 19th-century Orientalist paintings which hang on the walls of this room are souvenirs of the Algerian wine trade which had brought uncle Jules his fortune. But on entering the room it is another picture, on an easel in the corner, which catches your eye. An elegant- and frail-looking young man, dressed in the formal frock coat of the late 19th century and wearing a thin moustache, stares from the canvas with an air of blank incredulity. It is Marcel Proust himself, a copy after Jacques Émile Blanche, and well might he marvel at this house which, with its abundance of sights and smells to delight the senses, so easily conjures up in the mind of the visitor the feelings and memories whose recollection was for him the work of a lifetime.

Opposite and Above: Proust's bedroom is simply furnished. It was here that he would lie, trying in vain to escape the heat of the afternoon sun behind the drapes of the box bed. It was to no avail and the heat simply aggravated the writer's dissatisfaction with what he himself called a room "filled with things of no use".

Left: Here we find the bonnet of Felice, Proust's own cook, who was personified by Françoise in his narrative.

THE MARCEL PROUST MUSEUM,
ILLIERS-COMBRAY, NORMANDY
ARCHITECTURAL STYLE: VERNACULAR
CONSTRUCTION: UNKNOWN
SEE ALSO GAZETTEER, PAGE 170

Above: The entrance façade of the Villa Barbaro at Maser is a tour de force of Andrea Palladio's style. The elaborate capitals are taken from the temple of Fortuna Virilis at Rome. The façade is decorated with Ionic columns which support a broken cornice and project in front of the main body of the house. The two arcaded wings were designed to house the servants of the household.

Right: Inside, the entire villa is decorated with frescoes by the 16th-century Italian master Paulo Veronese. Here in the gallery, the artist cleverly employs illusionary images of classical maidens to give added credence to his own portrait and that of one of the Barbarini servants who appears to enter the room through the clever trompe l'oeil *doors.*

"As certainly 'tis highly creditable and convenient for a gentleman to have a house in the city . . . so perhaps he may receive no less pleasure and advantage from a house in the country." So wrote the architect Andrea Palladio in 1569 in his celebrated treatise "I Quattro Libri dell'Architettura". He was not merely theorizing. Since 1550, Palladio had been engaged in constructing just such a house for two country gentlemen. But this was no ordinary house. The villa which Palladio built for the brothers Daniele and Marcantonio Barbaro on the slopes of the Asolo hills at their estate at Maser, some 50 kilometres (19 miles) north-west of Venice, is one his most elegant creations. The Villa Barbaro is an affirmation of the characters of its owners. The Barbaro brothers were true Renaissance men. While on the one hand, farmers of a considerable estate, they were also men of learning and sophistication. Both were personal friends of Palladio and both moved in the eclectic artistic circles that characterized Venice at that time. Daniele Barbaro had also been a close friend of the poet and Latin scholar Pietro Bembo, had translated Vitruvius's classic ten-volume treatise on architecture "De Architettura", studied Aristotle and was Patriarch elect of Aquilea of the Venetian Republic. Marcantonio, for his part, combined a similarly scholarly mind with a high public office as an ambassador and a shrewd business sense. However, notwithstanding these considerable talents, both brothers also had a working knowledge of farming. The Barbaro brothers may have been gentlemen farmers but they understood the agriculture on which their livelihood depended. While other Venetian noblemen of the period might be content to construct country houses as weekend retreats, Daniele and Marcantonio Barbaro made their country villa a permanent home.

Employing their friend Palladio to design their house was the first demonstration of such an intention. The architect's plan for the Villa reflects the essential communion between culture and nature that permeated not only the minds of his clients but the wider spirit of Humanism which was abroad in 16th-century Venice. In his treatise,

Villa Barbaro

Palladio was later to write: "Since architecture, like all the other arts, imitates nature, nothing [in it] can satisfy that [which] is foreign from [that] which is found in nature". The tenacity with which Palladio adhered to this tenet would have been evident from the moment that the 16th-century visitor approached the house. The arcades which link the central block of the house to its two flanking pavilions provided accommodation for the servants and they are also a simple and efficient means of communication between all parts of the house in all weathers. Palladio, while emphasizing the harmonious aspects of classical form, also had a gift for the practical. Although clearly visible from the gate, it is not the service arcades that greet you today, but the jutting entrance hall of the house which projects toward the front and is open to the light from three sides, thus further emphasizing that harmony with nature which was the architect's goal. This projecting facade is fancifully decorated with Ionic columns and broken cornices and capitals based on those of the temple of Fortuna Virilis in Rome.

However, it is not until you enter the main hall that you become aware of the true magnificence of the Villa. Before you are the first of a series of frescoes by the Venetian painter Paolo Veronese which run throughout the entire house. A contemporary of Andrea Palladio and friend of Marcantonio and Daniele Barbaro, Veronese was commissioned by the brothers at the same time as the architect to decorate the villa with what have come to be regarded as some of his finest works. While it is possible that Palladio might not have approved of this tampering with his architecture, as, uniquely, his writings make no mention of his painterly collaborator, the resulting blend of architecture and decoration cannot be denied its consummate success. Veronese uses Palladio's elegant structure with sensitivity as the framework for some of the most ambitious *trompe l'oeil* murals ever attempted.

Beginning in the vaulted main salon, Veronese worked his way through the villa room by room toward the front, where, in the flanking chambers of the facade he painted the scenes from the story of Bacchus which meet us today. His overall theme, ingeniously concocted by his patrons from ancient Greek texts by Pausanias and others, typically concerns the workings of a Humanist universe presided over by Love, Peace and Fortune.

In the square salon Veronese painted the ceiling with an image of a celestial divinity in an effulgence of light, surrounded by Olympian deities. Below, figures representing the elements and the seasons once again evoke the theme of harmony with nature established by the architect. Not all of the artist's images are quite so lofty in their aspirations and the more human side of "truth to nature" is to be found in Veronese's sensitive portraits of Marcantonio's wife Giustiniana, their children, nanny and pets – a cat, a dog, a parrot and a monkey. Beyond them, through arches both real and illusionary, we see vignettes of the very countryside which surrounds the house, intermingled with a fanciful landscape of antiquity.

After the salon's awesome Olympian glories, the gallery, with its *trompe l'oeil* classical maidens, seems relatively restrained in appearance. But this contrast is carefully calculated as we proceed into a chamber decorated with an *Allegory of Conjugal Love* which is intended to reflect the happiness of the household. On the north side of the house, in a room which overlooks the wide courtyard, Veronese has painted a didactic Christian cycle of the Virtues which emphasizes the sort of Christian Humanism which meant as much to the owners of the Villa Barbaro as it did to the artist and architect alike.

Above: It is often difficult to discern the real from the imaginary in this extraordinary interior. Here a genuine plaster door case is set off by intricately modelled architecture which the artist has painted before a landscape vista. In the foreground, Veronese has included one of his patron's favourite dogs.

Left: The painted decorations are continued throughout the villa, filling each of the rooms with a different atmosphere. Astride the cornice of the door sit Pan and Pomona, the gods of pleasure. The eye is also drawn toward the fanciful countryside of ancient ruined landscapes which decorates the walls. Even on the ceiling Veronese continues his deception with a complex trompe l'oeil architectural schema that incorporates several different levels of painted decoration – from realistic tableaux to painted cornicing and sculpture.

At the rear of the villa, the garden room, with its frescoes of mountainous landscapes, seascapes and scenes from an imaginary ancient world, leads out to a small garden and semi-circular fountain recess in which the classical figures of Veronese's frescoes appear to have been transformed into marble. This is the Nymphaem, created by the sculptor Alessandro Vittoria, an ornate confection of elaborate festoons and cornices containing statues of the ancient deities, each one accompanied by an appropriate epigram.

Walking back inside the house it is possible that your eye might for an instant be captured by the figure of a young gentleman who enters the corridor through an open door. It is Paulo Veronese himself who greets us, complete with doffed cap and coy smile. But he is merely a painted illusion. As a parting gesture the artist has depicted himself in paint, and seems to want us to remain a little longer in this enchanting, witty world in which humanist principles and the skills of both artist and architect are so perfectly combined to unite nature with artifice.

VILLA BARBARO, MASER, TREVISO
ARCHITECT: ANDREA PALLADIO
CONSTRUCTION: 1550-1560
SEE ALSO GAZETTEER, PAGE 174

Far left: Visitors to the Villa Barbaro might be forgiven for taking this door for a painted illusion. In fact it is real. The extent to which the door blends into the surrounding painted decoration is a tribute to the mastery of Veronese and indirectly to the architect Andrea Palladio, whose magnificent structural creation the artist took as the ground for his own work.

Above and Left: Quite apart from the wealth of painted decoration, the villa is given its sense of classical proportion and harmony by the careful design of Palladio. A typical example is this long corridor which passes through numerous rooms and emphasizes the sense of scale and proportion which underlies the entire house. Even here Veronese is unable to resist adding his own witty touch to Palladio's creation with a figure at the end of the corridor.

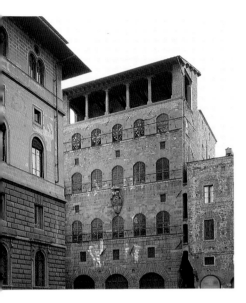

Above: The facade of the Palazzo Davanzati, with its open loggia, towers above the narrow Florentine street which it has dominated since its construction toward the middle of the 14th century. The coat of arms that decorates its walls is that of the Davanzati family, who, in 1578, bought the building from the successors of the Davizzi family for whom it had originally been built.

Right: To enter the Palazzo is to step back 400 years to the Florence of the early Renaissance. The walls of the Parakeet Room are painted with geometric patterns, interlaced with birds, which give the walls of this medieval house their air of opulence. As the decoration reaches the ceiling it becomes more elaborate with trompe l'oeil castellations and foliate vignettes. In contrast to the outside of the house, it is the Davizzi coat of arms that dominates the fireplace of this room, which is filled with 16th-century Florentine furniture.

Florence is a city of palaces. Her many *palazzi* reflect the struggles that lasted from the 14th to the 19th centuries in which noble families strove to out-do each other's material wealth. In the via Porta Rossa, close to the Mercato Nuovo, stands one such palace. The Palazzo Davanzati is unique among Florentine houses. While around it other palaces have changed with the centuries, embracing each new fashion in interior decoration to reflect the good taste and ever-increasing budget of their owners, this palace is stuck in a moment in time. To enter its walls is to journey back five centuries to the early Renaissance of the 1400s. But the Palazzo Davanzati has greater significance than this. It provides a link across 500 years between two men. On the surface Bernardo Davanzati, a 16th-century man of letters, and Elia Volpi, the early 20th-century antiques dealer had little in common. However, the one conviction that they did both share was their love for the Palazzo Davanzati. This link seems all the more extraordinary when you realize that neither man was the architect. Nothing is known of the man that built the Palazzo for the Davizzi family toward the end of the 14th century, but the presence of the family that commissioned him is still felt today. Despite the many changes in ownership which the house has undergone in its chequered history, and the fact that the Davanzati coat of arms hangs above the entrance gates, it is still the Davizzi who look down upon you today as you enter the courtyard of what was originally their house.

The main feature of the irregularly shaped courtyard which lies beyond the entrance gates is the covered staircase that runs through the middle of the building to the high loggia which crowns its roof. In the courtyard, below a relief of the Papal coat of arms, an inscription on a pillar points to the illustrious past of the Davanzati family. It commemorates the investiture of Niccolò Davanzati, who did much to enlarge the Palazzo, as Knight of the Golden Spur by Pope Eugenius IV. His elevation was not the first honourable milestone in the history of the family. A Davanzati had fought against the Guelphs at Monteperti in 1260 and Niccolò himself had been responsible for

Davanzati Palace

Above: On the upper storeys of the house, water is drawn up from the well by a system of pulleys.

Bottom right: The main feature of the courtyard is the covered staircase which carries you up into the heart of the house. Close to its foot a column bears an inscription commemorating the investiture of Niccolò Davanzati as a Knight of the Golden Spur.

Far right: The studded wooden shutters of the great hall reflect the mood of austerity which pervades the house. This cannot have been a comfortable place in which to spend the winter and at any time of year the palace would have been lacking in creature comforts.

founding the convent of Doccia in 1413. However, it was a later member of the family, Bernardo, who was to secure the place of the Davanzati in the pages of Florentine history.

Born in 1529, Bernardo spent the first years of his adult life developing a thriving mercantile business in Florence and France. Having made his fortune in this way, he was then free to indulge in his true passion for classical literature, philosophy and art here in the magnificent *palazzo* that he bought from the Davizzis' successors in 1578. Bernardo's chief achievements in later life were two works which together show his love of learning and his passion for life: he translated Tacitus and he wrote a standard treatise on viniculture.

It is not strictly true to say that the house which we see today is exactly as Bernardo would have known it. Having been sold by the Davanzati family in 1838, following the suicide of the last in their line, the house changed hands many times until it was bought by the renowned antiques collector Professor Elia Volpi in 1904. It was Volpi who began the restoration work that was later to be completed by the Florentine Museums commission.

Climbing the staircase from the courtyard you find yourself in the heart of Elia Volpi's vision. The characteristic, calculated austerity of the 15th-century Florentine *palazzo* is exemplified here in the Great Hall, with its painted stone walls, coffered ceiling and studded wooden shutters. Like the rest of the house, the room contains good examples of furniture of the 14th and 15th centuries. A few everyday artefacts, scattered around the room, give the visitor a clue as to the lifestyle of its inhabitants during the early Renaissance. Here are an hour glass and a lute, there a compass and a backgammon board.

Next door we find the dining room, dark by contrast, and next to it two rooms named after the murals which are their only decoration – the Peacock Room and the Parakeet Room. Climbing upstairs we reach the bedrooms. The main bedroom, known as the bridal chamber, boasts walls painted with a patchwork of family crests in contrasting colours, topped with an impressive 14th-century frieze. Probably painted for the wedding of Tommaso Davizzi to Catelana degli Alberti in 1395, it depicts the French medieval romance of the Chastelaine de Vergi. All the wall decorations in the house were uncovered by Volpi, who removed the whitewash that had concealed them for hundreds of years. Other revelations are the inscriptions that cover the walls, recording in detail the history of the Palazzo's original owners.

The general impression that strikes you during your tour of the Palazzo Davanzati is the house's general lack of comfort. Although the polychrome wallpaintings fill the rooms with colour, this is not by any means an opulent interior. Apart from these murals the decoration consists of few busts and fewer pictures. Most of the wall decoration takes the form of tapestry, and floors are largely of natural, uncovered stone. The rooms are draughty, providing a cool haven in the hot Florentine summer, but offering no protection whatsoever from the freezing winters that often descend on Tuscany. It must have been a comfortless existence for the inhabitants of the Palazzo, lightened only by the warmth generated by the large open fires that dominate each room. The scorch marks above the fireplace in the Parakeet Room and the smoky appearance of the frieze above testify to the fire's importance in this otherwise cheerless dwelling.

Further evidence of the lifestyle of the Palazzo's original occupants is provided by the trapdoors in the floor. These were not a means of entrance but a method of defence. We should not forget that the Palazzo Davanzati was built in an age when Florence was a city beset by raging vendettas between rival families. As well as being the family seat, every *palazzo* also had to serve as an impregnable fortress. It was down these trapdoors in the floor that in times of attack the Davizzi, and in due course their successors, the Davanzati, would drop heavy cannonballs or pour boiling oil over their attackers. Another trapdoor in the floor leads to the well-hole which originally would have supplied the entire house with water.

Climbing the last few steps of the central staircase we reach the roof. Here, in a long, open loggia you are able to gaze out over this romantic early Renaissance city, its skyline punctuated by the towers of its many historical palaces, knowing that you have been allowed a small but revealing glimpse into the rich and varied past which hides behind its doors.

DAVANZATI PALACE, FLORENCE
ARCHITECT: UNKNOWN
CONSTRUCTION: MID-14TH CENTURY
SEE ALSO GAZETTEER, PAGE 174

Above: Even the smallest closets are decorated with wall paintings.

Far left: The main bedroom is decorated with an heraldic pattern linking the coat of arms of Francesco Davizzi to that of his bride Catelana degli Alberti, who were married from this house in 1395. Above, the coats of arms of illustrious families with whom the Davizzi had a link are displayed against a background of trees and peacocks. The splendid bed dates from the late 17th century.

Left: The kitchen displays the awesome selection of levers and pulleys that were required for medieval cooking.

*Above: Pilate's House in Seville is
protected from the outside world by a high
wall. Passing through the central arch, the
visitor should not forget to look at the
jasper cross that is fixed to the wall. It is a
relic from the Holy Land, brought back
by the builder of the house, Don Fadrique
Enriquez de Ribera, in 1521 and
represents the guiding force behind the
creation of this remarkable house.*

*Right: In the main courtyard of the house
stands a white marble fountain, supported
by dolphins, which is observed from the
four corners of the square by classical
statues of ancient deities. The trelliswork
that decorates the balcony serves to
emphasize the Moorish influence in
Spanish architecture of the period.*

I n October 1521 Don Fadrique Enriquez de
Ribera, first Marqués de Tarifa, returned from
a pilgrimage to the Holy Land to his native city of
Seville. With him he brought a cross made from
jasper and this he nailed to the wall of the house
which his father had begun some 40 years before
in 1480. It was the first act in the continued
construction of the Casa de Pilatos, the house of
the Enriquez family, which Don Fadrique named
after Pontius Pilate's headquarters in Jerusalem,
the ruins of which he had visited on his travels.
The placing of the cross was more than a caprice
on the part of the Marqués. Don Fadrique was a
deeply religious man and positioned the cross after
careful calculations. The distance between the
jasper cross in the Casa de Pilatos and the great
cross of the Cruz de Campo in Seville is exactly
the same as the distance between the ruins of
Pontius Pilate's house in the Holy Land and the
hill of Calvary on which Christ was crucified.

However, apart from his unquestionable piety
Don Fadrique also had a considerable capacity for
intellectual matters. He was a generous and
informed patron of the arts and at the splendid
house which he and his successor Don Per Afan,
first Duque de Alcalà, embellished over the next
ten years he entertained the wits and cognoscenti
of 16th-century Spain. Here at the Casa de Pilatos
the Mannerist painter, poet, sculptor and priest
Pablo de Cespedes rubbed shoulders with, among
others, such contemporary cultural figures as the
Herreras – Antonio the historian and the poet
Fernando – together with the lyric poet Don Luis
de Góngora y Argote and even Miguel Cervantes,
author of *Don Quixote*. Don Fadrique and many
of his immediate successors truly believed that the
Spanish aristocracy of the 16th century was following in the artistically philanthropic footsteps of the
15th-century Medici in Florence.

Today their house survives as a demonstration
in stone of the depth of that belief and displays the
considerable connoisseurship of its owners in its
eclectic blend of architectural styles. The house is
a pleasing fusion of the Moorish, Renaissance and
Gothic styles that flourished in Mediterranean
Europe during the 16th century.

Pilate's House

The simple exterior of the outer walls does not betray the sumptuous flights of fancy which lie within. Here is Don Fadrique's jasper cross, fixed to the wall on the left of the marble gateway.

Beyond the doors is a courtyard, dominated by the striking blue and white roof tiles of the staircase tower, with its painted escutcheon of the ducal coat of arms. The house has a Moorish ground plan with an inner courtyard, two storeys and guest chambers. Beyond the second gateway lies the central courtyard of the plan, surrounded by shady arcades. In the middle sits a magnificent fountain carved from white marble, topped by a bust of Neptune and supported by leaping dolphins. The painted and inlaid decoration of the walls and arches is clearly influenced by that of the nearby palace of the Alcazar, although it also incorporates elements of the late Gothic and Renaissance styles. In each of the four corners of the courtyard stands a huge classical sculpture of the late Roman period, most notably of the goddesses Ceres and Pallas Pacifer, and the arcades themselves are adorned with niches which contain busts of Roman emperors. However, undoubtedly the most impressive aspect of the main courtyard is the use of Moorish-inspired *azulejos* (tiles) in gentle blue, white and yellow to decorate the lower half of the walls.

On the righthand side of the courtyard is the garden, which is reached through a vestibule that contains carved Moorish *ajaraca* (trelliswork) and *jameces* (window shutters) under a coffered ceiling. The garden is particularly Moorish in appearance, with its towering jacaranda tree, fountains and palm trees, although it also reveals a European influence in its yellow roses and hedges.

Other rooms off the courtyard are lined with colourful *azulejos* typical of Moorish Seville and richly carved stonework. As you proceed up the imposing staircase, past walls faced with more *azulejos*, look up at the cupola-style ceiling whose dome was copied from the famous Salón de los Embajadores in the Alcazar. Sadly, most of the works of art and the library, once the focal point of the upstairs rooms, have now been transferred to Madrid. However, the house still preserves something of the taste of its owners in its small museum of antiquities. Reflecting the character of its founders, the Casa de Pilatos is even today filled with beautiful things, including a series of mural decorations on the theme of Daedalus and

Icarus by the Sevillian painter, writer and poet Francisco Pacheco. The copy of Murillo's *Virgen de la Servilleta* reminds us that among all this grandeur, Don Fadrique and Don Per Afan were essentially religious men.

Descending again to enter the little tiled chapel, with its Gothic arch and *plateresco* ceiling, you arrive at the spiritual heart of the house. The short pillar inside is a copy of the pillar at which Christ was supposedly scourged and its original once stood in the house of Pontius Pilate in Jerusalem. The pillar, which was presented to Don Per Afan by Pope Pius V, was the inspiration behind the design of this hidden jewel of Seville: the physical expression of one man's faith.

Above: With its proliferation of leafy vegetation, the garden courtyard provides a welcome foil for the ordered architecture of the arcade.

Left: Around the courtyard runs an arcade lined with the busts of Roman emperors. However, its main attraction is the dazzling and colourful tilework which covers the lower half of its walls. This element works well with the classic Moorish stone carving which decorates the underside of the arches.

PILATE'S HOUSE, SEVILLE, ANDALUCIA
ARCHITECTS: DON FADRIQUE ENRIQUEZ DE
RIBERA AND DON PER AFAN
CONSTRUCTION: 1480-1531
SEE ALSO GAZETTEER, PAGE 178

Above: The exterior of the palace of Charlottenhof in the park of Sanssouci at Potsdam is characteristic of the simple style espoused by its architect Karl Friedrich Schinkel in his mature period. The porch, designed in the severe Doric order of Greek architecture, is perfectly complemented by the plain white stone in which it is built. A keynote of colour is provided by the blue shutters.

Right: The large hall, which forms the heart of the house, is a celebration of neoclassicism. It is hung with brightly coloured watercolours, taken from Raphael's frescoes in the Vatican, and furnished with pieces of antique sculpture, including a statue of David by Johann Josef Imhof and Ganymede by August Wredow. A Roman-style lantern is suspended from the ceiling above a console table, the marbled top of which is supported by lions linked by stretchers of light Etruscan-style filigree.

I n March 1826 Crown Prince Frederick William of Prussia received a belated Christmas present from his father, King Frederick William III. It was a country estate – a house set within a landscaped park close to King Frederick the Great's palace of Sanssouci outside Potsdam. The Prince was a man of sophisticated tastes, particularly in the spheres of architecture and design. Not only had he carried out an extensive study of classical antiquities but he had also travelled to Paris at the first opportunity after the fall of Napoleon in 1815 in order to meet the French neoclassicist designer Pierre François Fontaine. Together with his colleague Charles Percier, Fontaine had virtually created the Empire style which had taken Europe by storm over the previous 20 years.

It was clear from the outset that Prince Frederick William would make considerable alterations to the unfashionable manor house on his newly acquired estate. Built in the 1750s, it had come to be known as Schloss Charlottenhof, after the previous owner Charlotte von Gentzkow. However, despite his admiration for Fontaine, it was not to the French architect that the Prince turned to renovate the house, but to Karl Friedrich Schinkel, a native German designer who had just returned from a visit to Britain.

Schinkel was a talented all-rounder, architect, decorator and artist. Although he began his career as an apostle of the Gothic school, the simplicity of classicism quickly came to dominate his work. However, Schinkel's talents were not limited to those of a great neoclassical architect. He is also recognized as the designer who tempered the excesses of the Empire style with his countrymen's natural restraint, hinting at the cool chic of the Biedermeier style which was to come in the 1830s. With the commission to re-model Schloss Charlottenhof, Schinkel was able to put his ideas into practice.

For his framework Schinkel took the shell of the 18th-century building. Having demolished the mansard roof, he went on to create a new frontage with deep windows and an imposing stepped and pedimented Doric entrance porch. "The building

Charlottenhof

plan", he wrote, "had to utilize as much of the existing structure as possible". Yet, within this constraint the new building was, in Prince Frederick's words, to have "the loveliest possible form" and become that ideal place which throughout his life he was to refer to as "Siam, the land of the free". It is clear, even on approaching the house, that Schinkel was completely successful in satisfying his patron's exacting brief.

The house rises above a small, tree-enclosed lawn, its facade presenting a stark classical contrast to the surrounding foliage. The severity of the white stone is cleverly articulated by the painted shutters. Outside, a pair of bronze deer stand guard alongside two stone seats in the form of lions, also designed by Schinkel.

Beyond the two exterior sliding doors, cleverly conceived by the Crown Prince himself, lies the vestibule, the central focus of the palace, which unites the servants' quarters at street level with the apartments on the upper floor. The discreet entrance to the servants' hall is through a double door adorned with bronze panels. Before this, dominating the vestibule, is an ornate fountain which was designed by Schinkel in 1829.

On the upper landing, up stairs painted to resemble marble, the walls are decorated in a simple Etruscan-inspired style with coloured lines, a dado and harpies above. From here, central doors lead to the large hall, which is painted

cream to set off the bright red of the doors and the red and blue of the two niches in the west wall. These niches demonstrate Schinkel's taste for the exotic – the first contains a statue of David with the head of Goliath by Johann Josef Imhof, while the second houses Ganymede by August Wredow. Since his much-lauded set designs for the Berlin production of Mozart's *The Magic Flute* in 1815, Schinkel had discovered the decorative possibilities of perspectively aligned rows of gold or white stars set against a blue semi-dome of the night sky. He was to use this device extensively throughout his career and employed it to great effect here in the niches of the great hall, above a wall painted to his own instructions: "the colour of the scarlet curtain, with a matte finish like the fresco colours in pictures from Pompeii".

Next door, the bright-blue painted living room, hung with oil paintings of Roman views, separates the hall from the Crown Princess's writing room. Looking from the door of the living room through the corridor of rooms, you can observe the effect of Schinkel's use of colour. His clever juxtaposition of pink, blue, white and red in a perspective view is both pleasing to the eye and evocative of what he imagined to be the pure colours of the ancient world. Painted in 1828, the writing room was one of the first rooms to be completed. The soft pink of the walls is set off by a subtle contrast of green, gray and silver moulding.

Far left: The tent room has recently been restored to its original appearance and reflects the military style of decoration which, largely as a consequence of the 20 years of the Napoleonic Wars, pervaded much of European decoration in the first half of the 19th century. In Prince Friedrich's time, it would have been used as a bedroom for the Crown Princess's ladies-in-waiting.

Above left: Designed by Schinkel in 1829 for the Technical College of Berlin, the fountain in the vestibule was moved to the palace in 1843, two years before Schinkel's death. The bowl is exuberantly Greek in design, ornamented with nereids, sea horses and acanthus leaves.

Bottom left: The Crown Prince's bedroom is an exercise in restraint. Its satinwood bed, which is set against green walls, is framed by two cast-iron pillars topped with imperial eagles which point both to the ancient world and to the recently vanquished empire of Napoleon.

Above: Looking through the house from the Crown Prince's writing room, the simplicity of Schinkel's plan becomes evident. The desk to the left demonstrates Schinkel's virtuosity as a furniture designer. Executed with his characteristic delicacy and attention to detail, it blends in perfectly with the chair beside it and also complements the doors which are cast in iron and silvered.

Right: The Red Room at the end of Schinkel's central corridor serves to link the house to the garden through a colonnaded arbour.

The Pompeiian influence mentioned by Schinkel in his description of the hall is carried through into the writing room in the paintings executed on the frieze, which were added some time after 1834, possibly by B. W. Rosendahl. They were taken from the ancient paintings of dancers in the Villa of the Mysteries at Pompeii in Italy. The bold colour schemes that are featured in the classical villa provided inspiration for much of Schinkel's decoration. Further evidence of this influence can be seen in the painted decorations of the portico which, apart from a similar series of dancers, also contain images of sea monsters and human figures intertwined with foliate designs. Along with other such motifs in the palace, these classical decorations clearly indicate the influence

of the architect Robert Adam, whose work Schinkel had admired on his visit to Britain.

In the decoration of the Crown Prince's bedroom, Schinkel's approach was more restrained, probably at the behest of his patron. Here, against green walls, he set a large satinwood bed beneath an engraving of Raphael's painting of the *Transfiguration*, the original of which hangs in the Vatican. In deference to his patron's admiration of the full-blown Empire style, Schinkel included a fluted Ionic column on either side of the bed, topped with an imperial eagle. In one corner stands a deeply upholstered armchair, complete with attached bookrest, made from satinwood and horsehair in the simplified Empire style for which Schinkel was famous.

Along the corridor, the striped tent room was originally intended as a bedroom for the Crown Princess's ladies-in-waiting and it might strike us as curious that it should be decorated in such an overtly military style. However, such was the fashion of the period that this was perfectly appropriate, even down to the severity of the folding iron chairs, campaign beds and the warlike spears which serve as supports to the canopies. It was subsequently used as a guest room and Schinkel himself was one of its occupants on several occasions.

At the end of Schinkel's corridor of rooms lies the Red Corner Room, which opens out onto a colonnaded arbour that leads to the rose garden and the extensive grounds of the palace in which the architect even erected a Roman bath. Indeed, gazing out across this ideal view you might imagine yourself to be in some Roman villa. This is precisely what Schinkel intended and so this vista is the culmination of the decorative scheme inside the palace.

While many of Schinkel's buildings and interiors were destroyed in the devastation of Berlin which followed the Second World War, this gem of a palace has survived remarkably intact and remains so today; a corner of Prussia that is forever Rome.

CHARLOTTENHOF, POTSDAM, BRANDENBURG
ARCHITECT: KARL FRIEDRICH SCHINKEL
CONSTRUCTION: 1826
SEE ALSO GAZETTEER, PAGE 172

Goethe's Houses

When the young poet Johann Wolfgang von Goethe came to Weimar in November 1775 at the age of 26, he insisted that it was only to be a fleeting visit. Weimar was an agricultural town of some 6,000 people which seemed to have nothing to offer the poet compared to the bustling city of Frankfurt from which he had come. However, within a few years Goethe had transformed Weimar into a centre of culture whose court was filled with the leading writers and wits of the late 18th-century German states. He wrote to his friends in Frankfurt: "You would not believe how many good fellows and good heads there are gathered here".

The young Duke of Weimar, Karl August, enjoyed the company of the young poet and in a controversial move appointed him a member of his Privy Council. Along with the position went a house. It was a fitting home for a poet who was only then discovering his affinity with nature: a rustic *Gartenhaus* set in leafy solitude on the far side of the Ilm valley. In May 1776 Goethe wrote: "I have a dear little garden on the Ilm outside the gate . . . there is a little old house which I am having repaired. . ."

Goethe was to remain here for another ten years before commencing his travels. When he departed he left behind many friends. He also left the "little old house", together with a town house on the Frauenplan which he lived in at the same period in order to be closer to the Duke's side. It was to the town house that Goethe returned at the end of his travels. Today, the two houses form a living museum of the poet's life and work.

It is perhaps best to start, as Goethe himself did, by visiting the garden house. The building itself is unremarkable; its principal feature is the garden. Inside there is just enough furniture for the poet to be comfortable. His study is simply furnished and bathed in clear light. Here Goethe would sit at his desk and work into the evening. The heating in this modest dwelling was provided by a small cast-iron stove and by the large kitchen range. The only decorations are a few black and white engravings and some interesting pieces of late 18th-century furniture.

Above: The town house of the German poet Johann Wolfgang von Goethe lies behind the austere, yellow-painted facade of a typical late 18th-century dwelling.

Left: Goethe's study seems to emphasize the cerebral nature of his work. In this room, which opens off the poet's bedroom, the table is set with quill pens and ink and all seems ready for the occupier to begin the day's work.

Goethe's town house is altogether different. As you pass through the elegant pedimented doorway of its sombre yellow facade, you enter the environment of the poet's mind. Every aspect reveals an element of Goethe's multi-faceted character. The most striking feature is the preponderance of antique sculpture. Goethe studied classical art in Italy where he embraced the ancient civilizations as the antithesis of his country's own gloomy Gothic heritage. In Rome he wrote: "Here I follow the counsel I find in the works of the ancients. Turning them busily o'er, daily with pleasure renewed". Back in Weimar, Goethe was able to prolong that pleasure endlessly in the contemplation of copies, and a few original fragments, of classical statuary. He wrote: "In my room I already have the most beautiful bust of Jupiter". It is this which faces you today as you enter Goethe's dining hall. Beyond it, in his small dining room, a cabinet packed with classical pieces is on view, together with a copy of a magnificent late Greek head of Athena which sits on the manuscript cupboard.

Wherever you look, other statues will catch your eye. The most impressive of these has a room dedicated to its name. In the Juno Room, a huge head of the goddess, some five feet (1.5 metres) high, is mounted on a plinth. It was one of the poet's most treasured possessions. In fact, the original, which now stands in Rome, was the subject for a letter to his beloved Frau von Stein in January 1787: "Thou has but one rival, a colossal head of Juno". It was with ecstatic joy that he later wrote that he himself had acquired "A colossal Juno, great and glorious beyond all expression". Today she presides over the Juno Room. Before her, a pale Empire-style table supports a small statue of a winged Nike, above which a sculpture of an eagle seems to refer not only to the ancient gods so beloved of the poet, but also to the contemporary world of the early 1800s in which it had become the adopted symbol of the French Emperor Napoleon Bonaparte. For all his philosophising, Goethe was compelled to live in the real world where Weimar was at war with France. In 1806 he sat in his house and listened to

Above: Goethe's garden house, a present from his patron the Duke of Weimar, lies away from the town centre amid tranquil parkland grounds.

Bottom left: The furnishings of the garden house are simple compared to those of Goethe's town house, the only concession to style being individual pieces of furniture such as this Empire-style chair upholstered in striped silk. The heating for the house was provided by a curiously shaped cast-iron stove.

Opposite: The garden house was the ideal place for leisurely reflection and the composition of new work, much of which was created here in the poet's small study. The room is lit by a soft light which filters through the thin muslin drapes.

Above: The most sumptuously decorated of the rooms in Goethe's town house is the Juno Room, which was named after the massive 5-foot (1.5-metre) high bust of the goddess that stands at the doorway. The walls of the room are coloured in an idiosyncratic hue of pale blue which seems to suit the exuberance of the ancient artefacts it contains.

Right: Classical sculpture takes pride of place in Goethe's small dining room, as it does throughout the rest of the house. On a cupboard filled with manuscript books and portfolios sits a cast of Athena. The glass-fronted, veneered cabinet alongside contains the poet's own services of porcelain and glassware.

the cannonballs whistling over his roof, as the light from the burning houses around the town flickered on his walls. It was here also in the previous August, after the rout of the Prussian army at Jena, that Goethe had provided quarters for 16 French hussars and where he had been threatened with the loss of his life, before receiving a personal apology from Marshal Ney.

However, for Goethe, the war was but a passing storm cloud. His mind was preoccupied with greater, eternal questions and it was here, in the little study of his town house, that he sat and pondered. Next door lies Goethe's modest bedroom with painted wallhangings and a plain quilted bedspread. However, it was not in bed that Goethe found peace, but in his study. He was both poet and investigator, endowed with the ability to see God in nature. As he wrote, "If art and science one possess, one hath religion too". It is possible that Goethe would have approved of our brief investigation into his house where the tangible evidence of his life stimulates our own intellect. As Goethe himself said, it is "Productive imagination with greatest possible reality".

GOETHE'S HOUSES, WEIMAR, THURINGEN
ARCHITECTURAL STYLE: VERNACULAR
CONSTRUCTION: MID-18TH CENTURY
SEE ALSO GAZETTEER, PAGE 172

Horta Museum

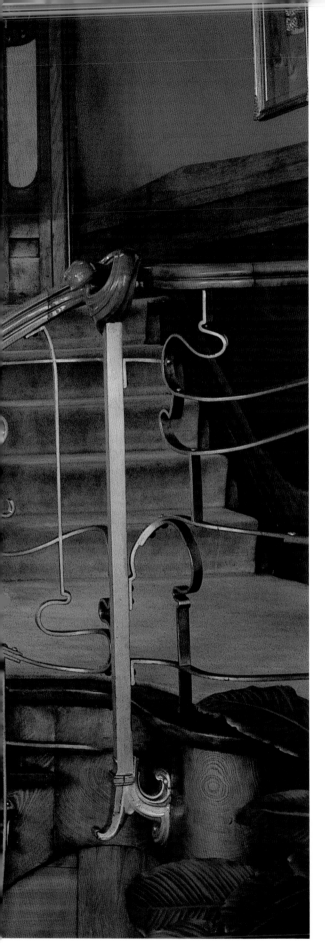

A profile of the architect Victor Horta in *l'Art Decoratif* in 1902 summed up his approach to his work: "Reason, feeling, logic, these are the elements which Victor Horta knows how to add to Nature and they are the secret of the perfect appearance, of the irreproachable homogeneity, of all the projects he has created".

The writer of the article need not have looked at "all the projects he has created". Had he but walked through Horta's own house, as we are able to today, on the rue Americaine at St Gilles in Brussels, Belgium, he would have detected all of Horta's key principles encapsulated in this one sublime expression.

The house which Horta designed for himself in 1898 is a perfectly preserved example of the style known as Art Nouveau. Its origins lay in William Morris's Arts and Crafts movement in England and the interest in Japanese art which swept through Europe in the late 19th century and which is typified in the paintings of the French Impressionists of the 1870s. By the 1890s in France Art Nouveau had found its expression in Emile Galle's glasswork and the furniture of Eugène Gaillard and Alexandre Charpentier, all of whom worked in a style characterized by sinuous line and stylized organic motifs. However, Horta's approach was different. His Belgian Art Nouveau looked elsewhere for its distinctive qualities. He was inspired not only by natural form but also by the architectural heritage which he saw all around him in his home country of Belgium and also in northern France. This was the heartland of the great Gothic edifices of the Middle Ages and it was to these that Horta looked for inspiration and, more importantly, to the architect who had championed the revival of the Gothic style in the 1850s and 1860s, Eugène Viollet le Duc. Horta wrote: "To study the past as much as one can, to discover its acquired truths, the fundamental principles, to use them as part of a common heritage of knowledge – I have the right to do this".

It was a right which the architect exercised in all of his designs and never more prominently than in that of his own house. From the outside it is clear at once that this is no ordinary building.

Above: Having designed numerous houses and hotels in the Art-Nouveau style at the beginning of the 20th century, the architect Victor Horta took great care to create the right impression with the facade of his own house in Brussels. Using an ingenious system of suspension, he achieved an apparently impossible effect of unnatural mannerism with a top-heavy overhanging bay. The sinuous, twisted shapes that decorate the wrought-iron balcony were inspired by natural forms and this inspiration is repeated in details throughout the rest of the house.

Left: The staircase in the entrance hall echoes the serpentine forms of the stylized tendrils which twine around the balcony. Beyond, the dining room opens out in a bright mass of white-glazed brick.

For the facade, Horta suspended a decorative wrought-iron balcony on three rods which project from an overhanging bay. Although the resulting graduated top-heavy overhang looks as if it would be physically impossible to achieve, it was made possible by Horta's masterly use of a sophisticated system of support similar to that used in high Gothic architecture. The design of the wrought iron is itself classic Horta, taking its inspiration from twining plant forms and insect wings, namely the flag iris on the balcony and the dragonfly's wing at the top of the building. The facade also has another function. Horta's house is in fact two buildings – the one residential, the other a place of work – and he stresses the difference between home and studio in the contrast of the two facades, that of the house on the left, ornate and decorative, and that of the studio on the right, bare and businesslike.

Entering the domestic house, the eye is immediately drawn by the echo of the flowing designs of the balcony outside repeated in the sinuous serpentine line of the ironwork within. Such mimicry was a favourite trait of Horta and runs throughout the interior. In his design for the living area of his house, Horta was strikingly revolutionary. He broke down the traditional walls between rooms and combined sitting and dining areas in one huge room divided by small side partitions.

You enter the hall through double doors decorated with the cloudy-coloured "American Glass" that Louis Comfort Tiffany invented in 1880. This was designed to let in light, while at the same time providing necessary privacy and

seclusion. The double doors lead to a staircase of creamy Carrara marble and soft-pink and white walls finished with gold borders. Up the stairs lies the mezzanine floor which, although originally planned as a music room and dining room, was extended by Horta in 1906 to include a sitting room. The music room is furnished with a suite of Art-Nouveau furniture designed by Horta and set on a plush gray carpet. However, the dining room was the architect's real masterpiece. The walls and vaulted ceiling of this extraordinary room are lined with enamelled bricks which subtly reflect the gilt of the Gothic-inspired metal supporting arches. The principal feature in this room is a splendid buffet made, like all the furniture in the dining room, from American ash. Horta was a perfectionist at selecting the right wood for a room, employing a number of exotic woods. The effect of the carefully chosen ash that he used here is to emphasize the warmth of this room which Horta wanted to fill with light.

On the upper shelves of the buffet, Horta displays a fine collection of porcelain. Below is a serving hatch from the kitchen and at floor level stands an elaborate gas-powered radiator which was used to heat the serving dishes. The whole is crowned by a magnificent bas-relief depicting the Muses, by the sculptor P. Braecke, which support

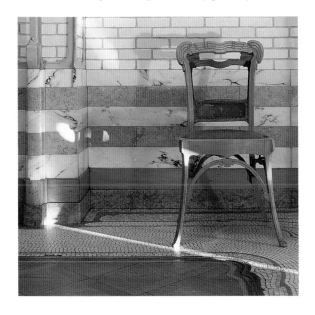

Above: Horta's attention to detail extended even to the design of the beds in his house. This stylized rose was a favourite motif.

Bottom left: The white tiles which decorate both the dining room and the sitting room form a good backdrop for the furniture. The American-ash wood furniture in this room can be seen as a tour de force of all Horta's skills as a designer.

Opposite: At the rear of the dining room, the sitting room, which was added to the house by Horta in 1906, is filled with light from the high, curved-top windows which lead to the garden. On the right, a three-part, glass-fronted buffet contains an assortment of the architect's oriental porcelain.

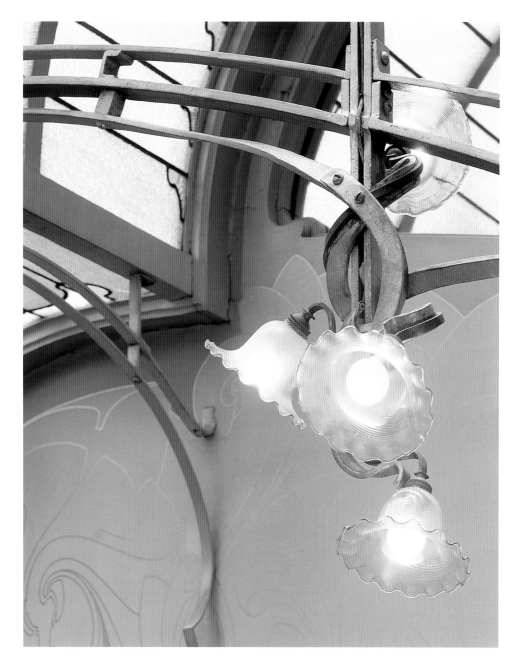

Back in the hall, ascend the stairs to the first floor, pausing on your way to notice the highly finished curve of the banister rail, carved and turned in the shape of interlocking plant stems, and the walls which are decorated with mural paintings in a typical Art-Nouveau motif of billowing floral patterns in white and gold. Off the stairwell are the small sitting room used by Madame Horta, with its leaf-patterned wallpaper in the manner of William Morris, and bedrooms filled with further examples of Horta's furniture. Even the beds in Horta's house continue the organic theme of the decoration. However, it is not until you reach the very top of the house that you find the appropriate apotheosïs of Victor Horta's style. The top of the stairwell is a palace of light. The murals, which become increasingly elaborate as you climb ever higher, now emerge into full-blown floral beauty. The light, which falls from above, changes with the times of day, and by night transforms the stairwell into a shaft of subtle artificial yellow light which in turn is reflected in the clouded glass of the roof.

Realizing that up here he had found the completion of his delicate dream of light and structure Horta wrote: "I had reached the summit of my happiness".

HORTA MUSEUM, BRUSSELS
ARCHITECT: VICTOR HORTA
CONSTRUCTION: 1898-1906
SEE ALSO GAZETTEER, PAGE 165

Above: One of Horta's personal conceits was to design lamps in the form of flowers which, twining on a brass stem, open out in petals of subtly coloured clouded glass.

Right: The contorted plant forms which give the Art-Nouveau style its character are found in all aspects of the house's decoration, including this banister rail twist.

Opposite: At the top of the staircase, Horta's creativity reaches its apotheosis in a palace of glass which is flooded with light. The light which filters through the clouded windows is reflected in the mirrors and polished brass before tumbling down into the deep well to illuminate the floors below.

in their hands a model of Horta's own master-piece, the Hotel Aubecq in Brussels. On the plain dining table stand a pair of twining silvered-bronze Art-Nouveau candelabra by Fernand Dubois. From the ceiling hang classic Horta lights in the form of lilies whose stems, made from brass, twine around the central rod.

Beyond the dining room, through stained-glass doors of "American Glass", lies the sitting room, with its huge curve-topped French windows which lead out onto glass steps that descend to the garden. On the right of the room is a large three-part buffet, originally made for Horta's Turin exhibition of 1902 and now used to house just a small part of the architect's renowned collection of oriental porcelain.

Above: Hvitträsk, the home and studio of Finnish architect Eliel Saarinen and his partners, rises castle-like from the hill above the Vitträsk lake which had first inspired him.

Right: The dining room is an embodiment of Saarinen's fascination with ancient Norse motifs. The vaulted ceiling is painted with a spiralling design to accentuate the span of its arches. This design is echoed in that of the ornately decorated stove in the corner of the room, which is covered in blue tiles. A ryijy rug, designed by Saarinen in 1914, covers the long, single-piece window seat, creating the medieval feeling for which the architect was aiming, while stained glass completes the atmosphere of Nordic romanticism.

I n late October 1907 the composer Gustav Mahler paused in Finland en route to a concert performance in Russia. Mahler was exhausted. His young daughter had recently died of an unexpected illness and it seemed as if his life had sunk into impenetrable shadow. Mahler stayed at a remote and picturesque spot overlooking a lake, just outside Helsinki. He described the building he stayed in as "charming", but "more of a castle" than a house and the whole experience had a remarkable effect upon his spirits. In a letter to his wife, Alma, he wrote: "When it got dark, we sat in the twilight in front of the open fire, where huge logs blazed and glowed as though in a smithy. . ." Around that fire with Mahler were gathered three Finns, an artist, Axel Gallén, and two architects – Herman Gesellius and Eliel Saarinen. The house which the composer thought was such a charming castle was Saarinen's architectural masterpiece, Hvitträsk, which still stands today as a lasting memorial to his genius.

Eliel Saarinen had been inspired to build his house in 1901 when, while working on a nearby building project with Gesellius and the third member of their architectural practice, Lindgren, he had come upon a tranquil, wooded hillside overlooking the Vitträsk lake. So immediate was his decision to live there that only one year later the first trees had been felled and a few months after that the first building of the complex which was to become his home was complete.

From the start Saarinen conceived his house as a castle – Mahler's initial reaction had not been far wide of the mark. Hvitträsk is in fact a cross between a medieval manor house and a castle straight from the pages of the *Tales of Hoffmann*. Rounding the bend from the forest today, you are still met by a fairy-tale dwelling from the world of Hansel and Gretel. The house is a jumble of towers, balconies and arched windows, sited in and around walls which seem to grow organically from the very rock of the ridge. The effect is intentionally dramatic. Saarinen has achieved in architecture what his friend Jean Sibelius had in music. The desire to evoke Finland's heroic past of Norse myth and legend lay at the heart of both

H v i t t r ä s k

men's art. In Saarinen's architecture this heroism is translated into a rugged formalism in which he made optimum use of plain, unstripped wood and rough-hewn stone.

Although Hvitträsk was eventually occupied by Saarinen alone, after the other two architects had moved on, it was originally planned as a residence for all three men. Apart from Saarinen's house in the South Wing, there was also a small house for Lindgren and another for Gesellius.

On entering Hvitträsk today, it is in Saarinen's South Wing that you find yourself. The dwelling is constructed on a number of different levels. Directly underneath the distinctively wide gable lies the cavernous living room. It was here that Mahler found his blazing fire and it is easy to see how the lure of this cozy yet capacious room, with its huge tiled stove, would have been hard to resist on a cold October night. The decoration is based on myth and folklore, in keeping with the character of the house, and originally consisted of animal skins and unadorned country furniture. However, over the years of Saarinen's residency the contents gradually became slightly more sophisticated and this is the interior style that we are greeted with today.

From this central living space you can walk through to the dining room which, although more compact than the living room, seems to reflect more succinctly Saarinen's interest in traditional Nordic motifs. The ceiling is vaulted to give an almost cave-like feeling to the room and each of the great spandrels which make up the groin are decorated with traditional stylized plant motifs. The blue-tiled corner stove echoes these designs in its fine cupola, which is decorated with an intricate swirling pattern of Celtic spirals in blue and orange. The colours of the mural decoration are reiterated in those of the simple Finnish *ryijy* rugs which are draped across the sofa and fall down to the floor. Like most of the lighting in the house, the central ceiling lantern was designed by Saarinen himself. The stained-glass window reveals the tale of two men and a woman. More precisely, the woman is Mathilda, and the men are her husband, Eliel, and his partner Herman Gesellius, who later became her lover. Following the collapse of both their marriages, Saarinen and Gesellius both remarried in March 1904 – Eliel Saarinen married Louise Gesellius, and Mathilda Saarinen wedded Herman Gesellius.

In contrast to the simplicity of these two living areas, the decoration of the other rooms in the South Wing seems relatively sophisticated. The furniture in the small boudoir (known as the Flower Room), adjacent to the master bedroom, dates from 1908 and matches the double bed next door which was designed by Saarinen. The dressing table, with its exaggeratedly tall mirror, is particularly striking.

No detail is neglected in this building since it was also intended to be a work of art. Apart from providing a home for the architects, Hvitträsk was to be their office and every aspect was designed to aid the contemplation which, it was believed, would eventually produce great architecture.

However, it would be wrong to believe that the architects, and later Saarinen and his family, were cut off from the world in their peaceful, lakeside retreat. Eliel and his second wife Louise enjoyed entertaining and, quite apart from such unexpected guests as Gustav Mahler, their visitors included the composer Jean Sibelius, the German art historian Julius Meier-Graefe, Geza Maroti, the Hungarian sculptor, Charles Rennie Mackintosh, the architect, and Maxim Gorky, the Russian writer who visited the house in the winter of 1905.

The house was designed for conviviality and standing in the living room you can imagine the light of the fire and the smell of cooking drifting up from the kitchens. The talk would undoubtedly have been of art, music and architecture. But there would never have been any pretension. No one cared to stand on ceremony here. Eliel Saarinen had achieved the goal that so many artists strived after – the perfect blend of family house with work of art. One visitor, Gustave Mahler, was only too aware of how hard it was to achieve this inner peace and it must have been with no little longing and some reflection on his own tragic life that he told his wife: "In spite of the warm welcome they were never for one moment officious. I even lay down in the next room for a nap on the sofa, without a word said, and there was not a sound to disturb me."

HVITTRASK, BOBACK, UUSIMAA
ARCHITECT: ELIEL SAARINEN
CONSTRUCTION: 1901
SEE ALSO GAZETTEER, PAGE 168

Above: The spiralling designs which embellish the dining-room stove are characteristic of those used by Saarinen to create a feeling of traditional decoration in a house which, in reality, was a triumph of modern simplicity.

Left: The furniture that gives the small boudoir (or flower room) such a different character to the reception rooms of the house was designed by Saarinen himself in 1908. It forms part of a suite of furniture, including a bed and an extraordinary tall mirror, which takes its inspiration from the form of a gothic arch.

Above: The Swedish painter Carl Larsson designed his house at Sundborn to harmonize with the traditional architecture of Dalarna, a style at the heart of Sweden's folk tradition. The heart shapes which adorn its exterior are an outward demonstration of the love which Larsson believed to be the essence of the family life inside.

Right: The dining room is perhaps closest in style to the Arts and Crafts movement of which Larsson's own taste can be said to be a derivative. The dining chairs and old Dalecarlian table are made to a simple geometrical design. A note of individual character is provided by the lamp shades, designed by Larsson in the shape of a flower, and the wide, tapestry-covered bench at the head of the table. At mealtimes, this bench was the artist's own seat, while guests and children occupied the other chairs. All of the furniture in this room, as in the entire house, was either found locally or made to Larsson's designs by local craftsmen.

"Only something like this little idyll would suit an artist," wrote the Swedish painter Carl Larsson in the 1880s. "Here I experienced that unspeakably sweet feeling of seclusion from the clamour and noise of the world that I had felt only once before." Larsson's idyll was a country log cottage, *Lilla Hyttnäs*, in the Swedish province of Dalarna. Home to the painter and his large family for 30 years, the house stands today as a living memorial to his unique philosophy of art as a complete way of life.

From the outside the house, a modest wooden building in the town of Sundborn, does not seem particularly special. It stands on waste ground on a bend in the Sundborn river, in the mining area of Dalarna which is also, paradoxically, the cultural heartland of Sweden. Larsson himself described it as an "unpretentious, rather ugly, insignificant building" and such it seems.

Built on two floors, the house is decorated externally in the traditional Dalecarlian style, with red-painted woodwork articulated with bands of blue and white. However, the recurring motif of a heart is everywhere, an indicator, even before you enter, that love is paramount in this house. It was, in Larsson's own words, "A little house of one's own, for my sweet wife and children" and between 1889, when he and his wife inherited the house from her aged aunt, and the artist's death in 1919 he produced countless exquisite watercolours of this idyllic sanctuary.

From the moment you enter through the covered porch, beneath the inscription "Welcome Dear Friend, to the House of Carl Larsson and his Spouse!", you begin to appreciate the nature of Larsson's philosophy. A sliding door leads to the painter's workshop which is lit by an enormous window and filled with the tools of the talented and industrious family. In one corner stand the spinning wheel and loom on which Larsson's wife, Karin Bergöö, herself an artist, and their daughters would weave the multi-coloured rugs and tapestries which are on view throughout the house. The cupboards, which are of traditional Dalecarlian design, come from the houses of local miners. On the back of the door Larsson painted

Carl

Larsson's House

VET DU HVAD:VA

Above: As you enter the house you are met by a picture of Larsson and his wife Karin Bergöö, herself an artist, seen in profile apparently through the arch of a window. Such a whim is typical of this house in which painted decoration is used with wit and sensitivity.

Right: The workshop was not only the domain of the painter but that of his entire family. While Larsson painted, his wife and children would work busily at the loom and spinning wheel, making the colourful tapestries that can be found throughout the house. Against one wall, a bench stands alongside a pillar which supports a caricature of Larsson.

Far right: Looked at in detail, the simple craftsmanship of the furniture becomes apparent – from the geometrical patterning of the wood to the bold colours that make up the woven tapestry, made by Karin Bergöö.

his wife, as if she is looking in at him, while alongside her a portrait of their son Pontus hangs on the wall.

The workshop leads into the dining room which, with its austere furniture, seems perhaps closest in spirit to the International Arts and Crafts style of the period. Larsson was keen to spread his stylistic doctrine, manifested throughout the house, and this didactic impulse was one of the reasons why he published his watercolours of the house in such books as *At Home* and *The House in the Country*. The essence of Larsson's style was a restrained gaiety in which symmetry and harmony of pattern were forever kept in mind, reflecting a homegrown philosophy of domestic harmony and ordered sensibility. As Larsson himself said of the room: "You open the door and "God's Peace" greets you from the wall where it is written. In the cupboards you can see all the tableware, shining and glimmering through glass doors. Bottles and jugs containing a selection of your favourite beverages are lined up on the sideboard".

At mealtimes, while children and visitors would sit in the red-painted chairs, Larsson would sit in the splendid tapestry-covered throne at the head of the table, above which hangs another

tapestry by Karin depicting the elements. Over his private cupboard containing liquor and cigars, Larsson, with characteristic wit, has inscribed "*Liberté, Egalité, Fraternité*". On the door, a portrait of the painter's daughter, Brita, typifies the vivid painted decorations which cover the walls of the house. The strength of colour is particularly evident in the red and green walls in the sitting room, situated off the dining room.

The white-painted furniture in the sitting room is of Swedish Gustavian design and its blue gingham covers are in keeping with the period feel of the room. The *escritoire* (writing desk), too, dates from the reign of King Gustavus III (1746-1792). In the corner nearest the door stands a tiled stove, dating from 1754, which Larsson found in an outhouse and, much to the amusement of his family, painstakingly reconstructed.

Larsson had many artist friends, including Prinz Eugen and Ivan Arosenius, and you will see some of their work displayed on the walls as you climb the stairs to the top floor. Upstairs, together with the library and a room crammed with the country antiques which Larsson collected with magpie-like obsessiveness, are the bedrooms. Larsson's bedroom is a good example of the northern Arts and Crafts style, although the painter

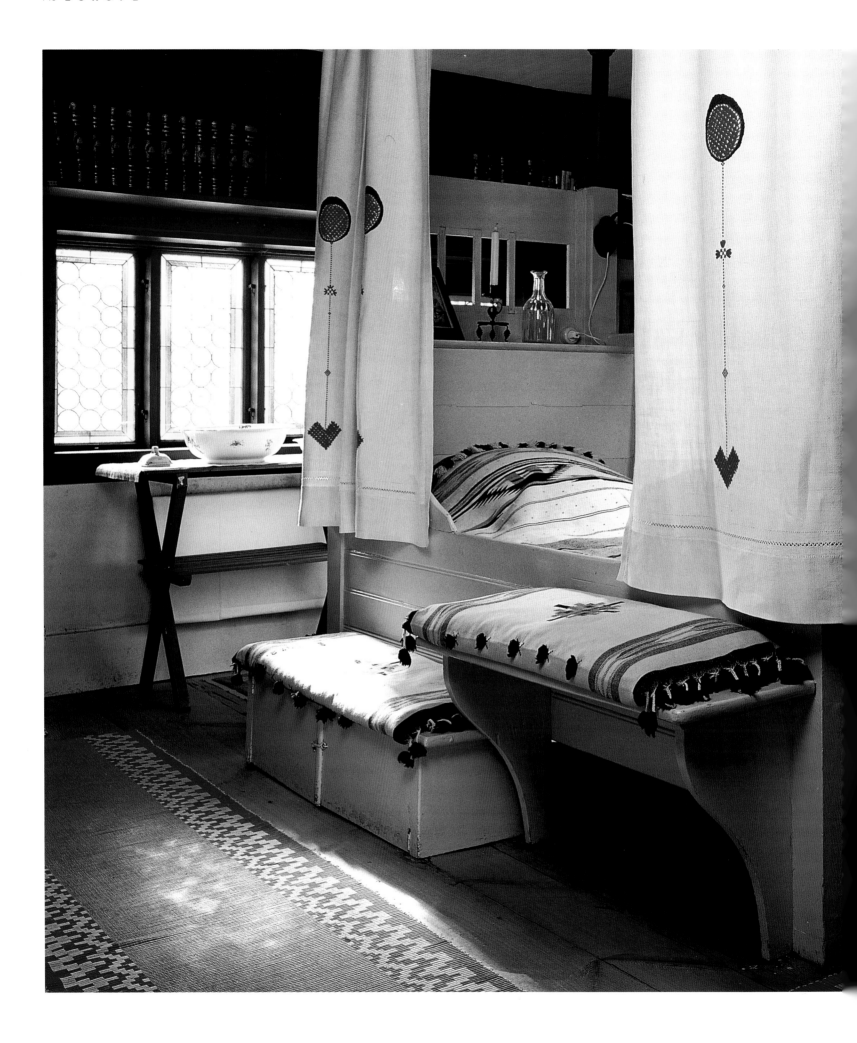

Far left: Larsson's bed is hung with bold draperies in a style close to the European Arts and Crafts movement. The artist was well acquainted with such design influences through the international magazine The Studio, *which was particularly prominent in promoting such stark simplicity as that seen here.*

Left: Looking from the bedroom corridor of Larsson's house, the sense of geometric simplicity becomes clear although this is always relieved by the little painted details which give the house its highly individual character.

would have learned of developments in other European countries from the famous design periodical *The Studio*, to which he subscribed. The bed certainly has a German feel to it, with its stark whiteness and the stylized embroidered designs on its hangings. Larsson wrote of this room: "This is my room. . . In my simple bed, on my straw mattress, I sleep well and deeply, like a king lying 'in state'."

The other bedroom belonged to Karin and the younger children. Inside we find a classic Swedish box bed covered in red gingham under a pretty frieze of bows, painted by Larsson, and, looking down upon his wife, a self-portrait of the artist.

Back at ground level, the temptation is to wander enraptured through Larsson's rooms, but most visitors are inevitably drawn back to the dining room, the cradle of household life. Here, above Larsson's drinks cupboard, is another inscription which seems to sum up the spirit of this artist's hideaway best of all: "Love each other children, for love is all".

CARL LARSSON'S HOUSE,
SUNDBORN, DALARNA
ARCHITECT: CARL LARSSON
CONSTRUCTION: 1889-1919
SEE ALSO GAZETTEER, PAGE 178

*F*ar *E*ast &
*A*ustralasia

Above: The exterior of Rouse Hill house features wide eaves such as those you would normally expect to find on a building of the English Regency period, rather than an Australian house of the same era. However, there is no doubt that the design was useful in providing shade from the blisteringly hot sun of the outback. The verandah is another shady refuge, added in the 1850s, some 50 years after work was begun on the house.

Right: The sitting room of Rouse Hill might easily be that of any English country house of the early Victorian era. All of the furniture here dates from the 1860s and was of colonial manufacture.

Richard Rouse was the typical Australian settler – hard-working, honest and devout. And Rouse Hill, the house which he designed and built for himself and his family near Vinegar Hill, between Parramatta and Windsor, encapsulates the simple dictums by which he lived his life.

Rouse came to Australia from England in December 1801 and settled in Hawksburg with his wife and two children. Architecture was a way of life for him. Between 1801 and 1805 Rouse was Superintendent of Public Works at Parramatta and from 1810 he took charge of many public buildings in the area. Built between 1813 and 1818, Rouse Hill is the only substantial surviving example of early Australian colonial architecture from this period.

A simple, four-square Georgian block made from local red sandstone, Rouse Hill stands in its own grounds, surrounded by huge fig trees. The wide eaves, an unusual feature for an Australian house, might look more in keeping on an English Regency building. And before the verandah was added during the 1850s, the original structure would have seemed even closer in appearance to the sort of house that Rouse had left behind in rural Oxfordshire, England. However, although it dates from the 1810s, the house is essentially Victorian in feel and the furnishings, for the most part, date from the 1870s. The decoration is unremarkable throughout, except for its very understatement and the nature of its conservation. Rouse Hill was a family house, occupied until the 1990s, and the character which has evolved during the past 100 years, since it was last decorated, has been deliberately preserved. This is no polished period showcase, but a true "living museum" in which the curators have sought to show the way in which a house can take on a character of its own. Great thought has been devoted to the techniques of its restoration since the house was "resumed" by the government in 1978 and although Rouse's descendants had lived there until 1993, and still own half of it, nothing had been over-cleaned or substantially mended. Shutters had, for the most part, been kept closed which prevented the strong sunlight from causing the

Rouse Hill House

Above: The drawing room is the epitome of the Victorian obsession with clutter. Objects of all sorts cover every available surface – from the boxes and vases on the low table to the cabinet filled with porcelain and glass. A notable feature of this room is the heavy bullion fringing of the pelmet.

furnishing fabrics and wallcoverings to fade unduly. In effect, the interior has remained unchanged since the early 20th century.

The conservators followed the opinion of John Ruskin: "restoration" was "a lie from beginning to end . . . Your model may have the shell of the old walls. . . but the old building is destroyed, and that more totally and mercilessly than if it had sunk into a heap of dust." Following Ruskin's advice, those responsible for the preservation of Rouse Hill have, little by little, repaired only the badly damaged pieces and applied a little careful use of modern craftsmanship to ensure that their dilapidation will be retarded. Wherever possible,

they have made use of original materials and nothing alien has been introduced. Their idea was not to "age" new additions, as is the custom in many country houses today. On the contrary, wherever re-paintings or repairs were undertaken, they were carried out not by matching new paint to faded colours, but by using as close as possible a match to the original unfaded tones. Of course, the results are not necessarily visually pleasing but Rouse Hill, like its builder, is honest. There is no attempt here at visual deceit. It is as if the house continues to live on.

As you enter the hall you are made aware of the sense of a living presence. A drawer has been left open, its bric-a-brac on full view, as if an inhabitant of the house has been rummaging through its contents, desperately searching for something. Might that something be the leather-bound diary which lies in another half-open drawer, or possibly one of the unpaid bills or letters whose compartments in the writing desk are so carefully defined in a bold Victorian copperplate handwriting?

The walls of the hall are painted in imitation yellow marble, part of the original decoration from the great spring-clean that was undertaken in the 1870s by Edwin Rouse's wife, Eliza. Above the doorway to the sitting room, a stag's head gives you the impression that, if externally the house is English domestic Regency displaced to a colonial setting, inside it might be any small English country house from the West Country to the Highlands of Scotland. Here in the hall, and next door in the sitting room, the customary black and white engravings by English Victorian artists hang among the plethora of objects brought home from the Grand Tour, exemplified by a 19th-century oil painting of the Madonna and Child, after Carlo Dolci. On the sitting room mantelpiece is a collection of Parian ware figures and in the middle of the table a rare piece of Worcester porcelain. All of the furniture in the sitting room, including the two Louis-XV-style *fauteuils* (armchairs), upholstered in a Persian-style tapestry, dates from the 1860s and is of colonial manufacture. The eclecticism of the decoration is particularly evident in the curtains or drapes, which, while they hang from the original 1860s poles with their elaborate brass finials, are themselves made from a Japanese material and date from the early 20th century.

Back toward the house, the picturesque bath house hides behind a trellis of flowers and latticed verandahs, with the summer house beyond. Dating from the 1870s, this airy structure is clearly derived from an architectural pattern book. However, on close inspection you will see that it is constructed from local wood and corrugated iron, a symbolic indication of the marriage of aesthetics with resourcefulness which is the abiding impression created by this fascinating chronicle of a family's changing taste.

ROUSE HILL HOUSE, VINEGAR HILL,
PARRAMATTA, NEW SOUTH WALES
ARCHITECT: RICHARD ROUSE
CONSTRUCTION: 1813-1818
SEE ALSO GAZETTEER, PAGE 163

Left: In the sitting room hangs a painting after an original by Carlo Dolci depicting the Madonna and Child. It was a perennial favourite and is frequently found in Victorian country houses throughout the British Isles as well as here in Australia.

Bottom: The dining room features a fascinating paper frieze, printed with a landscape scene, which extends around the room. Below, hang an eclectic collection of paintings and engravings which are typical of the wide-ranging taste of the Victorian owners of the house.

The drawing room is filled with all the clutter that is characteristic of any Victorian house. The side table and cabinet are crowded with small porcelain objects; the table lamps covered with hangings of fringed silk. The windows are shaded with a heavy gold-bullion fringed pelmet or valance and early 20th-century lace drapes. While it may be eclectic, the decoration at Rouse Hill is not at all provincial. Until the tide of nationalism at the turn of the 20th century, there was no objection to the importation of furniture into Australia and the latest designs were no more outdated than the time it took to sail from Europe.

The happy blend of 1870s fashion with earlier and later styles is best seen in the dining room. Here an 1860s floral wallpaper has been enhanced by a later generation of decorators with a deep frieze printed with a pastoral landscape.

Rouse Hill was originally conceived as a working farm and the careful conservation policy extends to many of the original outbuildings. While the interior of the house chronicles the taste of several generations of the family, in the outbuildings the pattern and foundation of their everyday lives can be felt. The farm's livelihood was based on cattle and the two functional uses of these animals are evident in the view from the chicken houses. From here you can see both dairy and slaughterhouse and beside the latter an early horseless carriage. The new wooden struts which support the roof of the slaughterhouse are clear evidence of the Ruskinian policy to restore only with modern materials.

Above: Harry Seidler's masterpiece, the house that he built for his mother at Wahroonga in Australia, is a classic example of 1950s architecture inspired by the Bauhaus. Its glass-window walls are the perfect device to integrate nature into the living environment.

Right: The living room is divided into two areas by the stone-clad pillar, which also serves to bring the natural world inside. Its muted pink-gray colours are echoed in those of the walls and furnishings, the only highlight being the bright geometric patterns of the sundeck mural. The chairs, made from tubular steel and plywood, were designed by Charles Eames in 1954 and manufactured in the United States, as was much of the furniture in the house.

"Where does nature stop and architecture begin?" asked the architect Harry Seidler in 1949. Only one year later he was to realize the answer in the house he built for his parents Rose and Max at Wahroonga, Australia, which today stands as evidence of the vision of this antipodean champion of Modernism.

Seidler was an Austrian Jew, born in Vienna in 1923. His family had moved to Australia in the 1930s, fleeing the Nazi occupation. Harry had followed, but he had come via the "scenic route" by way of England, Canada, North Carolina and New York. Far away from his homeland, Harry began to study architecture. He had the good fortune to study under three of the greatest founding fathers of the Modernist movement, also in exile: the German designer Josef Albers, the German architect Walter Gropius and Marcel Breuer, a Hungarian. All three men were influential in Seidler's work, but it was Gropius's teachings at Harvard that lit the spark of Modernism in him, confirming Seidler's belief that he had a part to play in what his master had called "transforming the visual man-made world".

Harry Seidler was, through his teachers, a true disciple of the Bauhaus – the school of arts and crafts that Gropius established at Weimar in 1919 and later moved to Dessau in 1925. Gropius, Albers and Breuer had all taught at the Bauhaus and, although the school was destroyed as subversive by the Nazis, its legacy lived on in their teachings. The original manifesto of the Bauhaus had been directed toward "the building of the future" and Gropius's intent was to unite all the arts under the banner of architecture. He wanted "to achieve in a new architecture the unification of all training in art and design" and so produce a harmonious whole – the "Gesamtkunstwerk" – a German equivalent of the ideal that William Morris had sought in 19th-century Britain.

During the 1930s and 1940s the teachings of the Bauhaus were disseminated around the world through its banished professors, changing the course of modern architecture. Seidler's house at Wahroonga can be seen as the most far-flung outpost of this international phenomenon.

Rose Seidler House

Above: The focal point of the kitchen, which is divided from the living area by a glass-panelled partition, is a large refrigerator in the classic rounded style that was so popular in the 1950s. Beside it stands a Kenwood mixer, another typical feature of prosperous 1950s homes.

Below right: The sun deck in the central wall of the house features a large abstract mural, painted by Harry Seidler himself in a riot of primary colours and swirling geometric forms.

The legacy of that austere, simple severity which characterized the mature "Bauhaus" style is immediately evident in the exterior of Rose Seidler House. The glass-curtain walls allow an almost uninterrupted view of the surrounding grounds. As Seidler himself explained: "The desire to avoid a single outlook only, resulted in a building which is freely exposed on all sides so that varying views of the surroundings become part of the interior." Seidler envisaged his house as an almost sculptural form that would become part of the surrounding landscape. It was equally important to him that people should be able to walk around the house and see into it from all sides as to experience it from within. In the climate of Australia he was able to realize this goal. Although designed to make life as simple as possible, Rose Seidler House is no mere "*machine à habiter*". By means of its glass-curtain walls the surrounding colours effectively become an integral part of the house's interior decoration. The colours of the living room are deliberately restrained to muted tones of pale-yellow, gray and brown. Similarly, the roughly hewn stone cladding of the central pillar which dominates the room has the effect of bringing the outside indoors. The very monumentality of its single bulk might be seen as something of a homage by Seidler to Gropius.

Seidler was a forceful Modernist visionary and it is fortunate that his taste was shared by his mother Rose, whom he persuaded to dispose of most of the furniture which she and his father had brought from Vienna. Instead, Harry filled her house with the fashionable Modernist pieces that he had discovered in New York. The simple "Grasshopper" chairs, made from laminated plywood to a late 1940s design by the Finnish designer Eero Saarinen (son of Eliel Saarinen) and manufactured by Knoll, bear a close resemblance to the revolutionary plywood chairs that Marcel Breuer designed in 1935. If he could not find the piece that he wanted, as was the case with the couch, Seidler would design it himself and have it made in Australia by a local carpenter, a fellow Austrian émigré.

The adjoining dining area, which has an airiness achieved by the ceiling's apparent lack of support, contains a suite of tubular steel and plywood chairs designed by Charles Eames in 1945 and manufactured by the American company Herman Miller.

The house embodies the "open plan" concept that was to be more fully embraced in Britain and America in the later 1950s – the living space is designed to be adaptable between the private and public rooms. Sliding doors and curtains or drapes can be used to either extend or limit the size of the

various areas. For example, a brown curtain or drape divides the playroom and sun deck from the dining room. When open, it creates a huge living space for parties and receptions, while closed, it opens up the master bedroom into a large private living room. Behind sliding doors lies the bedroom itself, dominated by a low bed covered in the fake fur that Seidler used in so many soft furnishings throughout the house.

Another key area in the open plan is the kitchen, divided from the dining space by a low "servery" with sliding panels of frosted glass. The kitchen contains all the latest high technology gadgetry that was on offer in the early 1950s, from the time-saving Kenwood food mixer to a huge, imported American Frigidaire. There is even a waste- or garbage-disposer.

Outside on the sun deck, beneath an abstract mural designed and painted by Seidler himself, sit three copies of Hardoy chairs, designed in Argentina in 1948 and produced by Knoll. The

mural provides an ingenious summation by Seidler of the colour scheme that he used throughout the house – mixing the gray of the walls and the brown of the bathrooms, bedroom and drapes with the red and yellow of the doors and the blue of the studio. Perhaps it is here that the visitor is best able to understand what Seidler was striving for and it seems likely that, as he painted this wall, he might have been thinking of those words of his master Walter Gropius which seem to echo throughout the house: "The ultimate if distant goal of the Bauhaus is the collective work of art – the Building – in which no barrier can exist between the structural and decorative art."

ROSE SEIDLER HOUSE, WAHROONGA,
NEW SOUTH WALES
ARCHITECT: HARRY SEIDLER
CONSTRUCTION: 1950
SEE ALSO GAZETTEER, PAGE 163

Above: Although the bedroom is the most restrained room of the Seidler house, its furnishings are nevertheless typical of the period. Behind the sliding doors that divide the room from the rest of the house lies a low, wide bed, draped in a covering of gray fake fur and lit from above by a pair of steel spotlights.

T he H ouse on the

The big box-office hit of 1951 was a musical. Audiences flocked to see "The King and I", a story about the meeting of two cultures in which an Englishwoman travels to Siam (now Thailand) to become a governess at the court of King Mongkut. The audiences can have had little idea that the splendid costumes which filled the stage originated from quite another overseas visitor to Siam. They were from the Thai silk factory of Jim Thompson, an American businessman who first came to Thailand during the war and had stayed on not to teach, but to learn. Captivated by the country, its people and its arts and crafts, Thompson expanded Thailand's small silk-weaving industry into an international business. Using the profits from this venture, he amassed together a breathtaking collection of oriental art, which has been preserved until this day in his house in Bangkok.

Thompson arrived in Thailand (which he always chose to call Siam) just after the surrender of Japan in 1945, as an officer in the Office of Strategic Services, aiding the Thai resistance. Thailand had been left virtually unscathed by the war and Thompson's first experience of the country – staying in the ancient Suan Kulab palace of King Chulalonghorn – was to change his life. Thompson fell in love with Thailand. Bangkok in the late 1940s was very different from the modern city of today. Thompson was greeted by a mysterious world of high traditional wooden houses, fantastical steeply roofed temples and dark-watered *klongs* (canals). Filled with brightly coloured barges, these canals had earned the city its title of "Venice of the East". The streets echoed with the cries of market-traders and the jingle of bell-hung rickshaws. Immediately on his arrival, Thompson began to buy works of art, paintings, sculptures and, most significantly, textiles. It was through his enthusiasm for Thai arts and crafts that Thompson discovered the country's small silk-weaving industry and within a few years he had transformed it into a successful business.

In the early years, Thompson lived in a hotel but with his new-found wealth he soon set about building himself a house. It was to be no ordinary

Above: Using three separate houses transported from different parts of Thailand for the shell of his house, silk-trader Jim Thompson created this idyllic "Siamese" house. Today his home serves as the perfect showcase for his magnificent collection of Far-Eastern antiquities. A characteristic feature of Thai houses, which Thompson himself admired, is their steep gables, three of which rise high above his own house on the banks of the klong (canal).

Left: The sitting room of Thompson's house opens out onto the garden and the klong. The waxed teak walls originally formed the external walls of a 19th-century weavers' house, which Thompson painstakingly dismantled and rebuilt to form his own home. Niches contain Burmese figures of deities. The chairs, although modern in form, are constructed from traditional bamboo and covered with the Thai silk with which Thompson made his fortune.

Klong

house, but a traditional Thai dwelling that would be appropriate in stature to his magnificent collection of Thai artefacts. Thompson began constructing the house in September 1958, on a carefully selected piece of land sandwiched between one of the *klongs* and a park. It was to be set in a compound filled with trees – the famous Thai flame of the forest tree and the broad-leaved mango were to create a shady garden.

Today, Thompson's house is still approached through this garden. The visitor steps from a boat on the *klong* and enters the world of old Bangkok. According to tradition, the buildings that make up his house tower one level above the ground as a precaution against flooding. They are built from teak and their deep-red painted and creosoted facades form a startling contrast to the verdant foliage which encloses them. Thompson's house is constructed from six separate buildings, which were moved to the plot from different parts of the

Above: In one of the guest bedrooms, three framed photographs of Jim Thompson sit on a carved chest beside a stone figure of Buddha which waits to welcome him back should he ever return.

Left: The Chinese altar tables which make up the table in the dining room were once used as gaming tables at the court of the Siamese King Chulalonghorn. The blue and white porcelain which fills the cabinets and adorns the table was Thompson's passion and his knowledge of it was extensive. Here, as throughout the rest of this extraordinary house, Buddha surveys the scene.

neighbouring countryside and reconstructed to Thompson's plan. The oldest section, in the middle, is appropriately a silk-weaver's house and dates from 1800, while the kitchen wing to the left dates from the 1850s. Work was finished in April 1959 and the house remained Thompson's home until his unsolved disappearance in the Malaysian jungle in 1967.

Before entering the house, the visitor today should walk through the sculpture-filled garden which is paved with 17th-century bricks from Ayudhya and has an 18th-century pieced-stone parapet. Enter the house through the tranquillity of the entrance hall, paved with Thai marble. Between the late 1940s and his disappearance, Thompson became quite a connoisseur of oriental art and wherever you look every surface is decorated with the fine eastern artefacts that he found on his frequent visits to the Nakorn Kasem market area in the Chinese part of Bangkok.

The sitting room, upstairs, is the focal point of the house. Thompson deliberately reversed the walls of the original weaver's house so that the woodcarving, which traditionally decorates the outside of a Thai house, now appears on the inside, waxed to a lustrous finish. Burmese figures from Amarapam look down from niches which were once windows, while another Burmese piece, a magnificent gold-lacquered Buddha, sits on the low, carved table. Another image of the Buddha, this time a fine example of U-Thong stone sculpture, stares out across the room from the top of a lacquer cabinet. Although one entire side of the room is left open to look out over the *klong*, the glass chandelier which Thompson bought from one of Thailand's old royal palaces provides a source of artificial light. Thompson had an unerring colour sense and it is perhaps this which explains his harmonious integration of modern armchairs, upholstered in understated yellow Thai silk, in an otherwise traditional room.

The sitting room is flanked by the study and the *Bencharong* room, which is named after the collection of porcelain which it houses. *Bencharong* in Thai means "five colours" and the room sparkles with many pieces of fine polychrome porcelain, made in China between the 17th and 19th centuries to designs by Thai artists.

Opposite the *Bencharong* room is the dining room, which overlooks the waterfront. Thompson became an authority on blue and white porcelain and this room is filled with his considerable collection, garnered from all over Asia, which includes several fine pieces of Ming. On the wall, paintings illustrate the most popular of the 547 Jataka fables, the story of Prince Vessantara who gave away all his possessions – even his wife – in an attempt to achieve perfection.

The sleeping quarters are grouped on the west side of the house. The walls of the bedrooms are deliberately enclosed to prevent the intrusion of mosquitoes from the *klong*. Thompson was a generous host and his house guests included Truman Capote, Cecil Beaton and Barbara Hutton. Never one to make his visitors feel uncomfortable, Thompson made sure that each room had its own modern bathroom. However, in essence, the house was built for show rather than for comfort and Thompson was renowned for his faith in traditional Thai methods. Thus, although the house has modern plumbing, cooking was always carried out on a charcoal stove rather than the gas and electric varieties favoured by his neighbours. Equally, electricity seems anathema here and the house still looks its best at night, lit by the flickering light from coconut-oil torches. Many of the locals might still hope that on one such night Thompson will return to his house on the *klong*. But it does not seem likely. Numerous theories have been advanced for his disappearance and in 1974 he was declared legally dead. Now no

candle is kept alight for Jim Thompson, but in one of the bedrooms, on a low carved chest, sit three framed photographs of him. If they are there to reassure him should he one day return, they are unnecessary. While he would not recognize the rest of modern Bangkok, Thompson could not fail to feel at home here in his own house which remains a reminder of a world which, like its owner, seems to have vanished forever.

Above: On one wall of the sitting room, opening out onto the klong, *a lacquer cabinet supports a head of Buddha, an outstanding piece of U-Thong stone sculpture. It is testimony to Thompson's natural sense of design and colour harmony that the modern armchairs here should blend in so easily with the antique furniture around them, even though separated in age by hundreds of years.*

THE HOUSE ON THE KLONG, BANGKOK
ARCHITECT: JIM THOMPSON
CONSTRUCTION: 1958-1959
SEE ALSO GAZETTEER, PAGE 178

ALGERIA

ALGIERS
Museum of Popular Arts and Traditions
Rue Soggema
Casbah
Algiers
The former royal palace of the Princess Nefissa is filled with furniture and textiles.

ANDORRA

ORDINO
Areny de Plandolit House (Maison Plandolit)
Ordino
Principat d'Andorra
A family mansion of the late 19th century.

ARGENTINA

ALTA GRACIA
Manuel de Falla Museum
Alta Gracia
The house of the composer (1876-1946) best known for his ballet The Three Cornered Hat. *Interiors with period furnishings, library and memorabilia.*

Virrey Liniers House
Calle Saenz Pena 45
Alta Gracia
A 19th-century house with period furnishings.

BUENOS AIRES
Enrique Larreta Museum of Spanish Art
Obligada 2139
Buenos Aires
A collection of 16th- and 17th-century Spanish paintings and tapestries are housed in the former residence of the 19th-century collector Enrique Larreta.

Mitre Museum
San Martin 336
Buenos Aires
The home of the great patriot and governor of Buenos Aires, General Bartolomé Mitre (1821-1906), has been preserved as it was during his lifetime and contains a collection of documents on the development of Argentina.

Ricardo Rojas House (Casa Rojas)
Charcas 2837
Buenos Aires
The former home of writer Ricardo Rojas (1882-1959) is filled with 19th-century period interiors, a library and a collection of curios.

Yrurtia House (Casa Yrurtia)
O'Higgins 2390
Buenos Aires
The home of sculptor Rogelio Yrurtia (1879-1950) contains a collection of sculpture and memorabilia. It is decorated in period turn-of-the-20th-century style.

CORDOBA
House of the Viceroy Sobremonte (Museo Histórico Provincial Marqués de Sobremonte)
Calle Rosario de Sante Fe 218
Córdoba
An 18th-century house with 18th- and 19th-century furniture, pictures, porcelain and objets d'art.

Leopoldo Lugones Museum
Avenida H. Yrigoyen 645
Córdoba
The writer's life (1874-1938) and work are traced through a collection of memorabilia in the family home. Paintings and artefacts.

GUALEGUAYCHU
Andrade House
Gualeguaychú
Entre Rois
Home of the poet Professor Olegario V. Andrade (1839-1882), featuring 19th-century furnishings and items of personal memorabilia.

LA PLATA
Dardo Rocha Museum
Calle 50, No 933
La Plata
The house of the Argentinian hero Dardo Rocha (1838-1921), with memorabilia and period furniture.

LOSA CORRAL
Fernando Fader House
Losa Corral
An extensive library and a fine collection of antique furniture are housed in the home of the artist Fernando Fader (1882-1935).

MORON
Domingo Vittoria Museum
Calle Jose M. Torres Y Salvador del Camil
Moron
Memorabilia and art collections are preserved in the house and studio of the sculptor Domingo Vittoria (b. 1894).

QUILMES
W. H. Hudson's Birthplace
Florencio Varela
Near Quilmes
The birthplace of the naturalist W. H. Hudson (1841-1922) has been recreated in the style of the 1840s and filled with period furnishings and antiques.

SALTA
House of Jose F. Uriburu
Careros 421
Salta
The family house of the early Argentinian president (in power 1930-1932). Built in 1773, it contains a collection of relics of the War of Independence.

SAMAY HUASI
The Regional Museum
Samay Huasi
La Rioja Province
Local collections of furniture and memorabilia are housed in the restored home of the founder of the University of La Plata, writer Joaquin V. Gonzalez (1863-1923).

SAN ANTONIO DE ARECS
Riconto Guitalder Museum
San Antonio de Arecs
A recreation of an Argentinian ranch, which demonstrates the traditional lifestyle of the gaucho.

SAN ISIDOR
Brigadier General Juan Martin de Pueyr-Redon Museum
Saenz Pena y Rivera In Dalle
San Isidor
Former house of Brigadier General Juan Martin de Pueyr-Redon, who died in 1850. Period furnishings and interiors.

SAN JORE
Regional Museum
Palacio San Jore
The house of the Argentinian patriot hero, General Urquiza, who overthrew the government in 1853, is filled with period furnishings and items of personal memorabilia.

SAN MARTIN
Jose Hernandez-Chacra de Peuyredon Museum
San Martin
Birthplace of the Argentinian poet, Jose Hernandez-Chacra, who was born in 1806. Depicts rural family life of the early 19th century.

TUCUMAN
Bishop Colon Bres's House
Parque 9 de Julio
Tucuman
The 19th-century bishop who introduced sugar cane to Tucuman lived in this house, which features period furnishings and memorabilia.

AUSTRALIA

ADVANCETOWN
Pioneer House
Numinbah Valley Road
Advancetown
Gold Coast
Queensland
An original pioneer "iron-bark" cottage with 1800s furnishings and period relics.

ALBANY
The Old Farm
Strawberry Hill
Albany
W. Australia 6332
A restored settler's farm with period furnishings and outbuildings that contain original farming implements (c.1800).

Old Jail
Stirling Terrace
Albany
W. Australia 6332
The restored town jail contains a collection of convict memorabilia and dates from 1800.

Patrick Taylor Cottage
31 Duke Street
Albany
W. Australia 6332
Built in 1832, the cottage contains period furnishings and memorabilia that date from the early colonial period.

BALLARAT
Montrose Cottage
Ballarat, Victoria 3350
A late 19th-century mining cottage, containing original period furnishings and memorabilia.

Sovereign Hill
PO Box 294
Ballarat, Victoria 3350
A complete gold-mining town of the 1850s, restored to its original appearance with attention to period detail.

BATHURST
Bathurst District Museum
Bathurst
New South Wales 2795
Special features include a settler's cottage dating from 1817.

Macquarrie House
1 George Street
Bathurst
New South Wales 2795
An early 19th-century townhouse with period interiors and antiques.

BERRIMA
Museum of Baking
Wingcarribee Street
Berrima
New South Wales
This recreated baker's shop of the late 19th century features working ovens and period implements.

BEXLEY
Lydham Hall
Lydham Avenue
Bexley
New South Wales
A prosperous late 19th-century house with lavish interiors in the style of the 1870s.

BRISBANE
Early Street
75 McIllwraith Avenue
Norman Park
Brisbane
Queensland 4000
An authentic pioneer settlement, complete with pub, houses and an Aboriginal dwelling.

High Barbaree
109 Albany Creek Road
Aspley
Brisbane
Queensland 4000
A mid-19th-century colonial home with period furniture and memorabilia.

Miegunyah
31-35 Jordan Terrace
Borden Hills
Brisbane
Queensland 4000
The hardships faced by the outback settlers are evident in this beautifully restored early 19th-century pioneer house with period interiors.

Old Court House
Cleveland
Brisbane
Queensland 4000
The original town courthouse, built in 1853, now containing memorabilia of the early Australian judiciary.

Wolston House
Wacol
Brisbane
Queensland 4001
Dating from 1852, this house is filled with period furniture. A butcher's shop of the same period is situated next door.

BROKEN BAY
Henry Kendall's Cottage
West Gosford
Broken Bay
New South Wales
The home of the poet Henry Kendall (1839-1882), displaying items of personal memorabilia.

BUDERIM
Pioneer Cottage
Ballanger Crescent
Buderim
Sunshine Coast
Queensland 4556
A restored early 19th-century cottage, furnished in the style of the period.

BURNIE
Pioneer Village
Burnie, Tasmania
An entire Tasmanian town dating from the turn of the 20th century, restored to its original appearance. Features include a blacksmith's store, post office and inn.

CANBERRA
Blundell's Farmhouse
Wendouree Drive
Canberra, ACT 2601
The pioneer farmer Richard Campbell built this settler's cottage for his ploughman in 1858.

FRANKSTON
Ballam Park Housestead
Cranbourne Road
Frankston
Victoria 3199
A restored farmhouse of c.1843, furnished in the style of the period with antiques.

GERALDTON
Russ Historical Cottage
Dongara
Near Geraldton
W. Australia
A pioneer cottage of the 1870s with period furnishings and memorabilia.

GLEN INNES
Lord of the Beadies
Glen Innes
New South Wales
Dating from 1874, this house features period furnishings.

GOULBURN
Riversdale
Goulburn
New South Wales 2416
An 1840s colonial Georgian house is situated alongside a neoclassical mansion of the mid-19th century with original period furnishings and antiques.

GRAFTON
Schaeffer House
Fitzroy Street
Grafton
New South Wales
The home of a Mr Schaeffer, a local government architect, built for him in 1906.

HARTLEY
Court House
Hartley
New South Wales 2786
The old town courthouse, built in 1837 by Mortimer Lewis, contains a collection of colonial furnishings.

LANE COVE
Carisbrook
Lane Cove
New South Wales
A restored and refurbished 1860s house, featuring period 19th-century interiors.

LAUNCESTON
Entally House
Bass Highway
Hadspen
Near Launceston
Tasmania 7257
An early colonial house with period furniture, antiques and a collection of memorabilia.

Franklin House
Hobart Road
Franklin Village
Launceston
Tasmania 7250
The home of Britton James, a Launceston brewer, built in 1838. Features lavish interiors of the mid-19th century.

LITHGOW
Esk Bank House
Inch Street
Lithgow
New South Wales
An 1841 house, restored and furnished in the style of the period.

MAITLAND
Grossman House Museum
Church Street
Maitland 2320
A house of the 1860s, filled with period furnishings and artefacts.

MERRIWA
Colonial Cottage
Bettington Street
Merriwa
New South Wales 2329
Dating from 1857, this colonial cottage features a parlour and bedroom with 1880 furnishings.

NEW TOWN
Runnymede
61 Bay Road
New Town, Tasmania
Built in the mid-1840s, this colonial house is furnished in 1860s style.

PARRAMATTA
Experiment Farm Cottage
9 Ruse Street
Parramatta
New South Wales 2150
An early settler's cottage, dating from 1798.

Hambledon Cottage
Hassall Street
Parramatta
New South Wales 2150
Dating from 1824, this cottage is filled with period furnishings.

Old Government House
Parramatta Park
Parramatta
New South Wales 2150
The lavishly decorated mansion house of the ex-Viceroy of New South Wales (1799-1855).

PERTH
Old Mill
Narrows Bridge
South Perth
W. Australia
The mill has been restored to its original 1835 appearance with working machinery.

SOUTH ESK
Clarendon House
South Esk, Tasmania
A large 1830s colonial house, notable for its formal gardens.

TOOWOOMBA
Tawa Pioneer Cottage
9 Boulton Street
West Toowoomba
Queensland
An 1880s pioneer house with period interiors.

VAUCLUSE
Vaucluse House
Olola Avenue
Vaucluse
New South Wales 2030
This colonial mansion belonged to William Charles Wentworth, a local businessman, and features period interiors.

VINEGAR HILL
Rouse Hill House
Vinegar Hill
Parramatta
New South Wales
Richard Rouse's understated home, built in 1813-1818, has been maintained as it was in the 1870s. (See pp.150-153.)

WAHROONGA
Rose Seidler House
71 Clissold Road
Wahroonga
New South Wales 2076
Architect Harry Seidler's 1950 creation displays austere Bauhaus style both inside and out. (See pp.154-157.)

WILBERFORCE
Australian Settlers' Village
Wilberforce
New South Wales
A recreation of an entire early 19th-century settlers' village, housed in a large open-air museum.

AUSTRIA

ALPL BEI KRIEGLACH
Peter Rosegger's Birthplace (Peter Rosegger Geburtshaus)
Alpl 42
Kluppeneggerhof
A-8671 Alpl bei
  Krieglach
Steiermark
Peter Rosegger, the novelist, was born in this alpine farmhouse in 1843. The house was restored in 1927 and today it features personal items of memorabilia and two recreated period rooms.

ANSFELDEN
Bruckner Museum (Anton Bruckner Gedenkstätte)
Augustiner Strasse 3
A-4052 Ansfelden
Oberösterreich
Birthplace of the composer Anton Bruckner in 1824. Bruckner's father was the local schoolmaster and the building, an old schoolhouse, contains a period 1830s schoolroom, mementos of the composer's life and the musical instruments that Bruckner played as a young boy.

ARNSDORF
Franz Xavier Gruber Museum
A-5112 Arnsdorf 46
Salzburgerland
Home of the composer of the Christmas carol Stille Nacht ("Silent Night"). Contains original furnishings and items of memorabilia. Gruber, who was church organist at Arnsdorf, wrote "Silent Night" in 1818.

BAD DEUTSCH ALTENBURG
Carl Leopold Hollitzer Museum
A-2405 Bad Deutsch Altenburg
Berzirk Breck an der Leitha
Niederösterreich
The artist's works are displayed in his home which is furnished as it would have appeared during Hollitzer's lifetime (1874-1942).

BAD ISCHL
The Emperor's Villa (Kaiservilla)
Jainzen 38
A-4820 Bad Ischl
Oberösterreich
The summer palace of Emperor Franz-Josef II of Austro-Hungary. Original furniture and Habsburg memorabilia are housed alongside 19th-century paintings, sculpture and porcelain.

Franz Lehar's Villa
Franz Lehar Kai 10
A-4820 Bad Ischl
Oberösterreich
House of the composer of the Merry Widow, bought by him from Count Kalnoky in 1830. Contains Lehar's furniture and personal effects, together with paintings and manuscripts.

BARNACH BEI VOITSBERG
Alt Kainach Castle
Burges Kundliches Museum
Schloss Alt Kainach
Hamptstrasse 68
A-8372 Barnach Bei Voitsberg, Steiermark
Dating from the early Renaissance, this castle features preserved interiors with period furnishings.

BRANDHOF
Archduke Johan Hunting Museum
Jagdschlossen Seeberg
Brandhof
Bezirk Brick an der Mur
Steiermark
Former hunting lodge of the Archduke, restored to its 19th-century appearance. Includes his elaborate period writing room and his personal possessions.

EIBISWALD
Kloepfer Museum
A-8552 Eibiswald 36
Bezirk
Deutschlandsberg
Steiermark
The birthplace of the doctor and poet Hans Kloepfer (d. 1944) contains original furnishings and items of personal memorabilia.

EISENSTADT
Haydn Museum
Joseph Haydngasse
A-7000 Eisenstadt
Burgenland
The house in which the composer Joseph Haydn lived between 1766 and 1788. Musical instruments and Haydn memorabilia are housed alongside paintings, letters and manuscripts. There is also a small museum to the composer Franz Liszt and the dancer Fanny Eisler.

FESTENBURG
Kernstock Museum
Schloss Festenburg
Bezirk Hartberg
Steiermark
The priest and poet Ottokar Kernstock (d. 1928) lived in this house which is furnished in late 19th-century style and contains his personal effects.

GAADEN
Ferdinand Raimund Museum
Heiligen Kreuger
  Strasse 1
A-2531 Gaaden
Bezirk Modling
Niederosterreich
Summer house of the playwright Ferdinand Raimund (1790-1836), containing many of his personal possessions and items of memorabilia.

GLOGGNITZ
Karl Renner Museum
Rennergasse 4
A-2640 Gloggnitz
Neiderösterreich
This museum is housed in the former home of the Austrian president Karl Renner, first chancellor of the Austrian republic, who also wrote the Austrian national anthem. It traces Austrian history in the context of Renner's life from 1918 to 1950.

INNSBRUCK
Apothecary Museum
Herzog Friedrich-
  Str. 25
A-6020 Innsbruck
Tirol
A restored chemist's shop of the early 18th century.

KREUS AN DER DONAU
Kreuser Schuriat Museum
Steiner Landstrasse 122
A-3500 Kreus/Donau
Niederösterreich
House of the painter Martyn Johann Schmidt (1718-1801), restored to its original appearance and containing his works and memorabilia.

KRIEGLACH
Peter Rosegger Museum
Roseggerstrasse 44
A-8670 Krieglach
Steiermark
The home of the novelist and short-story writer Peter Rosegger (1843-1918). Features the bedroom where he died and his workroom, together with portraits and memorabilia.

LINZ
Stifter Memorial Museum (Stifter-Gedenkstätte)
Untere Donaulande 6
A-4020 Linz/Donau
Oberösterreich
A wing of the house in which the Austrian poet worked and died. Original furniture and belongings are housed alongside portraits, manuscripts and memorabilia.

MIESENBACH
Gauermann Museum
A-2761 Scheuchenstein
Miesenbach
Niederösterreich
The family home, dating from c.1800, of the Gauermann family of artists contains original furnishings and works by the Gauermanns.

MODLING
Schoenberg House Museum
Internationale
  Schöenberg-
  Gesellschaft
Bernhardgasse 6
A-2340 Modling
Niederösterreich
The composer Arnold Schoenberg lived in this apartment from 1918 to 1925. It contains furniture, musical instruments, manuscripts and memorabilia.

PERCHTOLDSDORF
Hugo Wolf Memorial Museum
Brunner Gasse 26
A-2380 Perchtoldsdorf
Niederösterreich
The house of the composer Hugo Wolf (1860-1903) and where he lived from 1888 to 1891, contains his personal possessions and documents.

POCHLARN
Oskar Kokoschka Centre
Regensburger Strasse 29
A-3380 Pochlarn
Niederösterreich
The painter (1886-1980) was born in this house which is now a museum of his art, with documentary information on his life and work.

RAIDING
Liszt Museum
Lisztstrasse 42
A-7321 Raiding
Burgenland
The birthplace of the composer (1811-1886) features period interiors and contains portraits, letters and memorabilia.

ROHRAU
Haydn's Birthplace (Haydn Geburtshaus)
Hauptstrasse
A-2471 Rohrau
Niederösterreich
The house where the 18th-century genius was born, now restored to its appearance in 1728 with period furnishings and instruments, including Haydn's piano.

SALZBURG
George Trakl House
Waagplatz 3
A-5020 Salzburg
Memorabilia of the poet (1887-1914) are assembled in the house where he was born.

Mozart's Birthplace (Mozart Geburtshaus)
Getreidegasse 9
A-5020 Salzburg
The house in which Mozart was born and where he wrote his early works. The composer's first violin and piano are displayed with documents relating to his life.

ST GEORGEN
Palace Museum
A-8413 St Georgen
Bezirk Leibnitz
Steiermark
The house of the poet Paul Ernst (d. 1933) contains many of his personal possessions, together with items of memorabilia.

VIENNA
Beethoven Memorial (Beethoven Gedenkstätte)
Pasqualatihaus
Molkerbastei 8
A-1010 Wien
One of the many apartments in Vienna in which the great composer stayed between 1804 and 1808 and again from 1810 to 1814.

Sigmund Freud Museum
Berggasse 19
A-1090 Wien
Consulting room of the doctor (1856-1939), now furnished with his own collection of antiques.

Haydn's House
Haydngasse 19
A-1060 Wien
Furniture, personal memorabilia and the composer's deathmask are assembled in the house where Haydn lived between 1797 and 1809, and where he composed The Seasons.

Mozart Memorial Room
Figarohaus
Schulerstrusse 8
A-1010 Wien 1
Mozart wrote his opera The Marriage of Figaro here, where he lived from 1784 to 1787. The room features many original decorations and items of memorabilia.

The Old Bakehouse
Langegrore 34
A-1080 Wien 8
An original 18th-century baker's shop, restored to look as it would have appeared in 1701, complete with a working oven and period equipment and machinery.

Schonbrunn Palace
Schloss Schonbrunn
A-1130 Wien
An Imperial family residence of the Habsburg dynasty. The house, which dates from 1743, contains a magnificent collection of 18th- and 19th-century furnishings and has remained unchanged since the end of the First World War.

Schubert Museum
Nussdorfer Strasse 54
A-1090 Wien
Birthplace of the composer Franz Schubert in 1797, restored to its original appearance at the time of his birth.

Johann Strauss Museum (Johann Strauss Wohnung)
Praterstrasse 54
A-1020 Wien 2
The house in which Johann Strauss composed The Blue Danube waltz in 1867 features many original items of furniture, together with Strauss memorabilia.

WAIZENKIRCHEN
Wilhelm Kienzl Birthplace
Gasthof Mayerhuber
A-4730 Waizenkirchen
Bezirk Griezkirchen
Oberösterreich
The birthplace of the composer and biographer of Richard Wagner, Wilhelm Kienzl (1857-1941), contains period furniture and memorabilia.

ZWICKLEDT
Kubin House
Zwickledt
Bezirk Scharding
Oberösterreich
The Blaue Reiter painter Alfred Kubin (1877-1959) lived in this house which still contains his personal possessions, together with works of art by him.

BELGIUM

ANTHISNESS
Castle Museum
B-4160 Anthisness
An attempt to recreate the interior of a castle, with an authentic dungeon and furnished 17th-century living quarters.

ANTWERP
Rockox House (Rockoxhuis)
Keizerstraat 12
B-2000 Antwerpen
The home of Nicolas Rockox, perhaps patron of the painter Peter Paul Rubens, restored to its 17th-century appearance.

Rubens's House (Rubenshuis)
Rubensstraat 9-11
B-2000 Antwerpen
A faithful period reconstruction of Sir Peter Paul Rubens's studio which was destroyed during the Second World War.

BRUGES
The Beguine House (Begijnhuis)
Monasterium de
  Wijngaard
Oud Begijnhof 30
B-8000 Brugge
West-Vlaanderen
A restored and refurbished convent which demonstrates how the Beguine order of nuns lived during the 15th century.

Folklore Museum (Museum voor Volkskunde)
Rolweg 40
B-8000 Brugge
West-Vlaanderen
Several houses in the old city of Bruges, restored to their 17th- to 19th-century appearance. Includes a 19th-century inn and an apothecary's shop.

Guido Gezelle Museum
Braine-le-Comte
Rolweg
B-8000 Brugge
West-Vlaanderen
Period furnishings and memorabilia are housed in the birthplace of the Flemish poet Guido Gezelle (1830-1899).

BRUSSELS
Erasmus's House (La Maison d'Erasme)
31 rue du Chapitre
B-1070 Bruxelles
The house in which the scholar and scientist lived during the 1530s, filled with period furnishings and collections relating to his life and work.

Horta's House (Musée Horta)
25 rue Américaine
B-1050 Bruxelles
Architect Victor Horta (1861-1947) designed this house for himself in 1898, epitomizing his distinctive Art Nouveau style. (See pp.132-137.)

GENT
Museum of Folklore (Museum voor Volkskunde)
Kraanlei 65
B-9000 Gent
Oost-Vlaanderen
Located in restored 14th-century almshouses, the museum illustrates daily life in Gent during the 19th century.

ITTRE
Forge Museum (Musée de la Forge)
11 rue Basse
B-1460 Ittre, Brabant
A restored blacksmith's shop of the 19th century, complete with working forge.

LIEGE
Ansembourg Museum (Musée d'Ansembourg)
En Feronstrée, 114
B-4000 Liège
The house of the banker Michel Willens, dating from 1735. Period furnishings are housed alongside family memorabilia of the 18th century.

Gretry Museum
34 rue des Recollets
B-4000 Liège
The birthplace in 1741 of the musician André Ernest Modeste Gretry who composed Richard Coeur de Leon. *Contains period 18th-century furnishings and memorabilia relating to the composer.*

OSTEND
James Ensor's House (James Ensorhuis)
Vlaanderenstraat 27
B-8400 Oostende
West-Vlaanderen
Home of the Post-Impressionist painter James Ensor, who was born in Ostend in 1860. Features personal memorabilia and works of art.

THIEU
Museum of the Central Canal (Musée vivant du Canal du Centre)
Ecluse No.1
69 rue des Peupliess
B 7058 Thieu
Haisaut Mons
A preserved section of the 19th-century canal, with Keepers' houses and various working exhibits.

VIEUX-GEMAPPE
The Caillou Farm
Caillou 8
B-1472 Vieux-Gemappe
The small farm where Napoleon set up his headquarters during the Waterloo campaign. Much of the farm has been restored as it would have looked at the time of the battle of Waterloo in 1815.

WATERLOO
Wellington Museum (Musée Wellington)
147 chaussée de Bruxelles
B-1410 Waterloo
Brabant
The wayside inn where Wellington had his headquarters during the battle of Waterloo. Maps, uniforms and memorabilia are on display, including Lord Uxbridge's wooden leg. Original furnishings.

BERMUDA

ST GEORGE'S
The Confederate Museum
The King's Parade
St George's
An early 19th-century house, furnished as it would have appeared in 1861, at the time of the American Civil War.

Historical Museum
Kent Street
St George's
An early 1700s Bermuda house.

The Old Rectory
St George's
A restored colonial cottage dating from 1715 and filled with period furnishings.

Henry Tucker House
Water Street
St George's
The house of the President of the Council of Bermuda during the American War of Independence. Features restored 18th-century interiors.

SMITH'S PARISH
Verdmont
Smith's Parish
A 17th-century colonial house, complete with period furnishings and antiques dating from 1815.

Winterhaven Cottage
Harrington Sound Road
Smith's Parish
A restored and refurbished 18th-century Bermudan farm cottage.

BRAZIL

BLUMENAU
Museum of a Colonial Family
Alameda Duque de Caxis
Blumenau
Santa Catarina
A 19th-century mansion featuring colonial interiors.

CACHOEIRA
Nobre House (Praca da Aclamacao Cachoeira)
Cachoeira
The former residence of the Brazilian writer features period furnishings and items of memorabilia.

FLORIANOPOLIS
Vitor Merles House
Florianopolis
Birthplace of the painter Vitor Merles with period interiors and a collection of Merles' work.

LENCOIS
Afrânio Peixoto House (Casa de Afrânio Peixoto)
Praca Afrânio Peixoto
Lencois, Bahia
Personal possessions and memorabilia are housed in the home of the writer Afrânio Peixoto (1876-1947).

RECONCAVO
Wanderley Pinho Museum
Engenho da Fregnesia
Reconcavo, Bahia
An 18th-century house which was formerly the home of the aristocratic Wanderley Pinho family.

SALVADOR
Rui Barbosa House
Rua Rui Barbosa 12
Salvador, Bahia
The birthplace of the Brazilian patriot Rui Barbosa (1849-1923) features period interiors and items of memorabilia.

House of the Seven Cardeiros
Rua Sao Francisco 32
Salvador, Bahia
A 17th-century Brazilian house with period furnishings and decorations.

Nelson de Sousa Oliveira Collection
Av. 7 De Setembro 172-4
Salvador, Bahia
The house of professor Nelson de Sousa contains a diverse collection of pictures, sculpture, jacaranda furniture and porcelain.

SAO PAULO
Casa do Grito
Parque do Ipiranga
Sao Paulo
An early 19th-century Brazilian house filled with period furnishings.

Manor House Museum
Praca Monteiro Lobato
Sao Paulo
An 18th-century house, restored with period furnishings and decoration.

Portinari House
Praca Cándido Portinari
Brodosqui
Sao Paulo
The house of the artist Cándido Portinari (1903-1962), with original works and personal items of memorabilia.

VICOSA DO CEARA
Amelia Bevilacqua Museum
Viçosa do Ceará
The birthplace in 1813 of the jurist Clovis Bevilacqua, restored to its original appearance during his lifetime.

BULGARIA

BANSKO
Nikola Vaptsarov House
9 Place Vaptsarov
Bansko
The birthplace and house of the revolutionary poet (1909-1942), much of it preserved as it was during his lifetime.

KARLOVO
Vasil Levski House
Karlovo
Memorabilia of the 19th-century Bulgarian patriot (1837-1873) is gathered together in his birthplace.

KOPRIVSHTITSA
Georgi Benkovski House
Koprivshtitsa
Birthplace of the early Bulgarian revolutionary, Georgi Benkovski (early 1840s-1876), the 1831 house contains period furnishings and memorabilia.

Dimco Debeljanov House
Deganska ul.
Koprivshtitsa
The 1830s home of the poet Dimco Debeljanov (1887-1916), filled with memorabilia, documents and furniture.

Todor Kablesov House
Koprivshtitsa
An 1850s house, filled with period furnishings and memorabilia relating to the life of the 19th-century revolutionary Todor Kablesov.

Ljuben Karavelov House
Koprivshtitsa
The house of the revolutionary poet Ljuben Karavelov (1835-1879), with personal possessions, furniture and memorabilia.

Oslekov Museum
Koprivshtitsa
A museum of life in Bulgaria before its liberation in 1878 is housed in 19th-century entrepreneur Nenco Nikolov Oslekov's house, built in 1856.

LOVEC
Vasil Levski Museum
Lovec
The house where the 19th-century revolutionary Vasil Levski took refuge is now filled with his personal possessions and memorabilia.

PAZARJIK
Stanislav Dospevsky Museum
B.G. Dimitrov 50
Pazarjik
House of the painter Stanislav Dospevsky (1826-1876), with 19th-century furniture, paintings and memorabilia.

SOFIA
Dimiter Blagoev Museum
Ul. Kossuth 33
Sofia
The founder of Bulgarian Communism, Dimiter Blagoev (1856-1924), lived in this house, which is now a shrine to his memory and filled with personal possessions and documents.

Georgi Dimitrov Museum
Opalcenska 66
Sofia
The simple house where the communist leader Georgi Dimitrov lived between 1888 and 1912 contains furniture, memorabilia and documents.

ZHERAVNA
Tordan Yovkov House
Zheravna
Memorabilia, first editions of Yovkov's works and documents relating to his life are housed in the author's home.

CANADA

AINSWORTH HOT SPRINGS
Silver Ledge Hotel
Ainsworth Hot Springs
British Columbia
A Canadian frontier hotel, furnished in late 19th-century style.

ALLISTON
South Simcoe Pioneer Museum
Riverdale Park
Alliston, Ontario
The museum of Canada's frontiersmen is housed in an 1851 pioneer cabin, fitted out in the style of the period.

ALVINSTON
A. W. Campbell House
Rural Route 2
Alvinston
Ontario
Named after the family that built the house, this rural dwelling of the 1890s is filled with period furnishings and Campbell memorabilia.

AMHERSTBURG
Park House
Dalhousie Street
Amherstburg
Ontario
A collection of 1890s furnishings, in a classic colonial house of the period.

ANNAPOLIS ROYAL
O'Dell House and McNamara House
Historic Waterfront
Lower Street and George Street
Annapolis Royal
Nova Scotia
The mid-19th-century inn and schoolmaster's house have been perfectly restored to their original appearance.

ARTHABASKA
Laurier Museum
16 rue Laurier
Arthabaska
Quebec
The former residence, from 1867 to 1896, of the Canadian statesman Sir Wilfrid Laurier, Prime Minister of Canada from 1896, contains period furnishings and memorabilia.

BERTHIERVILLE
Pioneer Village
Berthierville
Quebec
An entire 19th-century village, including the original chapel, dairy and manor house, restored to its original appearance.

BIGGAR
Homestead Museum
Highway 51
Biggar
Saskatchewan
The pioneer house and general store were both constructed in 1910. They have been restored to their appearance at the turn of the 20th-century.

BOWMANVILLE
Pioneer House
Darlington Provincial Park
Rural Route 2
Bowmanville
Ontario
A two-storey pioneer log cabin, built and furnished in the style of the 1820s to 1840s.

BRANTFORD
Bell Homestead
94 Tutela Heights Road
Brantford
Ontario
The house of the inventor of the telephone, Alexander Graham Bell, including the room from which he made the first ever telephone call in 1876.

BROUGHAM
Town of Pickering
Highway 7
Brougham
Ontario
An entire 19th-century town, including a school, a blacksmith's shop and a variety of barns, restored to its original appearance.

CANNIFTON
O'Klava Mill
Cannifton
Ontario
A typical mill, dating from 1848, built alongside a school constructed in 1811. Both buildings have been restored to their original condition.

CANNINGTON
Hewett House and Pioneer House
Cannington
Saskatchewan
Built during the early 19th century, these pioneer houses are equipped with period furnishings and memorabilia.

CAPE SPEAR
Lighthouse
Cape Spear
Newfoundland
A restored early 19th-century lighthouse with keeper's quarters, period furnishings, machinery and local memorabilia.

CARAQUET
Arcadian Historic Village
Near Caraquet
New Brunswick
The Arcadian people that came to Canada from France in the 18th century lived in this village which includes houses, a school, a store and an inn, dating from 1780 to 1880.

CAVENDISH
Anne of Green Gables House
Prince Edward Island
The 1880 house of novelist Maude Montgomery, author of Anne of Green Gables, furnished in the simple style of the book.

CHARLOTTETOWN
Strathgartney Homestead
Route 1
Charlottetown
Prince Edward Island
An 1846 farmhouse, furnished in the style of the period, with period decorations, memorabilia and antiques.

DARTMOUTH
Quaker Whalers' House
52-59 Ochterlorny Street
Dartmouth
Nova Scotia
This coastal house, which dates from 1785 to 1792, was owned by a Nantucket whaler and contains original furnishings and memorabilia from the age of Moby Dick.

DORCHESTER
Keillor House
Route 6
Dorchester
New Brunswick
The house of the local Keillor family, dating from 1813-1900 and filled with period furnishings and family memorabilia.

DOWNSVIEW
Black Creek Pioneer Village
Jane Street and Steele's Avenue
Downsview
Ontario
An entire pioneer village of the 19th century. 20 buildings date from 1793 to 1867, including a town hall, church, shops and other classic buildings.

DRESDEN
Uncle Tom's Cabin
Rural Route 5
Dresden
Ontario
The 1842 house of the Reverend Josiah Henson, who inspired the central character of Uncle Tom in Harriet Beecher Stowe's novel.

DUNVEGAN
Mission St Charles Alberta
Dunvegan
Alberta
The original log-built settlement church and neighbouring rectory of 1885, with original furnishings.

EDMONTON
Rutherford House
University of Alberta
11153 Saskatchewan Drive
Edmonton, Alberta
The first Premier of Alberta, A.C. Rutherford, lived in this house, which features early 20th-century interiors.

Ukranian Cultural Heritage Village
Near Elk Island Natural Park
Rural Route 1
Edmonton, Alberta
A complete village of 20 buildings in the Ukranian settlers' style of 1890-1930, with Russian-style furnishings of the period.

John Walter Historical Site
10627 93rd Avenue
Edmonton
Alberta
J. Walter, the owner of the local sawmill, built the houses that make up this village between 1874 and 1886. They all feature traditional 19th-century interiors.

GODERICH
Huron Historical Gaol
81 Victoria Street North
Goderich
Ontario
The original gaol (c. 1839-1842) and 1900 gaoler's house, all decorated in period style.

GRAFTON
Barnum House
Highway 2
Grafton
Ontario
An 1817 house with period rooms filled with agricultural tools.

GRAVENHURST
Bethune Memorial Museum
John and Hughson Streets
Gravenhurst
Ontario
The birthplace of Dr Norman Bethune. Built in 1901, the house is filled with its original period furnishings.

GUELPH
Colonel John McCrae Museum
102 Water Street
Guelph
Ontario
Colonel McCrae, the artist, doctor and poet, was born in this house. It dates from 1872 and contains his personal possessions, furniture and memorabilia.

HAMILTON
Dundurn Castle
Dundurn Park
York Boulevard
Hamilton
Ontario
Dating from 1832, this castle is filled with period furnishings installed by its former occupant, Prime Minister Sir Allan Macnab (1854-1856).

**Whitehern
(McQuesten) House**
41 Jackson Street West
Hamilton, Ontario
*A house of the 1840s, once
the home of local doctor
Calvin McQuesten.
Contains furniture and
memorabilia.*

HANTSPORT
Churchill House
Main Street
Hantsport, Nova Scotia
*The home of Ezra
Churchill, the shipbuilder,
dates from 1860 and is
filled with shipbuilding
tools and instruments, and
period furnishings.*

HARRISON MILLS
Kilby Historic Park
215 Kilby Road
Harrison Mills
British Columbia
*A collection of historic
buildings, including a
general store and hotel
dating from 1904, with
stock and furnishings of
the 1920s and 1930s.*

HOLLAND CENTRE
Comber Pioneer Village
Holland Centre
Ontario
*An entire pioneer village
restored to its original
appearance. Contains a
log cabin dating from
1841, a log barn, an inn
and a schoolhouse.*

ILE D'ORLEANS
Mauvide-Jenest Manor
Ile d'Orleans, Quebec
*A 19th-century French-
Canadian manor house,
containing a collection of
antique furniture from
the 18th and 19th
centuries.*

IROQUOIS
Carmen House
Carmen Road
Iroquois, Ontario
*Built in 1825, this house is
decorated in period style
and contains its original
furnishings and artefacts.*

ISLINGTON
Montgomery's Inn
Dundas Street
Islington, Ontario
*A restored travellers' inn
of 1830, with period
decoration and
furnishings.*

KELOWNA
**Father Pandosy
Museum**
Benvolin Road
Kelowna
British Columbia
*Dating from 1859, this
restored mission is made
up of log buildings with
period furnishings.*

KINGSTON
Bellevue House
5 Centre Street
Kingston, Ontario
*The home of Canada's
first Prime Minister, John
A. Macdonald, with 19th-
century interiors and
period furnishings.*

Old Fort
Henry Highway 2
Kingston, Ontario
*A 19th-century pioneer
fort with buildings
furnished in period style.*

KITCHENER
Homer Watson House
1754 Old Mill Road
Kitchener, Ontario
*The house of the artist
Homer Watson, furnished
in the style of his lifetime
(1855-1936) with 1830s
furniture and
memorabilia.*

Woodside Park
528 Wellington Street
  North
Kitchener, Ontario
*An 1870s house with
period decoration and
furniture, formerly the
home of William Lyon
Mackenzie King (1874-
1950), Prime Minister of
Canada 1921-1926.*

LAURENTIDE
**Sir Wilfred Laurier
House**
Laurentide, Quebec
*The 1840s home of the
statesman, Sir Wilfred
Laurier, first Catholic
premier of Canada.
Period furnishings and
memorabilia.*

LIVERPOOL
Simeon Perkins House
420 Main Street
Liverpool, Nova Scotia
*The 1766 house of the
diarist Simeon Perkins,
furnished in the style of
the period and filled with
Perkins memorabilia.*

LONDON
Eldon House
481 Rideout Street North
London, Ontario
*A house from c.1834,
restored and decorated in
the style of the period.*

MAITLAND
W.D. Lawrence House
Maitland, Nova Scotia
*The shipbuilder lived in
this 1870s house, which is
furnished in period style.*

MANOR
Hewlett House
Manor, Saskatchewan
*Once the home of English
settlers, this 1880s house
has original furniture.*

MIDDLEPORT
Chiefswood
Highway 54
Middleport, Ontario
*Birthplace of the
celebrated Native-
American poetess, E.
Pauline Johnson, this
Native-American house
dates from before the
Confederation.*

MONT CARMEL
**Arcadian Pioneer
Village**
Mont Carmel
Prince Edward Island
*An Arcadian pioneer
church, smithy, school,
house and store, furnished
in 19th-century style.*

MONTREAL
Chateau de Ramezay
Notre Dame Street East
Montreal 127, Quebec
*Owned by an 18th-century
governor of Montreal, this
1705 château contains
French furniture,
porcelain and silver.*

MOUNT UNIAKE
Mount Uniake
Mount Uniake
Nova Scotia
*The 1815 house of an
Attorney-General of Nova
Scotia, R. J. Uniake
(1797-1830).*

NEW LONDON
**Lucy Maud
Montgomery Birthplace**
New London
Prince Edward Island
*Home of the diarist and
writer (1874-1942), with
period furnishings.*

NIAGARA FALLS
Oak Hall
Portage Road South
Niagara Falls
Ontario
*Built between 1898 and
1928 for the Schollkop
family, Oak Hall features
impressive interiors with
period decoration and
panelling taken from
Hampton Court in
England.*

NIAGARA ON THE LAKE
McFarland House
Niagara Parkway
Niagara on the Lake
Ontario
*Dating from 1800, this
restored house is filled
with 1820s furnishings.*

Niagara Apothecary
5 Queen Street
Niagara on the Lake
Ontario
*A restored 1860s chemist's
shop, complete with its
original stock and
decorative features.*

ORILLA
Stephen Leacock House
Old Brewery Bay
Atherley Road
Orilla
Ontario
*Dating from 1927, the
home of the author
Stephen Butler Leacock
(1869-1944), best known
as a humorist for his
Nonsense Novels of
1911, contains furniture
and memorabilia.*

PERIBONKA
Louis Hemon Museum
Route 169
Peribonka
Quebec
*The former house of the
writer Louis Hemon.
Contains original
furnishings and period
decor of the early 20th
century.*

QUEENSTOWN
**Laura Secord
Homestead**
Queenstown and
  Partition Steets
Queenstown
Ontario
*Laura Secord, a local
celebrity, lived in this
house which is decorated
in period style with early
1800s furnishings.*

ST ANDREWS
Red River House
Junction of Highways
  238 and 410
St Andrews
Manitoba
*The Hudson's Bay trader
and explorer Captain
William Kennedy's
former home contains late
19th-century period
decoration, furniture and
memorabilia.*

ST GEORGE
**Adelaide Hunter
Hoodless Homestead**
Rural Route 1
St George
Ontario
*The former home of the
founder of the Women's
Institute, Adelaide
Hunter Hoodless.
Contains period
decorations of the 1860s.*

TORONTO
Colborne Lodge
Colborne Lodge Road
Howard Road
High Park
Toronto, Ontario
*The mansion, which dates
from 1836 and belonged
to a local figure, John G.
Howard, contains its
original decoration,
furniture and
memorabilia.*

Mackenzie House
82 Bond Street
Toronto
Ontario
*Toronto's first mayor, W.
L. Mackenzie, lived in
this house, which features
19th-century period
interiors.*

VICTORIA
Point Ellice House
2612 Pleasant Street
Victoria
British Columbia
*Built by the local O'Reilly
family in the 1860s, Point
Ellice House contains
original 1860s period
decoration and furniture.*

WINDSOR
Haliburton Museum
Clifton Avenue
Windsor
Nova Scotia
*The home of the writer
T. C. Haliburton, built in
1833, with period
interiors and furnishings.*

CHINA

BEIJING
Xu Beihong Museum
53 Xinjiekou
Beidajie
Xicheng District, Beijing
*The house of Xu Beihong
(d. 1953), the painter of
horses, features
memorabilia, the artist's
library and many of his
works and implements.*

CHENGDU
**Du Fu's Cottage
(Du Fu Caotang)**
Chengdu, Sichuan
*Home of the poet Du Fu
(712-70), this cottage
contains items of
memorabilia and Chinese
and Western editions of
his works.*

NANCHANG
Qing Yun Pu Monastery
Nanchang, Jiangxi
*The rooms that the
painter Bada Shanren
(1661-1687) occupied,
reproduced as they
appeared during his
lifetime.*

SHANGHAI
Lu Xun Museum
Hongkou Park
Shanghai
*The writer died in this
house in 1936. It contains
Lu Xun's personal
possessions, furniture and
memorabilia.*

SHAOSHAN
Mao's Birthplace
Shaoshan, Hunan
*The birthplace of
Chairman Mao Tse-tung
(1893-1976) features
furnishings and
memorabilia relating to
the leader of the Chinese
Communist party. Visitors
may even sleep in his bed.*

YANAN
Mao's House
Yanan, Shaanxi
*The cave house in which
Mao Tse-tung lived from
1935 to 1947, containing
his personal possessions
and memorabilia.*

COLOMBIA

BOGOTA
Jorge Eliécer Gaitán Museum
Calle 42, 15-32
Bogotá
Home of Gaitán, the left-wing liberal politician who was assassinated in 1948.

BUCARAMANGA
Garcia Rovira House
Calle 35, 8-68
Bucaramanga
Santander
The birthplace of the 19th-century artist Garcia Rovira contains colonial furniture.

POPAYAN
Valencia House Museum
Carrera 6, 2-69
Popayán, Cauca
Personal possessions and memorabilia are housed in the home of the poet Guillermo Valencia.

TUNJA
Juan de Vargas House
Calle 20, Carreras 8-9
Tunja, Boyaca
The house of writer Juan de Vargas contains 19th-century furnishings and memorabilia.

CUBA

BAYAMO
Carlos Manuel de Céspedes House
Bayamo
The birthplace of Céspedes (1871-1939), the first President of Cuba, contains period furniture, decoration and memorabilia.

HAVANA
Hemingway Museum
Finca la Vigia
Habana
San Francisco de Paula
The U.S. novelist Ernest Hemingway (1899-1961) lived in this house. It contains original furnishings and his personal possessions.

CZECH REPUBLIC

HUDLICE
Josef Jungmann Museum
Rodny domek
C.43, Hudlice
Former home of the natural historian, Josef Jungmann, with collections of natural history.

KRECOVICE U SEDLCAN
Josef Suk Museum
C.3 Krecovice u Sedlcan
Former house of the composer filled with period furnishings.

NELAHOZEVES
Antonin Dvorak Museum
Nelahozeves
The composer Antonin Dvorak (1841-1904) lived in this house. It is filled with late 19th-century furnishings, personal possessions and memorabilia relating to the famous composer.

STARA HUT U DOBRUSE
Karel Capek Museum
Na Strzi c.125
Stara Hut u Dobruse
The home of the author Karel Capek (1890-1938) is filled with his own items of furniture and collections of his work.

DENMARK

GLUD
Glud Museum
Museumsveij 44
Glud
DK-8700 Horsens
S. Jylland
A re-creation of a rural village including a barn, fisherman's house, three farmhouses and a working blacksmith's shop.

ODENSE
Hans Andersen's House (Hans Christian Andersen Hus)
Hans Jensens Straede 37-45
DK-5000 Odense C
Fyn
The birthplace of the writer of fairytales. 19th-century interiors with furniture and memorabilia.

OSLØS
Skjoldborg Museum (Skjoldborg Hus)
Skippergade 6
Osløs
DK-7742 Vestløs
N. Jylland
Johan Martinus Skjoldborg's childhood home, furnished as it was during the writer's lifetime (1861-1936).

PADBORG
Froslev Camp Museum (Froslevlejreus Museum)
Lejrvejen 97
DK-6330 Padborg
S. Jylland
The notorious prison camp where Danes were imprisoned for taking part in resistance activities against the Nazis in World War II, now restored to its appearance at that time.

PRAESTO
Thorvaldesen Collection (Thorvaldesen Samlingen pa Nyso)
Nysovej 5
DK-4200 Praestö
Sjaelland
Works by the Danish sculptor Bertel Thorvaldesen (1770-1844) are housed in the 17th-century manor house where he had his studio during the 1840s.

SKAGEN
Michael and Anna Anchers's House (Michael og Anna Anchers Hus)
Markvej 2
DK-9990 Skagen
N. Jylland
The Anchers family of painters lived and worked in this house during the late 19th century. It features period furnishings and collections.

SKIVE
Annine Michelsen Memorial Room (Frk. Annine Michelsen Mindestuen)
Ostergade 4A
DK-7800 Skive
N. Jylland
The home of the confectioner Annine Michelsen, which now contains memorabilia and documents on her art.

SVENDBORG
Svendborg Museum
Grubbemollevej 13
DK-5700 Svendborg
Fyn
The former town workhouse, now preserved as a museum to show the poor working conditions during the 19th century.

TERSLOSE
Terslose Manor (Den Holbergske Stiflelse Terslosgard)
Holbergvej 101
Terslose
DK-4293 Dianalund
Sjaelland
The home of the playwright Ludvig Holberg (1684-1754), preserved inside as it was during his lifetime. Personal possessions and memorabilia.

EGYPT

ALEXANDRIA
Montazah Palace Museum
Montazah
Alexandria
A 19th-century royal palace, complete with period furnishings and memorabilia relating to the Royal family.

CAIRO
Abdine Palace Museum
El Goumhouria Square
Cairo
A 19th-century royal palace, furnished in the style of the period.

Al Gawshara Palace Museum
Citadel
Cairo
Built in 1811 as a palace for the Royal family, the house features Middle-Eastern-style interiors and French and Far-Eastern furniture.

Manial Palace
Roda Island
Cairo
Dating from 1901, this Royal dwelling features a rare collection of fine antiques.

Rest House Museum
Helwan
Cairo
The rest house of ex-King Farouk, who abdicated in 1952, is filled with original furnishings.

ESTONIA

TALLINN
Peter the Great's Cottage
Kadriorg
Tallinn
The Tsar's country house has been preserved as it was during the 1710s, at the time of the construction of his St Petersburg palace.

FINLAND

BOBACK
Hvitträsk
SF-02440 Boback
Uusimaa
The house and studio of the architect Eliel Saarinen features original interiors with pieces designed by Saarinen. (See pp.138-141.)

ESPOO
Gallen-Kallelan Museum (Gallen-Kallelan Museo)
Gallen-Kallelantie 27
SF-02600 Espoo
Uusimaa
The home and studio of artist Akseli Waldemar Gallen-Kallelan (1865-1931), preserved as they were during his lifetime.

Glims Farmstead (Glims Talonmuseo)
Glimsintie 1
SF-02740 Espoo
Uusimaa
An entire 16th-century farmhouse, preserved with all its outbuildings and period furnishings.

HALIKKO
Halikko Museum (Halikko Museo)
Kirkkorinne 7
SF-24800 Halikko
Turku ja Pori
Intricately detailed reconstructions of traditional 18th- and 19th-century rural workshops.

HAMEENLINNA
Sibelius's Birthplace (Sibeliusken Syntymakoti)
Hallituskatu 11
SF-13210 Hämeenlinna
Häme
The 1830s house in which the composer Jean Sibelius was born in 1865.

HARJAVALTA
Emil Codercreutz Museum
SF-29200 Harjavalta
Turku ja Pori
The house of the 19th-century collector Baron Emil Codercreutz, filled with his collections of folk art displayed in period settings.

HELSINKI

Amos Anderson Museum (Amos Anderson Museo)
Yrjonkatu 27
SF-00100 Helsinki
Built in 1912, the house was once owned by the publisher Amos Anderson and contains his extensive art collections.

Seurasaari Open Air Museum (Seurasaari Ulkomuseo)
Seurasaari
SF-00250 Helsinki
A rural village made up of preserved 18th- and 19th-century windmills, houses and workshops.

IMATRA

Industrial Workers' Museum (Teollisuustyovaen a Suntomuseo)
Ritikanranta
SF-55120 Imatra, Kymi
A living museum which, in its buildings and furnishings, illustrates how workers lived from the 1890s to the 1960s.

JARVENPAA

Sibelius's House "Ainola"
SF-04400 Järvenpää
Uusimaa
The house in which the composer Jean Sibelius lived from 1904 until his death in 1957 contains original collections of furnishings and memorabilia.

KIMITO

Sagalund Museum (Sagalunds Museo)
Vreta
SF-25700 Kimito
Turku ja Pori
Various buildings, including a school, demonstrating rural life in Finland from the 1650s to 1900s.

KUOPIO

Kuopio Open Air Museum (Kuopion Museo)
Kauppakatu 23
SF-70100 Kuopio
A collection of five traditional buildings with period interiors dating from the 18th century to the 1930s.

KUUSAMO

Kuusamo Museum (Kuusamon Kotiseutumuseo)
Porkkatie 4
SF-93600 Kuusamo
A recreated farm with barns, stables, a dwelling house and other 19th-century buildings.

PORVOO

Johan Runeberg House (J.L. Runeberg Koti)
Runeberginkatu 20
SF-06100 Porvoo
Uusimaa
Where the poet lived from 1853 until his death in 1877, furnished in period style with memorabilia.

SAARIJARVI

Squire's House Museum (Saatylaiskotimuseo)
Saarijärven Museo
PL 13
SF-43101 Saarijärvi
Keski-Suom
A house of the 1780s, where the poet J. L. Runeberg was a tutor, furnished and decorated as it was during his lifetime.

TURKU

Luostarinmaki Handicrafts Museum (Luostarinmaen Kasityolaismuseo)
SF-20700 Turku
A Jugendstijl-style building filled with crafts and furnished in the distinctive sinuous manner of the style.

VAASA

Bragegarden
Sandviken
SF-65100 Vaasa
An 1810 dwelling house, a farm and other rural buildings of the same period are housed in this large open-air museum.

FRANCE

AIX-EN-PROVENCE

Cézanne's Studio (Atelier Cézanne)
9 avenue Paul Cézanne
F-13100 Aix-en-Provence
Bouches-du-Rhône
The home and studio of the great late-Impressionist painter Paul Cézanne (1839-1906). The house was built by him in 1901, and it is still furnished in the turn-of-the-20th-century style of his lifetime.

AJACCIO

House of the Bonapartes (Maison Bonaparte)
rue Saint-Charles
F-20000 Ajaccio
Corse
Restored childhood home of the Emperor Napoleon I (1769-1821). A humble dwelling, simply furnished in the style of the late 18th century.

AMBIERLE

Alice Taverne Museum (Musée Taverne)
F-42820 Ambierle
Loire
Exhibits on the history of local life are displayed in this mid-19th-century town house.

ARBOIS

Pasteur Family Home (Maison Pasteur)
83 rue de Courcelles
F-39600 Arbois
Jura
The small house in which the scientist and discoverer of vaccination (1822-1895) grew up is furnished as it was during the days of his childhood.

AVIGNON

Théodore Aubanel Museum (Musée Aubanel)
7 place Saint Pierre
F-84057 Avignon
Vaucluse
The 14th-century family home of the printer and publisher Théodore Aubanel, restored to look as it did during his lifetime. The museum's diverse contents include a working printing press.

BARBIZON

Barbizon School Museum (Musée Théodore Rousseau)
55 Grande Rue
F-77630 Barbizon
Seine-et-Marne
The home of the painter Théodore Rousseau (1812-1867) now tells the story of the mid-19th-century school of French landscapists. It features paintings, period furnishings and memorabilia.

BARR

Marco's Folly (Le Folie Marco)
30 rue Dr Sultzer
F-67140 Barr, Bas-Rhin
The mansion of a 1760s barrister has been restored to its original late 18th-century appearance and is filled with a large collection of faience.

BONNEUIL-MATOURS

Arcadian Farm Museum (Les Huit Maisons)
Archigny
F-86210 Bonneuil-Matours, Vienne
A late 18th-century farm which tells the story of the French settlers who were driven out of Canada during the 1770s.

BRUNOY

Dunoyer de Segonzac Museum (Musée Dunoyer de Segonzac)
Marie de Boussy-Sainte-Antoine
F-91800 Brunoy
Essonne
Birthplace of the realist painter André Dunoyer de Segonzac, restored to its appearance at the time of his birth in 1884.

CAGNES-SUR-MER

Renoir Museum (Musée Renoir)
Chemin des Collettes
F-06800 Cagnes-sur-Mer
Alpes-Maritimes
The house where Renoir lived between 1908 and 1919, restored to its appearance at the turn of the century, contains period furnishings, paintings and memorabilia.

CAMBO-LES-BAINS

Edmond Rostand Museum (Musée Rostand)
route de Bayonne
F-64250 Cambo-les-Bains
Pyrénées-Atlantiques
The poet and playwright (1868-1918), best known for Cyrano de Bergerac, lived in this mansion which contains period furnishings of the 1890s.

CHATEAUROUX

Bertrand Museum (Musée Bertrand)
2 rue Descente-des-Cordeliers
F-36000 Châteauroux
Indre
One of the Emperor Napoleon's most faithful generals lived in this house, which is now restored to its early 19th-century appearance.

CHATEAU-THIERRY

Jean de La Fontaine Museum (Musée Fontaine)
12 rue Jean-de-La-Fontaine
F-02400 Château-Thierry
Aisne
The house, which dates from 1559, was once occupied by the interpreter of Aesop's fables Jean de La Fontaine (1621-1695), and features early 18th-century furnishings and decoration.

CHATELLERAULT

Descartes's House (Maison Descartes)
162 rue Bourbon
F-86100 Châtellerault
Vienne
The 18th-century philosopher's family home, restored to its appearance at the time of his childhood.

COLMAR

Bartholdi Museum (Musée Bartholdi)
30 rue des Marchands
F-68000 Colmar
Haut-Rhin
The family home of the sculptor Auguste Bartholdi (1834-1904). Period furnishings and memorabilia.

COLOMBEY-LES-DEUX-EGLISES

La Boisserie
F-52330 Colombey-les-Deux-Églises
Haute-Marne
The house in which President Charles de Gaulle lived from 1934 to 1939 and later, after the Second World War, until his death. Early 20th-century interiors and memorabilia.

COMPIEGNE

Château de Compiègne
place du General-de-Gaulle
F-60200 Compiègne
Oise
An 18th-century Bourbon palace containing several important interiors of the Napoleonic period.

DENICE

Claude Bernard Museum (Maison Bernard)
Saint-Julien-en-Beaujolais
F-69640 Denice, Rhône
Birthplace of the physiologist (1813-1878), decorated in mid-19th-century French style.

ESBLY

Louis Braille Museum (Musée Braille)
rue Louis-Braille
Coupvray
F-77450 Esbly
Seine-et-Marne
Birthplace of the friend of the blind and inventor of braille (1809-1852).

EU

Louis-Philippe Museum
Château d'Eu
F-76260 Eu
Seine-Maritime
A 19th-century château, restored to its appearance at the time of the reign of Louis-Philippe (1830-1848).

GARGILESSE

George Sand's House
Aligra
F-36190 Gargilesse
Indre
The country retreat of Amandine Aurore Lucile Dupin (George Sand, 1804-1876), the novelist and infamous transvestite lover of Chopin.

GASNY
Monet's House
Giverny
F-27620 Gasny
Eure
The Impressionist painter Claude Monet (1840-1926) lived in this country house, which is set in the landscaped grounds he immortalized on canvas.

ILE D'AIX
Napoleonic Museum
Maison de l'Empereur
rue Napoleon
F-17123 Ile d'Aix
Charente-Maritime
Napoleon Bonaparte spent his last night in France in this house, before leaving for exile on St Helena in 1815. Period decoration.

ILE D'OUESSANT
Ouessant Museum
Maison du Niou Huella
F-29242 Ouessant
Finistère
A local 19th-century house containing original painted furniture.

ILLIERS-COMBRAY
**Proust Museum
(Maison de Tante Léonie)**
4 rue du Docteur Proust
F-28120 Illiers-Combray
Eure-et-Loire
The house of Tante Léonie, the character that Marcel Proust (1871-1922) immortalized in his works. Late 19th-century interiors. (See pp.98-103.)

JARD-SUR-MER
**Clemenceau Museum
(Maison Clemenceau)**
Saint-Vincent-sur-Jard
F-85520 Jard-sur-Mer
Vendée
The house in which George Clemenceau (1841-1929), premier during the First World War, spent his last ten years, complete with turn-of-the-20th-century decoration.

JUGON-LES-LACS
Historic Farm Museum
Le Saint-Esprit-des-Bois
Pledeliac
F-22270 Jugon-les-Lacs
Côtes-d'Armor
An 1810 farmhouse and other rural buildings.

LABASTIDE-MURAT
**Murat's House
(Maison Murat)**
place de l'Eglise
F-46240 Labastide-Murat, Lot
Birthplace of Napoleon's dashing Marshal Joachim Murat who, having been King of Naples, met his death before a firing squad. Empire interiors.

LA-CHATRE
George Sand's House
Château de Nohant
F-36400 La-Chatre
Indre
George Sand's home, decorated in 1860s style.

LA COTE-SAINT-ANDRE
**Berlioz Museum
(Maison Berlioz)**
69 rue de la République
F-38200 La-Côte-Saint-André, Isère
Birthplace of composer Hector Berlioz (1803-1869), featuring mid-19th-century interiors.

LE-PETIT-COURONNE
**Corneille's House
(Maison Corneille)**
Des Champs
502 rue Pierre-Corneille
F-76650 Le-Petit-Couronne
Seine-Maritime
The family home of the 17th-century dramatist Pierre Corneille (1606-1684), decorated in the style of the period with 17th-century antiques.

LILLE
De Gaulle's Birthplace
9 rue de la Monnaie
F-59000 Lille, Nord
Charles de Gaulle, the French patriot president, was born in this house in 1890. Features turn-of-the-20th-century interiors and memorabilia.

LIRE
Joachim de Bellay Museum
18 rue du Grand-Logis
F-49530 Lire
Maine-et-Loire
Joachim de Bellay (1522-1560), the poet and friend of Ronsard, grew up in this house. It contains 16th-century furniture and memorabilia.

LIVAROT
Fernand Léger Farm Museum (Musée Léger)
Lisores
F-14140 Livarot
Calvados
The family farm of the pseudo-cubist painter (1881-1955), with turn-of-the-20th-century interiors.

MAILLANE
Frédéric Mistral Museum
11 avenue Lamartine
F-13910 Maillane
Bouches-du-Rhône
The house of the Provençal poet (1830-1914) in the town where he was born, lived and died. Late 19th-century interiors.

MARNES-LA-COQUETTE
Pasteur Institute Museum
3 boulevard Raymond-Poincaré
F-92430 Marnes-la-Coquette
Hauts-de-Seine
The laboratory of Louis Pasteur (1822-1895), the discoverer of the vaccination.

MARSEILLES
**Cantini Museum
(Musée Cantini)**
19 rue Grignan
F-13006 Marseilles
Bouches-du-Rhône
The 18th-century mansion of the local aristocratic Cantini family, with period furnishings and decoration.

Grobet-Labadie Museum
140 boulevard Longchamp
F-13001 Marseille
Bouches-du-Rhône
19th-century mansion of a Marseilles industrialist, Alexandre Labadie, with period interiors.

MEDAN
**Emile Zola's House
(Maison Zola)**
26 rue Pasteur
Medan, Yvelines
The home of the man of letters Emile Zola (1840-1902), with late 19th-century furnishings.

MEUDON
**Rodin Museum
(Maison Rodin)**
19 avenue Auguste-Rodin
F-92190 Meudon
Hauts-de-Seine
The realist sculptor lived and worked in this house from 1895 to 1917. Early 20th-century decorations.

MONTFORT-L'AMAURY
**Ravel Museum
(Maison Ravel)**
5 rue Maurice-Ravel
F-78490 Montfort-l'Amaury, Yvelines
The house in which the composer lived and created his masterpieces between 1921 and 1937. Features period decoration, furnishings and memorabilia.

MARNES-LA-COQUETTE
Pasteur Institute Museum

MONTMORENCY
**Rousseau Museum
(Maison Rousseau)**
4 rue du Mont-Louis
F-95160 Montmorency
Val-d'Oise
The philosopher Jean-Jacques Rousseau lived in this house from 1757 to 1762. Features mid-18th-century decoration and furnishings.

NICE
Palais Massena
65 rue de France
F-06000 Nice
Alpes-Maritimes
The mansion was built in 1900 for Victor Massena and features contemporary furniture and decoration.

ORNANS
**Courbet Museum
(Maison Courbet)**
1 place Robert-Fernier
F-25290 Ornans, Doubs
The birthplace of the realist painter Gustave Courbet (1819-1877) is located in the town which he captured on canvas.

PARIS
**Balzac's House
(Maison Balzac)**
47 rue Raynouard
F-75016 Paris
The house of the great realist novelist Honoré de Balzac (1799-1850). Period interiors of the early 19th century.

**Bourdelle Museum
(Musée Bourdelle)**
16 rue Antoine-Bourdelle
F-75015 Paris
The house of the sculptor Emile Antoine Bourdelle (1861-1929), Rodin's assistant, contains furnishings of the late 19th century, memorabilia and documents.

Branly's House
Institut Supérieur d'Electronique
21 rue d'Assas
F-75006 Paris
The physicist's laboratory, as he left it: early 20th-century interiors and equipment.

**Clemenceau Museum
(Maison Clemenceau)**
8 rue Franklin
F-75116 Paris
The imposing home of the World War I Prime Minister features turn-of-the-20th-century interiors and memorabilia.

**Delacroix Museum
(Atelier Delacroix)**
6 place de Furstenberg
F-75006 Paris
The former house of the Romantic painter Eugène Delacroix (1798-1863). Several rooms are intact and contain his works and memorabilia.

Victor Hugo's House
6 place des Vosges
F-75004 Paris
Home of the author of Les Misérables, *much as it was during his lifetime (1802-1885).*

Musée Gustave Moreau
14 rue de la Rochefoucauld
F-75009 Paris
Home of the artist, displaying his work, maintained as it was during his lifetime (1826-98). (See pp.92-97.)

Nissim de Camondo
63 rue de Monceau
F-75008 Paris
This 20th-century building houses a collection of 18th-century antiques, with special emphasis on Louis XVI style. (See pp.86-91.)

**Pasteur Museum
(Institut Pasteur)**
25 rue Docteur Roux
F-75015 Paris
The scientist's apartment, preserved as it was during his lifetime (1822-1895).

PAU
Château de Pau
F-64000 Pau
Pyrénées-Atlantiques
Château with 19th-century interiors.

PLEYBEN
**Cornec House
(Maison Cornec)**
Ecomusée des Monts d'Arrée
F-29190 Saint-Rivoal
Pleyben, Finistère
A 1700s house with period furnishings and memorabilia of the era.

PONTE LECCIA
Pascal Paoli Museum
Morosaglia
F-20218 Ponte Leccia
Haute-Corse
Birthplace of the Corsican patriot, a modest house of the 19th century.

PRIVAS
Museum of the Protestant Vivarais
Le-Bouchet-de-Pranles
F-07000 Privas, Ardèche
The birthplace of the Calvinist martyr, pastor Pierre Durand (1700-1732).

ROCHEFORT
**Pierre Loti's House
(Maison Loti)**
141 rue Pierre-Loti
F-17300 Rochefort
Charente-Maritime
The family home of the novelist Louis Marie Julien Viaud (1850-1923), whose story Madame Chrysanthème *was the inspiration for* Madam Butterfly. *Interiors of the late 19th century and memorabilia.*

ROUEN
Corneille Museum
4 rue de la Pie
F-76000 Rouen
Seine-Maritime
The birthplace of the 17th-century dramatist (1606-1684) features period interiors and memorabilia.

Flaubert and Medical History Museum
Hôtel-Dieu
51 rue de Lecat
F-76000 Rouen
Seine-Maritime
The house in which the novelist Gustave Flaubert was born in 1821, now a museum of medical history.

RUEIL MALMAISON
Château de Malmaison
avenue du Château
F-92500 Rueil
    Malmaison
Hauts-de-Seine
The house of Napoleon's Empress Josephine. Lavish First Empire interiors and antiques, with memorabilia.

SAINT-CERE
Jean Lurcat's Studio (Atelier Lurcat)
Saint-Laurent-Le-Tours
F-46400 Saint-Céré, Lot
Bought by the artist in 1945, the house is decorated in suitably surrealist style with many of his tapestries.

SAINT-JEAN-CAP-FERRAT
Ephrussi de Rothschild House
Villa Ile-de-France
F-06230 Saint-Jean-
    Cap-Ferrat
Alpes-Maritimes
A magnificent villa in the Italian style, owned by the Rothschild millionaire. Antiques and pictures.

SAINT-QUENTIN
Antoine Lecuyer Museum
28 rue Antoine-Lecuyer
F-02100 Saint-Quentin
Aisne
The mansion of a local banker features 19th-century interiors.

SAULZAIS
Le Grand Meaulnes Museum (Musée Fournier)
Ecole d'Epinueil-le-
    Fleuriel
F-18360 Saulzais, Cher
The school that Alain-Fournier (1886-1914), author of Le Grand Meaulnes, *attended — restored to its 1890 appearance.*

SENLIS
Henri Barbusse Museum (Villa Sylvie)
Aumont
F-60300 Senlis, Oise
The World War One novelist, author of Under Fire, *lived in this house between 1910 and 1935. It contains his personal effects and memorabilia.*

SERIGNAN-DU-COMTAT
Fabre's House (Musée d'Histoire Naturelle)
F-84830 Serignan-du-
    Comtat, Vaucluse
Owned by the entomologist J.H. Fabre (1823-1915), the house is furnished in the Provençal style of the 1880s and contains memorabilia and personal possessions.

SIZUN
Kerouat Mills (Ecomusée des Monts d'Arrée)
Commana
F-29237 Sizun, Finistère
A unique exhibit of two working monastic mills of the 19th century.

TARBES
Foch's Birthplace (Maison Foch)
2 rue de la Victoire
F-65000 Tarbes
Hautes-Pyrénées
Memorabilia of the World War I Marshal of France, collected together in the house where he was born in 1851.

TOURS
Anatole France's House (La Bechellerie)
Saint-Cyr-sur-Loire
F-37100 Tours
Indre-et-Loire
Home of Anatole France (1844-1924), the novelist and author of Les Dieux ont Soif, *from 1914. Period interiors and memorabilia.*

GERMANY

AUGSBURG
Brecht Museum (Bert-Brecht-Gedenkstätte)
Auf dem Rain 7
D-8900 Augsburg
Bayern
The birthplace of the playwright Bertolt Brecht (1898-1956) is filled with furnishings and memorabilia that tell the story of his life and work.

BAD DRIBURG
Weber's House (Weberhaus)
Weberplatz
D-3490 Bad Driburg-
    Alhausen
Nordrhein-Westfalen
The poet Wilhelm Weber (1813-1894) was born in this house, which features decoration, memorabilia and documents of the time.

BADEN-BADEN
Brahms's House (Brahms-Haus)
Maximilianstrasse 85
D-7570 Baden-Baden
Baden-Württemberg
Johannes Brahms (1833-1897) spent his summers betwen 1865 and 1874 in this house. The rooms, which are decorated and furnished in period style, contain the composer's memorabilia and documents.

BAD HONNEF
Adenauer's House (Stiftung Bundeskanzler-Adenauer-Haus)
Rhondorf
Konrad-Adenauer
    Strasse 8c
D-5340 Bad Honnef 1
Nordrhein-Westfalen
Built in 1937 by Konrad Adenauer (Chancellor of West Germany from 1948 to 1963), the house has been restored to its appearance at the time of his occupancy.

BAD SAAROW
Gorky Museum
Ulmenstrasse 20
1242 Bad Saarow
Bezirk
Frankfurt/Oder
A Russian-style house with 1920s furniture.

BAMBERG
Hoffman's House (E.T.W. Hoffmann-Haus)
Schillerplatz 26
D-8600 Bamberg
Bayern
Documents and memorabilia relating to Ernst Theodor Wilhelm Hoffmann (1776-1822) are housed in the home of the writer, composer and caricaturist famed for his fantastical tales.

BAYREUTH
Wagner Museum
Haus Wahnfried
Richard-Wagner-
    Strasse 48
D-8580 Bayreuth
Bayern
Richard Wagner (1813-1883) designed this house and lived in it from 1874 until his death. Restored in the 1970s, it contains some of the composer's personal effects.

BERLIN
George Kolbe Museum
Sensburger Allee 25
D-1000 Berlin 19
The sculptor George Kolbe (1877-1947) built this house in 1928 and used it as his home and studio. Today it houses a collection of Kolbe's art and that of other German artists of the 1920s.

BONN
Beethoven's House (Beethoven-Haus)
Bonngasse 20
Postfach 2563
D-5300 Bonn 1
Nordrhein-Westfalen
The birthplace of the composer Ludwig van Beethoven (1770-1827). Built in 1715, the house is filled with furnishings from Beethoven's lifetime as well as personal possessions and memorabilia.

BREMEN
Roselius House (Roselius-Haus)
Bottcherstrasse 6
D-2800 Bremen
The restored 1920s home of the patron of the arts and inventor of decaffeinated Café Hag, *Ludwig Roselius.*

BRUNSWICK
Wilhelm Raabe Museum (Wilhelm-Raabe-Gedächtnisstätte)
Leonhardstrasse 29a
D-3300 Braunschweig
Neidersachsen
The house in which the novelist died has been restored to its appearance during his lifetime (1831-1910) and contains his personal possessions, drawings and watercolours.

BUDINGEN
Schloss Museum
D-6470 Büdingen
Hessen
The former home of the Princes of Ysenburg and Büdingen features late 19th-century furnishings and decoration.

BURLADINGEN
Village Museum (Dorf-Museum und Albpfad)
Maichle-Hof
D-7453 Burladingen-
    Melchingen
Baden-Württemberg
An open-air museum that includes a 19th-century Alpine farm.

DARMSTADT
Artists' Colony Museum (Museum der Kunstler-Kolonie)
Europaplatz 1
D-6100 Darmstadt
Hessen
The studios and homes of artists of the German Art-Nouveau movement at the turn of the 20th century. Restored after war damage, the museum now contains decorative art of the period.

DRESDEN
Schiller's Cottage
Schillerstrasse 19
Dresden, Sachsen
The house in which the poet wrote his epic poem Don Carlos *in 1787 contains Schiller memorabilia.*

EISENACH
Bach House
Fraunplan 21
59 Eisenach, Thüringen
Johann Sebastian Bach's family home, filled with memorabilia.

ESCHERSHAUSEN
Raabe Museum (Wilhelm-Raabe-Gedenkstätte)
Raabestrasse 5
D-3456 Eschershausen
Niedersachsen
Memorabilia, personal possessions and Wilhelm Raabe's works are contained in the house where the novelist was born in 1910.

ETTLINGEN
Ettlingen Museum
D-7505 Ettlingen
Baden-Württemberg
Home of Sibylla Augusta, widow of the Margrave of Baden, from 1727 to 1733.

EUTIN
Palace Museum (Schloss-Museum)
D-2420 Eutin
Schleswig-Holstein
Home of the local Oldenburg family, with 17th- to 19th-century interiors.

FRANKFURT AM MAIN
Goethe's House (Goethe-Haus)
Grosser Hirschgraben
    23-25
D-6000 Frankfurt am
    Main 1
Hessen
The birthplace of the poet Johann Wolfgang von Goethe (1749-1832), restored after war damage to its appearance during his lifetime.

FRIEDRICHSRUH
Bismarck Museum
D-2055 Friedrichsruh
Schleswig-Holstein
Former home of the Prussian politician and general Otto von Bismarck (1815-1898), with late 19th-century furnishings and art collections.

GIESSEN
Liebig Museum
Liebigstrasse 12
Postfach 11 03 52
D-6300 Giessen
Hessen
The laboratories of the chemist Justus Liebig (1803-1873), restored to their appearance during the 1850s.

GRIMMA
Goschen House
Schillerstrasse 25
724 Grimma, Sachsen
*The former home of the
publisher Goschen, who
died here in 1828,
contains a collection of
Biedermeier furnishings.*

HALLE
Handel House
Grosse Nikolaistrasse 5
402 Halle
Sachsen-Anhalt
*The composer George
Frideric Handel (1685-
1759) was born in this
house, which is filled with
memorabilia.*

HERRNHUT
**Alt Herrnhuter Stube
Museum**
Comenius Strasse 6
8709 Herrnhut, Sachsen
*An 18th-century house,
furnished in 1830s
Biedermeier style.*

HUNXE
Pankok Museum
Haus Esselt
Otto-Pankok-Weg 4
D-4224 Hunxe/
  Drevenack
Nordrhein-Westfalen
*Dating from the 17th
century, this house
belonged to the artist Otto
Pankok (1893-1966) and
is filled with memorabilia.*

HUSUM
**Storm's House (Storm-
Haus)**
Theodor-Storm-
  Gesellschaft
Wasserreihe 31
D-2250 Husum
Schleswig-Holstein
*The house of the governor
of the area and poet
Theodor Storm (1817-
1888) is furnished in
period style and contains
his memorabilia.*

ILMENAU
**Gabelbach Hunting
Lodge**
Waldstrasse 24
63 Ilmenau
Thüringen
*Dating from 1783, this
former hunting lodge was
occupied for a short time
by the poet Johann
Wolfgang von Goethe
(1749-1832). It contains
Goethe memorabilia.*

JENA
**Goethe Memorial
Museum**
Goethe Allee 26
69 Jena, Thüringen
*Goethe memorabilia and
documents are contained
in the house where he
stayed in 1817 and 1822.*

**Schiller Memorial
Museum
(Schiller Gasschen)**
69 Jena, Thüringen
*The house in which the
dramatist Johann
Christoph Friedrich von
Schiller (1759-1805) lived
between 1797 and 1802.*

KAUB AM RHEIN
Blücher Museum
Metzgergasse 6
D-5425 Kaub am Rhein
Rheinland-Pfalz
*Field Marshal Blücher
conducted the Leipzig
campaign, which defeated
Napoleon in 1813, from
this small house.
Memorabilia of the
campaign is contained in
19th-century interiors.*

KLEVE
**Koekkoek Museum
(Stadtisches-Museum-
Haus-Koekkoek)**
Kavarinerstrasse 33
D-4190 Kleve
Nordrhein-Westfalen
*The house of the Dutch
landscape painter Barend
Cornelius Koekkoek
(1803-1862), with
paintings and
memorabilia.*

KONSTANZ
**John Huss House
(Johann-Hus-Haus)**
Hussenstrasse 64
D-7550 Konstanz
Baden-Württemberg
*The house in which the
religious heretic John
Huss (1369-1415) was
arrested in 1414 contains
memorabilia of the
German reformation.*

LUBECK
**Behn House Museum
(Behnhaus)**
Königstrasse 9-11
D-2400 Lübeck
Schleswig-Holstein
*Dating from the 1780s,
this merchant's house is
filled with 18th-century
furnishings.*

LUDWIGSHAFEN AM
RHEIN
Schiller's House
Schillerstrasse 6
D-6700 Ludwigshafen-
  Oggersheim
Rheinland-Pfalz
*The poet Johann
Christoph Friedrich von
Schiller lived in this house
in the 1780s. It contains
his documents and
memorabilia.*

MEININGEN
Baumbach House
Burgstrasse 22
61 Meiningen
Thüringen
*The home of the poet
Rudolf Baumbach, who
died in 1905, with 19th-
century furnishings and
the poet's possessions.*

MUNICH
Villa Stuck
Prinzregentenstrasse 60
D-8000 München 80
Bayern
*Dating from the 1890s,
the house of artist Franz
von Stuck (1863-1928)
features painted
decoration and
memorabilia.*

NEUKIRCHEN UBER
NIEBULL
Nolde's House
D-2268 Neukirchen
  über Niebull
Schleswig-Holstein
*Built by the Expressionist
painter Emil Nolde
(1867-1956), this building
houses his paintings.*

NORDERNEY
**Fisherman's House
Museum (Norderney
Fischerhausmuseum)**
Im Waldchen am
  Weststrand
D-2982 Norderney
Niedersachsen
*A restored 19th-century
fisherman's house with
period interiors.*

NURNBERG
**Dürer's House
(Albrecht-Dürer-Haus)**
Nürnberg, Bayern
*The house in which the
artist Albrecht Dürer
(1471-1528) lived from
1509 to 1528 features
original carvings and
reproduction period
furnishings.*

OBERURSEL
**Hans Thoma Museum
(Hans-Thoma-
Gedächtnisstätte)**
Marktplatz 1/
  Schulstrasse 22a
D-6370 Oberursel
  (Taunus), Hessen
*Personal possessions and
memorabilia are housed
in the summer residence
of the painter Hans
Thoma (1839-1924).*

PLAUEN
Vogel House
99 Plauen-Kreber
Sachsen
*The home and studio of
the artist Hermann Vogel
(1854-1921).*

POTSDAM
Sanssouci Park
Sanssouci
15 Potsdam
Brandenburg
*Built during the 1740s for
the ruling Hohenzollerns,
the Chinese teahouse
features 18th-century
interiors.
The Orangery was built
in the 1850s and is filled
with 19th-century
furnishings.*

Schloss Charlottenhof
Sanssouci
Potsdam, Brandenburg
*Crown Prince Friedrich
Wilhelm of Prussia's
palace was renovated by
architect Karl Friedrich
Schinkel in the 1830s in a
tribute to classicism. (See
pp.120-125.)*

RATZEBURG
Ernst Barlach Museum
Barlachplatz 3
D-2418 Ratzeburg
Schleswig-Holstein
*The family home of the
painter (1870-1938)
houses his original works
and memorabilia.*

REGENSBURG
**Kepler Museum
(Kepler-
Gedächtnishaus)**
Keplerstrasse 5
D-8400 Regensburg
Bayern
*Built in 1500, this house
belonged to astronomer
Johann Kepler (1571-
1630). It is filled with
documents on his
discoveries.*

TRIER
**Karl Marx House
(Karl-Marx-Haus)**
Brückenstrasse 10
D-5500 Trier
Rheinland-Pfalz
*The birthplace of the
founder of communism
contains documents and
memorabilia of Marx's
life and work.*

TUBINGEN
**Hölderlin Museum
(Hölderlinturm)**
Bursagasse 6
D-7400 Tübingen
Baden-Württemberg
*Documents and
memorabilia are housed
in the home of the poet
Friedrich Hölderlin
(1770-1843).*

WEIL DER STADT
Kepler Museum
Keplergasse 2
D-7252 Weil der Stadt
Baden-Württemberg
*The birthplace of the
astronomer Johann
Kepler, with documents
relating to his career.*

WEIMAR
Goethe's Garden House
Corona Schrotter
  Strasse
53 Weimar, Thüringen
*The poet lived in this
house between 1776 and
1782. It features 18th-
century furnishings and
memorabilia. (See
pp.126-131.)*

**Goethe's Town House
(Goethe's Wonhaus am
Frauenplan)**
53 Weimar, Thüringen
*The town house of the
poet, Wolfgang von
Goethe. (See pp. 126-
131.)*

Liszt Museum
Marienstrasse 17
53 Weimar, Thüringen
*The house where the
composer Franz Liszt
(1811-1886) lived is filled
with musical instruments
and memorabilia.*

Tiefurt Schloss
Hauptstrasse 14
53 Weimar, Thüringen
*A collection of porcelain is
contained in the 18th-
century summer house of
the Duchess Amelia.*

WESSELBUREN
Hebbel House
Osterstrasse 6
D-2244 Wesselburen
Schleswig-Holstein
*The birthplace of the
writer Christian Friedrich
Hebbel (1813-63), with
original manuscripts.*

WIEDENSAHL
**Busch's Birthplace
(Wilhelm-Busch-
Geburtshaus)**
D-3061 Wiedensahl
  Nr. 89 bei Stadhagen
Niedersachsen
*Personal effects are
preserved in the house in
which the writer and
artist Wilhelm Busch
(1832-1908) was born.*

WOLFENBUTTEL
**Lessing's House
(Lessing-Haus)**
Lessingplatz 1
Postfach 13 64
D-3340 Wolfenbuttel
Niedersachsen
*The playwright Gotthold
Ephraim Lessing (1729-
1781) died in this house.
Its 18th-century interiors
house his work.*

WOLFSBURG-
FALLERSLEBEN
**Hoffmann Museum
(Hoffmann-von-
Fallersleben-Museum)**
Schlossplatz
D-3180 Wolfsburg
  12/Fallersleben
Niedersachsen
*The birthplace of the poet
Heinrich Hoffmann
(1798-1874) is filled with
his personal possessions.*

WUPPERTAL
**Engels's House
(Historische Zentrum)**
Engelsstrasse 10
D-5600 Wuppertal 2
Nordrhein-Westfalen
*The family house of the
sociologist contains
memorabilia.*

ZWICKAU
Schumann House
Hautmarkt 4
95 Zwickau, Sachsen
*The composer Robert
Schumann (1810-1856)
was born in this house. It
contains 19th-century
furnishings, Schumann
memorabilia and editions
of his music.*

GREECE

AMBELAKIA
G . Schwartz Mansion
Ambelákia
Thessalia
A mansion of the late 18th century with period interiors and artefacts.

ATHENS
Kanellopoulos Museum (Odhos Mues i Kleoum)
Athens
Dating from the mid-19th century, this house has been restored to its former glory, with collections of antiques.

CORFU
Museum of the Achilleon
Near Corfu
Built in 1890 for the Empress of Austria, this restored house features pictures and memorabilia.

KALIMNOS
Vouvalina Mansion
Kálimnos
Dhodhekánisos
Dating from the late 19th century, this mansion is filled with period furnishings and memorabilia.

KOS
Casa Romana
Kos
A Roman dwelling house of the 3rd century AD, restored to its appearance at that time with fine mosaics.

MESSOLONGI
Palamas House (Ikia Ethnikou Puti Kostes Palamas)
Triantafillou Spondi 10
GR-302 00 Messolóngi
Stereá Eláda
The poet and patriot Kostes Palamas (1859-1943) lived in this house, which contains documents relating to his life and work, together with memorabilia.

MIKONOS
Lena's House
Laographiko Museio
GR-846 00 Mikonos
The 19th-century home of a ship's captain, as it would have appeared at the time.

HUNGARY

ALMOSD
Kolcsey House
Almosd
Hajdu-Bihar megye
Home of the local poet Kolcsey, with his personal possessions and memorabilia.

BADACSONY
Irodlami Museum
Badacsony
Veszprem megye
The 18th-century house of the poet Kisfaludy contains his manuscripts, memorabilia and original furnishings.

BUDAPEST
Nagyteteny Palace Museum
Csokasi utca 9
Budapest XXII
Dating from the 18th century, this palace is filled with 15th-, 16th- and 18th-century furniture.

ESZTERGOM
Mihaly Babits Museum
Utca 13
Esztergom
Komarom megye
The former country house of the poet Babits, who died in 1941, contains his personal effects and memorabilia.

SUKORO
Folklore Museum
Szilvas Sor 7
Sukoro, Fejer megye
A restored peasant dwelling of the 19th century, furnished with simple rural furniture and artefacts.

ICELAND

AKUREYRI
Matthias Jochumsson Museum
Eyearlandsvegur 3
Akureyri
Home of the poet and author of the national anthem, with his personal possessions.

INDIA

AMBER
Amber Fort
Amber, Rajasthan
The old palace of the Maharaja of Jaipur, in his ancient capital. State apartments with original painted and inlaid decorations.

GWALIOR
Jaivilla's Palace
Newtown, Gwalior
Madhya Pradesh
The Maharaja of Gwalior's palace is still inhibited by the present maharaja but this wing is open to the public. It houses collections of memorabilia of the Indian nobility in the 18th and 19th centuries.

JODHPUR
Meherangarh Fort
Jodhpur, Rajasthan
A series of palaces housing an impressive collection of possessions belonging to the Maharajahs of the 17th and 19th centuries. Furniture, paintings and original decorations.

KANTHALAPRA
Rishi Bankim Museum
Naihati
24 Parganas
Kanthalapra
West Bengal
The former home of the Indian writer Rishi Bankim, containing his personal possessions and memorabilia.

UDAIPUR
City Palace Museum
Udaipur, Rajasthan
A wing of the Maharana's Palace, as it would have appeared at the close of the last century. Spectacular inlaid and painted decorations.

IRELAND

BANTRY
Bantry House
Bantry
Co. Cork
This 18th-century house contains a collection of Russian icons, furniture, paintings and tapestries. A modern sculpture exhibition is held in the garden.

BLESSINGTON
Russborough
Blessington
Co. Wicklow
Constructed in 1741, this Palladian mansion houses a magnificent collection of paintings by Gainsborough, Goya, Rubens and Velázquez, together with fine displays of silver, furniture and tapestries.

BRUREE
De Valera Cottage
Knockmore
Bruree
Co. Limerick
The house where the first Irish president, Eamonn de Valera (1882-1975) grew up, restored to its appearance during his lifetime.

CAHERDANIEL
Derrynane House
Caherdaniel
Co. Kerry
The ancestral home of Daniel O'Connell (1775-1847), an early freedom fighter and politician, is decorated in 19th-century style.

GLENCOLUMBKILLE
Folk Museum
Glencolumbkille
Co. Donegal
Four cottages, each of them furnished in the style of a different period – from the 1700s to the 20th century.

GORT
Thoor Ballylee
Gort
Co. Galway
The writer W.B. Yeats (1865-1939) lived in this 16th-century tower house during the 1920s. It has been restored to look as it did during his lifetime.

KILLARNEY
Muckross House
National Park
Killarney
Co. Kerry
The one-time mansion of the Anglo-Irish Herbert family, now partly restored to its former glory.

RATHDRUM
Parnell Museum
Avondale House
Rathdrum
Co.Wicklow
The birthplace of the politician Charles Stewart Parnell (1846-1891) features early 19th-century furnishings.

ROSMUC
Patrick Pearse's Cottage
Rosmuc
Co. Galway
The restored summer retreat of the patriot leader Patrick Pearse (1879-1916).

SLANE
Ledwidge House
Jeanville
Slane
Co. Meath
The cottage of the poet Francis Ledwidge, who was killed in World War I, houses late 19th-century furnishings and memorabilia relating to Ledwidge.

WATERFORD
Rice Museum
Mount Sion
Barrack Street
Waterford
This 1802 house was home to the founder of the Christian Brothers, Edmund Ignatius Rice, and features 19th-century interiors.

ISRAEL

HAIFA
Mane-Katz Museum
89 Yefe Nof Street
Haifa
The Israeli painter's collection of works, together with items of memorabilia and furnishings.

TEL AVIV
Beit Bialik
22 Bialik Street
Tel Aviv
The former house of the poet Haim Nahan Bialik is filled with personal possessions and memorabilia.

Ben Gurion House
17 Ben Gurion
  Boulevard
Tel Aviv
The former house of the Israeli Prime Minister David Ben Gurion contains original furnishings and items of personal memorabilia.

Weizmann House
Rehovot
Tel Aviv
The home of Israel's first president, Dr Chaim Weizmann (1874-1952), contains original furniture, personal possessions and a collection of memorabilia.

*IT*ALY

AGRIGENTO

Pirandello's House (Casa di Pirandello)
115 Strada
Porto Empedocle
Contrada Caos
I-92100 Agrigento
Sicilia
Birthplace of the playwright Luigi Pirandello (1867-1936), author of Six Characters in Search of an Author, *restored to its appearance at the time of his birth.*

AREZZO

Vasari's House (Casa de Giorgio Vasari)
Via XX Settembre 55
I-52100 Arezzo
Toscana
Frescoes by the painter and historian Giorgio Vasari (1511-1574) decorate the house that he bought in 1540.

BAGNAIA

Villa Lante della Rovere
Via Jacopo Barozzi 71
Bagnaia
Lazio
This 16th-century villa was designed by Girolamo Vignola (d. 1544), a follower of Raphael, and is decorated with his frescoes and furnishings. The Renaissance ornamental gardens outside are famous for their ornamental fountains.

BUSSETO

Villa Verdi di Sant' Agata
Near Busseto
Emilia-Romagna
Country villa of the great operatic composer Giuseppe Verdi (1813-1901), and where he spent his retirement.

CAPRERA

Garibaldi Museum (Compendio Garibaldino)
I-07024 Caprera (La Maddalena)
Sardegna
Built by the patriot Giuseppe Garibaldi (1807-1882), this complex of six buildings has been preserved as it was during his lifetime.

CAPRESE MICHELANGELO

Michelangelo's Birthplace (Museo Michelangeolesco)
Castello
I-52033 Caprese Michelangelo
Arezzo, Toscana
15th-century furnishings decorate the simple room in which the great sculptor was born in 1475.

CASERTA

Royal Palace Palazzo Reale (Appartimenti Storici e Museo Vanritelliano)
Parco Reale
Caserta
Campania
Built for Charles III in 1752, the royal palace features magnificent apartments, decorated in the neoclassical style. Also gardens.

CASTELFRANCO VENETO

Giorgione's House (Casa di Giorgione)
Piazzetta Duomo
I-31033 Castelfranco Veneto
Treviso, Veneto
The restored house of the painter Giorgio Barbarelli (Girogione, 1478-1511) contains 15th-century furnishings and a series of still-lifes and documents relating to his life .

CATANIA

Bellini Museum (Museo Belliniano)
Piazza S. Francesco d'Assisi 3
I-95124 Catania
Sicilia
The birthplace of the opera composer Vicenzo Bellini (1801-1835) features 1830s decoration.

ELBA

Palazzina Napoleonica dei Mulini
Portoferraio
Elba
Converted from two old windmills, this small palace was home to the exiled Napoleon Bonaparte. The furnishings were originally installed at his sister Elisa's home in Piombino.

FERRARA

Palazzina di Marfisa
Corsa Giovecca 170
Ferrara
16th-century palace with grotesque decoration, furniture and bronzes.

FLORENCE

Museo Horne
Via dei Benci 6
Firenze
The house of English collector Herbert Percy Horne, with 15th- and 19th-century decoration and late 15th-century paintings.

Palazzo Davanzati
Via Porta Rossa 13
Firenze
Often referred to as the Florentine House Museum, this 14th-century merchant's house was restored by Elia Volpi at the turn of the 20th century. (See pp.110-115.)

St Mark's Monastery (Convento e Museo di San Marco)
Piazza San Marco
I-50121 Firenze
The monastery where the painter Fra Angelico (c.1400-55) was a monk. The cells, including his, are still as they were in the 15th century.

GARDONE RIVIERA

The Prioria
Vittoriale degli Italiani
12 via Vittoriale
I-25083 Gardone Riviera
Brescia, Lombardia
The residence of Gabriele D'Annunzio, extravagant 20th-century writer and poet, where he died in 1938. Preserved intact, with all the furnishings exactly as the poet left them, the Prioria is filled with sculptures, ceramics, Murano glass, carpets and over 33,000 books.

GENOA

Mazzini's House (Casa di Mazzini)
Via San Luca 13
I-16124 Genova
The former home of the Italian nationalist Giuseppe Mazzini (1805-1872) is filled with mid-19th-century furnishings.

LUCCA

Puccini's House (Casa Museo Puccini)
Corte San Lorenzo 9
I-55100 Lucca
Toscana
The family home of the composer of Madam Butterfly, *restored to its appearance during Puccini's lifetime (1858-1924).*

MANTUA

Ducal Palace (Palazzo Ducale)
Piazza Sordello 39
I-46100 Mantova
Lombardia
Magnificent frescoes and trompe l'oeil paintings by Andrea Mantegna (1431-1506) decorate the palatial home of the Gonzaga family. Dating from the 13th century, it also features furnished apartments of the 16th century.

Palazzo d'Arco
Piazza d'Arco 1
Mantova
Lombardia
Dating from 1784, this Palladian palace by architect Antonio Colonna preserves the atmosphere of a family house. It features late 18th-century decoration and furnishings.

MASER

Villa Barbaro
Maser
Treviso
Veneto
A Palladian villa, filled with frescoes by Paolo Veronese (c.1528-1588), 17th-century decorations and works of art. (See pp.104-109.)

MILAN

Manzoni's House (Casa di Manzoni)
Via Morone 1
I-20121 Milano
Lombardia
The home of Alessandro Manzoni, author of The Betrothed, *features the poet and novelist's workroom, bedroom and library, all of which have been restored to their appearance during his lifetime (1785-1873).*

Poldi Pezzoli Museum (Museo Poldi Pezzoli)

Via Manzoni 12
I-20121 Milano
Lombardia
This house was owned by a local 19th-century dignitary, Gian Giacomo Poldi. It has been restored to its appearance during his lifetime, with collections of furniture and paintings.

PESARO

Rossini's House (Casa di Rossini)
Via Rossini 34
I-61100 Pesaro, Marche
Birthplace of the composer Gioachino Rossini (1792-1868), restored to its original appearance during his lifetime.

ROME

Pirandello's House (Casa di Pirandello)
Via Bosio 15
I-00121 Roma
Home of the poet Luigi Pirandello from 1913 until his death in 1936. His workroom and library have been preserved intact.

Villa Farnesina
Villa della Lungara
I-00121 Roma
Built between 1508 and 1511, this fine Renaissance villa contains frescoes by Raphael.

STRA

Villa Pisani
Stra
Padua, Veneto
The villa where Hitler met Mussolini in 1934 features fine paintings and furniture. The 18th-century decoration is by Giovanni Battista Tiepolo (1696-1770).

TRIESTE

Civico Museo Mario Morpurgo de Nilma
Via Imbriani, 5
34121 Trieste
A typical Triestian aristocratic home, furnished in the eclectic style of the late 19th century with object d'arts, sculpture, ceramics and furniture by Gossleth.

URBINO

Casa di Raffaello
Via Rafaello
Urbino, Marche
Birthplace of Raphael (1483-1520). The large 14th-century house contains paintings by Raphael's father, Giovanni Santi, together with copies of his own work.

VENICE

Goldoni's House (Casa Goldoni)
S. Toma 2794
I-30125 Venezia
The house where the playwright Carlo Goldoni lived in the 1760s, restored to its original appearance.

Palazzo Querini-Stampalia
Castello 4778
I-30122 Venezia
An early 16th-century Venetian family mansion with lavish 19th-century decorations.

Raccolta Peggy Guggenheim
Palazzo Venier dei Leoni
Canal Grande
Dorsoduro
Venezia
The art collector Peggy Guggenheim's lavish apartments are filled with her collection of 20th-century paintings.

JAPAN

KAMEYAMA
Samurai Estate
545 Nishimaru-cho
Kameyama-shi
Mie-ken 519-01
A complete Edo-period
(1603-1868) samurai
estate, furnished in 19th-
century Edo-period style.

KANAZAWA
Seisonkaku
1-2 Eirokucho
Kanazawa-shi
Ishikawa-ken 920
Dating from 1863, the
home of the Maeda family
is decorated and furnished
in sumptuous 19th-
century style.

NAGOYA
Meiji Mura
Inuyama
Nagoya-shi
Aichi-ken 461
30 buildings dating from
the late 19th-century
reign of the Emperor
Meiji, including a bath-
house, a kabuki theatre
and Frank Lloyd Wright's
original Imperial Hotel,
moved from Tokyo.

TAKAYAMA
Sannomachi
Takayama-shi
Gifu-ken
A street of preserved Edo-
era merchants' houses
with high post-and-beam
ceilings, containing
implements and furniture
of the period.

TOKYO
Shitamachi Museum
(Shitamachi Fuzoku
Shiryokan)
Ueno Koen
Taito-ku, Tokyo
Reconstructions of a
merchant's house, a
coppersmith and a
sweetshop document life
in 1920s Tokyo.

TSUMAGO
Okuya Museum
(Okuya Kyodokan)
Tsumago
Nakiso-machi
Kiso-gun, Nagano-ken
An Edo-era inn,
containing utensils and
documents of the time, in
a complete Edo-era village
still inhabited today.

LIBERIA

TOTOTA
William VS Tubmann
Museum
Totota, Bong County
The house of President
William Vacanarat
Shadrach Tubman (1895-
1971).

LUXEMBOURG

VIANDEN
Victor Hugo Museum
Vianden
The house in which the
French novelist and
author of Les Misérables
(1802-1885) stayed while
in Luxembourg is filled
with his memorabilia and
personal possessions.

MALTA

MDINA
The Norman House
(Palazzo Falzon)
Villegaignon Street
Mdina
A classic example of a
Siculo-Norman-style
building of the late 15th
century.

VITTORIOSA
The Inquisitor's Palace
Main Gate Street
Vittoriosa
A late 16th-century
building with 16th-
century furnishings and
artefacts.

MOLDOVA

KISHINEV
Pushkin House
Antonskaya Ul.
Kishinev
The house in which
Alexander Pushkin (1799-
1837) lived from 1820 to
1823, and where he wrote
Eugene Onegin, *is*
decorated in 19th-century
style and contains
memorabilia relating to
the writer.

MEXICO

CUAULTA
Morelos House
Calle Morelos
Cuaulta
The house in which the
Mexican patriot Father
Maria Morelos y Pavón
(d. 1815) stayed during
the seige of Cuaulta in
1814 is filled with 19th-
century furnishings and
memorabilia.

DOLORES HIDALGO
Casa Hidalgo
Calle Morelos 1
Dolores Hidalgo
Chihuahua
The 1779 house of patriot
and priest Miguel
Hidalgo y Costilla (d.
1811).

MEXICO CITY
Frida Kahlo Museum
Calle Allende
Mexico City
Original furnishings,
works of art and personal
possessions are housed in
the home and studio of
Frida Kahlo (1907-1954)
and her husband Diego
Rivera (1886-1957), the
artists.

OAXACA
Juárez House
Calle de Garcia Vigil 43
Oaxaca
The house in which
President Benito Juárez
(1806-1872) grew up,
with 19th-century
furniture and personal
memorabilia.

NETHERLANDS

AMSTERDAM
Anne Frank's House
(Anne Frank Huis)
Prinsengracht 263
1016 GV Amsterdam
The house and attic in
which the Jewish
authoress lived in secret
and wrote her famous
diary during the Second
World War, restored to its
wartime appearance.

Rembrandt's House
(Museum het
Rebrandthuis)
Jodenbreestraat 4-6
1011 NK Amsterdam
The house where the
painter lived and worked
from 1639 to 1660,
furnished in the style of
the period.

Willet-Holthuysen
Museum
Herengracht 605
Amsterdam
The fine and decorative
art collections of Mrs
Abraham Willet are
displayed in her 1689
house.

APELDOORN
Het Loo Palace
(Paleis Het Loo)
Koninklijk Park 1
7315 HR Apeldoorn
Built for William of
Orange in 1685, this
palace features restored
decoration and
furnishings of the 18th
century.

BOSKOOP
Nursery Museum
(Boomwekerijmuseum)
Reyerskoop 54
2771 BF Boskoop
A gardener's house of the
17th century, complete
with furnishings and
implements.

DELFT
Prinsenhof Museum
(Stedlijk Museum het
Prinsenhof)
St Agathaplein 1
2611 HR Delft
The court of William of
Orange in the 1580s, at
one time a convent. The
chapter room, library and
dormitory are restored to
their 16th-century
appearance.

Tetar van Elven
Museum
Koornmarkt 67
2611 EC Delft
The 17th-century home of
the painter Paul Tetar
van Elven (1823-1896)
features original
decoration and panelling.

FRANEKER
Eise Eisinga
Planetarium
Eise Eisingastraat 3
8801 KE Franeker
The house of the
astronomer Eise Eisinga
(1744-1828), with his
personal planetarium.

HAASTRECHT
Bisdom van Vliet
Museum
Hoogstraat 166
2851 BE Haastrecht
The 1870s mansion of the
Bisdom family.

LEIDEN
De Valk Mill
(Stedelijkmolenmuseum
'De Valk')
2e Binnenvestgracht 1
2312 BZ Leiden
A typical 1740s windmill
with original workings
and living area.

MODDERGAT
Fisherman's House
(Museum't
Fiskerhuske)
Fiskerspaad 4-8A
9142 VN Moddergat
Three fisherman's cottages
from the 1790s onward,
filled with early 19th-
century furnishings and
tools.

RIJNSBURG
Spinoza's House
(Het Spinozahuis)
Spinozalaan 29
2231 SG Rijnsburg
The house of the
philospher and scientist
Benedict de Spinoza
(1632-1666).

STAPHORST
Farmhouse Museum
(Gemeentelijke
Museumboerderij)
Binnenweg 26
7950 AA Staphorst
An 1830s farmhouse,
restored to its mid-19th-
century appearance with
furnishings and
implements of the period.

NEW ZEALAND

AUCKLAND
Ewelme Cottage
14 Ayr Street
Parnell, Auckland
Dating from 1864, the
family home of the Lush
family features original
decoration, including
wallpaper by William
Morris.

Fencible Cottage
Unxbridge Road
Howick, Auckland
A cottage of 1848 with
19th-century furnishings
and memorabilia.

BLENHEIM
Riverlands Cob Cottage
PO Box 308, Blenheim
Marlborough Province
Built in 1865, this cottage
has its original furnishings.

LOVELLS FLAT
Old Sod Cottage
Milton-Balclutha
Highway
Lovells Flat
Otago Province
A 19th-century pioneer
cottage with period
furnishings.

NEW PLYMOUTH
Hurworth
New Plymouth
Taranaki Province
The 19th-century country
house of Sir Harry
Atkinson (1831-1892),
Prime Minister of New
Zealand, contains
furnishings and
memorabilia.

TAURANGA
The Elms
Middison Street
Tauranga, S. Auckland
Dating from 1838, this
group of buildings includes
a mission, a library and
shops, all with original
furnishings and effects.

WAIMATE NORTH
Waimate Mission
Te Ahuahu Road
Waimate North
Bay of Islands
Canterbury
Restored to its 1832
appearance, this mission,
the second-oldest house in
New Zealand, is filled
with 19th-century
artefacts.

NORWAY

ASGARDSTRAND
Munch's House (Munchhuset)
Munchsgate
N-3155 Åsgårdstrand
Vestfold
Home of the painter Edvard Munch from 1897 to 1944, preserved as it was during his lifetime.

DALEN
Grimdalen Museum (Anne Grimdalens Minne)
N-3880 Dalen
Telemark
An open-air farmstead museum comprising 11 buildings that date from the 17th to 19th centuries.

FOLLEBU
The Björnson House (Aulestad)
Karoline og
    Björnstjerne
    Björnsons Hjem
N-2620 Follebu
Oppland
The preserved farm of Björnstjerne Björnson (1832-1910), writer and composer of the national anthem.

GRIMSTAD
Ibsen's House (Ibsenhuset og Grimstad Bymuseum)
Henrik Ibsensgate 14
N-4890 Grimstad
Aust-Agder
The playwright Henrik Ibsen (1828-1906) lived here during his apprenticeship in the 1840s. 19th-century decoration and memorabilia.

HOP
Troldhaugen
N-5043 Hop
Hordaland
Summer residence of the composer Edvard Grieg (1843-1907), restored and furnished in 1880s style.

LYSEKLOSTER
Lysoen Museum (Museet Lysoen)
Lysoen
N-5215 Lysekloster
Hordaland
The house of the violinist Ole Bull (1810-80), built in 1872 by the architect C. F. von Lippe.

OSLO
Bogstad Manor (Bodstad Stiftelse)
Bogstad Gard
N-0758 Oslo
A Norwegian manor house, complete with 17th- to 19th-century interiors.

SKIEN
Venstop Farm (Fylkesmuseet for Telemark og Grenland)
Ovregate 41
N-3700 Skien
Telemark
Henrik Ibsen's childhood home, preserved as it was at the time of his occupancy in the 1830s.

STAVANGER
Ledaal
Ledaal Eiganes 75
N-4005 Stavanger
The 1800s manor house of the local Kielland family, now a royal residence, features 19th-century decoration and memorabilia.

SVARTSKOG
Amundsen's House (Roald Amundsens Hjem "Uranienborg")
Roald Amundsensvei
    192
N-1420 Svartskog
The house of the polar explorer Roald Amundsen has been preserved as it was when he left it in 1928.

PAKISTAN

LAHORE
Fagir Khana Museum
Lahore
A well-to-do Pakistani family home of the late 19th century.

TANDO MUHAMMAD KHAN
Talpur House
Tando Muhammad
    Khan
Near Hyderabad
The 19th-century furnished house of the last ruling dynasty of Sind.

PARAGUAY

ASUNCION
Museum of the Birth of Independence
Calle 14 de Mayo
Esquina Presidente
    Franco
Asunción
This 1770s house saw the birth of the independence campaign in 1871. It is filled with 18th-century furniture and memorabilia.

THE PHILIPPINES

BATANGAS
Talaga Mabini Shrine
Barrio Talaga
Tanauan, Batangas 4232
The birthplace of Apolinario Mabini (1864-1903), theoretician and spokesman of the 1896 revolution, contains his personal possessions and memorabilia.

POLAND

KRAKOW
Jan Matejko House
Ul. Florianska 41
Kraków
The picture collections of the artist Professor Matejko are now housed together in his home, which has been restored to its appearance during his lifetime.

TORUN
Hall of the Teutonic Knights
ul. Przedzamcze 3
Torun
A 14th-century hall, the dwelling place of the Knights, with original decoration and furnishing.

ZELAZOWA WOLA
Chopin Museum
Zelazowa Wola
The birthplace of the composer Frederic Chopin (1810-1849) houses his personal possessions and memorabilia in 19th-century interiors.

PORTUGAL

ALCOBACA
Alcobaça Museum (Museu de Alcobaça)
2460 Alcobaça, Leiria
The Cistercian monastery of Alcobaça, restored to its 17th-century appearance.

ALPIARCA
Dos Patudos House (Casa Museu dos Petudos)
Estrada National (EN)
    118
2090 Alpiarca
The country house of politician José Relvas (1858-1929) features a fine collection of porcelain.

PORTALEGRE
Jose Regio's House (Casa-Museu Jose Regio)
Rua Jose Regio
7300 Portalegre
Memorabilia and personal possessions are contained in the former home of the poet Jose Maria de Reis (Jose Regio, 1901-1969).

PORTO
Museum of the Romantic Era (Museu Romantico da Quinta da Macieirinha)
Rua Entre Quintas 220
4000 Porto
The house in which the King of Sardinia lived in 1849, converted to a museum of the Romantic period with mid-19th-century interiors.

SINTRA
Pena Palace (Palacio Nacional de Pena)
2710 Sintra
Lisboa
An 1885 building, the one-time home of the Portuguese monarchy, with late 19th-century interiors and furniture.

ROMANIA

BACAU
Georghiu Bacovia House
Strada G. Bavovia 13
Bacau
The house of the poet Bacovia (1881-1957) is filled with his memorabilia and furniture.

BALCESTI
Nicolae Balcescu House
Balcesti
The family home of the revolutionary Nicolae Balcescu (1819-52), with 19th-century furnishings and memorabilia.

BOTOSANI
Nicolae Lorga House
Strada N. Lorga 14
Botosani
The scientist Nicolae Lorga (1871-1940) was brought up in this house, which contains his personal possessions and memorabilia.

BRASOV
Muresianu House
Piata 23 August 25
Brasov
The house of a prominent 19th-century Romanian family, preserved intact with period decorations.

BUCHAREST
Theodor Aman Museum
Strada C. A. Rossetti 8
Bucuresti
The studio and house of the artist have been restored to their late 19th-century appearance.

G.L. Tatarescu Museum
Strada Domnita
    Anastasia 7
Bucuresti
Works by the painter (1818-1894) are housed in his home and studio, which is furnished in 19th-century style.

BUSTENI
Cezar Petrescu House
Strada Tudor-
    Vladimirescu 1
Busteni
Personal possessions and memorabilia fill the home of the writer Cezar Petrescu (1892-1961).

CERNA
Panait Cerna House
Cerna
The family home of the poet (1881-1913) has been preserved as it was during his early years.

CIMPINA
Nicolae Grigorescu Museum
Strada 23 August 170
Cimpina
The studio and house of the painter, who died in 1907, furnished in the style of the late 19th century.

IASI
Mihail Codreanu House
Strada Rece 5
Iasi
The house of the writer, furnished as it was in his lifetime (1876-1957) and containing his personal possessions.

MIRCESTI
Vasile Alexandri Museum
Mircesti
The poet (1821-1890) lived in this house, which is decorated and furnished in the style of the late 19th century.

TIRGU JIU
Ecaterina Teodoriu House
Bulerardül 1 May
270 Tirgu Jiu
The restored former home of Ecaterina Teodoriu (d.1917), the Romanian partisan killed in the First World War.

VINATORI
Mihail Sadoveanu Museum
Vinatori
The home of writer Mihail Sadoveanu (d.1961) is filled with personal possessions, memorabilia and early editions of his work.

RUSSIA

ABRAMTSEVO

Abramtsevo
Moskovskaya obl.
The houses that make up the painter's colony were inspired by Mantov, the industrialist, and were built on his estate in the late 19th century. They are preserved intact with original artwork and furnishings.

GORKI

Kashirin House
Pachtovyi Sjezdzi
Gorki
The home of the grandfather of writer Maxim Gorky (1868-1936) features early 19th-century furnishings and family memorabilia.

ILYICHOVO

Lenin's House
Ilyichovo
Peterburgskaya obl.
Vladimir Ilyich Lenin (1870-1924), the Russian revolutionary, lived in this house in 1917, the year of the Revolution. Original furnishings are contained in a recreated interior.

KISLOVODSK

N.A. Yaroshenko House
ul. Yaroshenko 3
Kislovodsk
Stavropolski, Krai
The home of the painter, Nikola Yaroshenko (d.1898) is filled with memorabilia and period furnishings.

KLIN

Tchaikovsky House
ul. Tchaikovsky 48
Klin, Moskovskaya obl.
Personal memorabilia and 19th-century furnishings are housed in the home of the composer Piotr Ilyich Tchaikovsky (1840-1893).

MOSCOW

Chekhov House
Sadovaya-
   Kundrinskaya Ul. 6
Moskva
The writer Anton Chekhov (1860-1904) lived in this house between 1886 and 1890. It has been restored to appear as it did in his lifetime.

F.M. Dostoievski Apartment
ul. Dostoievskoyo 2
Moskva
The apartment of the writer of The Brothers Karamasov, *and where he lived from 1823-1828.*

Gorky Apartment
Ul. Kachalova 6/2
Moskva
The small apartment in which the writer Maxim Gorky (1868-1936) lived from 1931 to his death is filled with early 20th-century furnishings and Gorky memorabilia.

·

Nemirovich-Danchenko Apartment
Ul. Nemirovicha-
   Danchenko 5-7
Moskva
The home of the co-founder of the Gorky theatre contains late 19th-century furnishings and personal possessions.

Skriabin Apartment
Vakhtangova II
Moskva
The apartment in which the composer Alexander Skriabin (1872-1915) lived and died contains his personal effects.

Leo Tolstoy Estate
Ul. Lva Tolstovo 21
Moskva
The preserved family home of the writer Leo Tolstoy (1828-1910) is complete with his personal possessions and late 19th-century furnishings.

Vasnetsov House
Per. Vasnetsova 13
Moskva
The studio and house of the painter Victor Vasnetsov (1848-1926), built in 1894 and filled with early 20th-century furnishings and personal possessions.

SPASSKOYE-LUTOVINOVO

Turgenev Estate
Spasskoye-Lutovinovo
Orlovskaya obl.
The family home of the writer Ivan Sergeevich Turgenev (1818-1883) contains 1880s furnishings and personal effects.

ST PETERSBURG

Brodski Apartment
Pl Iskusstv 3
St Petersburg
The small apartment in which the painter lived between 1924 and 1939 is filled with Brodski's personal possessions and memorabilia.

Peter the Great's Summer Palace
Letni Sad
St Petersburg
Built between 1710 and 1714, the tsar's magnificent residence was designed along neo-classical lines with a Russian influence. A collection of decorative arts is housed in the 18th-century interiors.

Pushkin Apartment
Nab. Reki Moiki 12
St Petersburg
The apartment in which the writer Alexander Pushkin lived between 1836 and 1837 has been restored to its appearance during his lifetime.

YASNAYA POLYANA

Tolstoy Museum
Yasnaya Polyana
Tulskaya obl.
A museum of Tolstoy's life and work is contained within the 19th-century interiors of his private estate.

SLOVAK REPUBLIC

BRATISLAVA

J. N. Hummel Museum
Klobucnicka ulice 2
Bratislava
Birthplace of the composer Johann Nepomuk Hummel (1778-1837), this house contains his piano, personal possessions and memorabilia.

DIVAKY

Mrstik Brother's Museum
C.57 Divaky
The former home of the writers, with period interior.

SOUTH AFRICA

CAPE TOWN

Groot Constantia Manor House
Cape Town 8000
Cape Province
A 1685 farmhouse with 19th-century additions, furnished with antiques of the 18th and 19th centuries.

DURBAN

The Old House
31 St Andrew's Street
Durban 4001, Natal
A house of the 1850s.

EAST LONDON

Gately House
1 Park Gate
East London 5201
Cape Province
The first mayor of East London, John Gately, lived in this house. The interiors have remained largely unchanged since 1875.

IRENE

General Smuts Museum
Doornkloof
Irene, Transvaal
General Jan Smuts (1870-1950), South African prime minister 1919-24 and 1939-48, bought the British officers' mess in Middleburg and moved it to this site in Irene where it became his home.

KIMBERLEY

Dunluce Lodge
Kimberley 8300
Cape Province
The home of the Orr family from 1902 to 1975. Now a museum of the 20th century, it features 1900s furnishings.

PRETORIA

Kruger House
60 Church Street West
Pretoria 0001, Transvaal
The house of President Kruger (1825-1904) has remained unchanged since his lifetime.

SPAIN

ANTEQUERA

Antequera Museum (Museo Municipal)
Coso Viejo 29200
Antequera, Málaga
A mansion of the 1700s, formerly the home of the Najara family.

AVILA

Birthplace of St. Teresa de Jesús
Carmelite Convent
Plaza de la Santa
Avila
The preserved room in which St. Teresa was born.

BARCELONA

Verdaguer House (Museo Verdaguer)
Villa Joana
Vallvidrera
08017 Barcelona
The house of the poet Jacint Verdaguer (1845-1902) contains original furnishings of the late 19th century.

EL TOBOSO

Dulcinea's House (Casa Dulcinea del Toboso)
Calle José Santonio
45820 El Toboso
Castilla-La Mancha
The La Mancha farmhouse that is supposed, by popular legend, to be the home of Dulcinea del Toboso in Don Quixote. Traditional regional furnishings and details.

FUENDETODOS

Goya's Birthplace (Casa Natal de Francisco de Goya)
Plaza de Goya
50142 Fuendetodos
Zaragoza, Aragón
The childhood home of the painter (1746-1828) is filled with late 18th-century furnishings.

GANDIA

Ducal Palace (Palacio del Santo Duque)
Santo Duque 1
46700 Gandia
Valencia
Original 16th-century furnishings are contained in the former home of the Borgias, a one-time Jesuit residence.

GRANADA

Manuel de Falla's House (Casa-Museo Manuel de Falla)
Antegueruela 11
18010 Granada,
Andalucía
The house in which the composer Falla (1876-1946) lived from 1922 to 1940 is filled with possessions and furnishings.

LA LOSA

Riofrio Royal Palace (Palacio Real)
Bosque de Riofrio
40420 La Losa, Segovia
Built in the 1750s for the widow of Philip V, this restored palace features period interiors and furnishings

LAS PALMAS

Pérez-Galdós House
Calle Cano 33
Las Palmas
The former home of the writer Benito Pérez Galdós (d.1920), with furnishings and memorabilia.

MADRID

Lope de Vega's House (Casa-Museo Lope de Vega)
Cervantes 11
28014 Madrid
The house of the playwright Lope de Vega between 1610 and 1635 features furnishings of the mid-17th century.

SANT SALVADOR DEL VENDRELL

Pablo Casals's House (Casa-Museo Pablo Casals)
Avinguda Palfuriana
   59-61
43130 Sant Salvador del
   Vendrell
Original furnishings and memorabilia are contained in the house of the cellist Pablo Casals (1876-1973).

SEGOVIA

Antonio Machado House
Calle de los
   Desampados, Segovia
The former home of the poet Antonio Machado (1875-1939), friend of Pablo Picasso, is filled with his original furnishing and possessions.

SEVILLE

**Murillo's House
(Casa-Museo Murillo)**
Santa Teresa 8
41000 Sevilla, Andalucía
*The home of the painter
Bartolomé Estebán
Murillo (1617-1682) is
filled with his work and
memorabilia.*

**Pilate's House
(Casa de Pilatos)**
Plaza de Pilatos 1
41003 Sevilla, Andalucía
*The 16th-century house of
the first Marqués de
Tarifa combines elements
of Moorish, Renaissance
and Gothic style. (See pp.
116-119.)*

SITGES

**Museum of the
Romantic Era (Museo
Romantico: Casa Llopis,
Sant Gaudenci)**
08780 Sitges, Barcelona
*Furnished in the
Romantic style of the
1820s, the Llopis House
contains 19th-century
memorabilia.*

TOLEDO

**El Greco Museum
(Casa y Museo del
Greco)**
Samuel Levi 3
45002 Toledo
Castilla-La Mancha
*House of the Cretan
painter El Greco
(Domenikos
Theotokopoulos, 1541-
1614) with 16th-century
furnishings.*

VALLADOLID

**House of Cervantes
(Casa de Cervantes)**
Calle del Rastro 7
47000 Valladolid
Castilla-León
*The home of the author of
Don Quixote from 1603
to 1606, with furnishings
of the 17th century.*

VILANOVA I LA GELTRU

**Museum of the
Romantic Era (Museo
Romantico: Can Papiol)**
Calle Major 32
08800 Vilanova i la
Geltrú, Barcelona
*Dating from the late 18th
century, the Papiol family
mansion is decorated in
19th-century Romantic
exotic style.*

SWEDEN

BUNGE

**School Museum
(Bunge Skolmuseum)**
Box 35, S620 Bunge
35 Fårösund
Gotlands län
*A preserved school dating
from the 1930s, including
a teacher's apartment.*

FÅRÖSUND

**School Museum
(Bunge Skolmuseum)**
Box 35
Bunge
S-620 35 Fårösund
Gotlands län
*An 1840s schoolroom with
contemporary equipment
and memorabilia.*

JULITA

**Julita Agricultural
Museum (Sveriges
Landbruksmuséum)**
Nordiska Muséet
Julitagård
S-640 25 Julita
Södermanlands Län
*An open-air museum of
farming through the ages
(17th to 20th centuries).*

KYLLAJ

Strandridaregården
Hellvi
Kyllaj
S-620 34 Ladrö
Gotlands Län
*Built for customs officer
Johan Ahlbom, this 1730s
Swedish manor house
features 18th-century
decorations and furniture.*

LIDINGÖ

**Carl Milles's House
(Millesgården)**
Carl Millesväg 2
S-181 34 Lidingö
Stockholms Län
*The house and studio of
the Swedish sculptor Carl
Milles (1875-1955) is
filled with early 20th-
century furnishings and
original works.*

LINKÖPING

**Old Linköping
(Gramla Linköping)**
Kryddbodtorget 1
S-582 46 Linköping
Östergötlands Län
*This open-air museum
consists of 80 buildings
that recreate the
atmosphere of a 19th-
century town.*

NORRKÖPING

**Dyer's House
(Fargargarden)**
St Persgatan 3
Norrköping
Östergötlands Län
*An open-air museum
which includes a 19th-
century dye works.*

SIGTUNA

Sigtuna Museum
Storgatan 55
S-193 00 Sigtuna
Stockholms län
*An 18th-century town
hall, preserved in its
entirety with decorations
and documents of the era.*

SIMRISHAMN

**Gislov Blacksmith's
Museum (Gislovs
Smidesmuséum)**
Gislov
S-272 92 Simrishamn
Malmöhus Län
*An original smithy with
equipment and tools.*

SUNDBÖRN

**Carl Larsson's House
(Carl Larssongården)**
S-790 15 Sundbörn
Kopparbergs Län
*The home of the Swedish
painter (1853-1919),
decorated by Larsson and
his wife in a variant of the
Arts and Crafts style.
(See pp.142-147.)*

UPPSALA

**Linnaeus's House
(Linnés Hammarby)**
S-755 98 Uppsala
*The farmhouse home of
the naturalist Carolus
Linnaeus (1707-1778)
features original late
18th-century furnishings.*

SWITZERLAND

BERN

**Einstein's House
(Albert Einstein Haus)**
Kramgasse 49
CH-3011 Bern
*The house in which the
scientist lived from 1903
to 1905, restored to its
original condition.*

BRIENZ

**Swiss Open Air
Museum (Schweiz
Freilichtmuseum)**
CH-3855 Brienze, Bern
*A collection of rural
dwellings from different
parts of Switzerland,
showing the traditional
lifestyle.*

EBNAT-KAPPEL

**Ebnat-Kappel Museum
(Heimatmuseum
Ebnat-Kappel)**
Ackerhusweg 16
CH-9642 Ebnat-Kappel
St Gallen
*The house of Albert
Edelman, a collector of
antiques and folksongs, is
filled with painted
furniture and folk art.*

ECHALLENS

**House of Wheat and
Bread (La Maison du
Blé et du Pain)**
Place de l'Hotel-de-
Ville
CH-1040 Echallens
Vaud
*A complete working
bakery of the 19th
century.*

GENEVA

Maison Tavel 6
rue du Puits-Saint-
Pierre
CH-1204 Genève
*Dating from the 1330s,
the oldest house in Geneva
has been restored to its
original 14th-century
appearance.*

**Voltaire Museum
(Institut et Musée
Voltaire)**
25 rue des Delices
CH-1203 Genève
*The house in which the
French philosopher
Voltaire (1694-1778)
lived from 1755 to 1765
contains his personal
possessions and original
works.*

HEIDEN

Henri Dunant Museum
CH-9410 Heiden
Appenzell-
Ausserrhoden
*The winner of the first
Nobel Prize spent his last
year in this house, which
has been restored to its
appearance at the time of
his death in 1910.*

MUSTAIR

**Convent Museum
(Klostermuseum)**
Kloster St Johann
CH-7537 Mustair
Graubünden
*Sculptures and
Romanesque artefacts are
housed in this restored and
reconstructed 12th-
century Benedictine
monastery.*

SCHWYZ

**Ital Reding House (Ital-
Reding Haus)**
Rickenbachstrasse 24
CH-6430 Schwyz
*The 1600s house of the
governor of Schwyz
contains painted rooms
and memorabilia.*

WARTH

**Ittingen Museum
(Kartause Ittingen)**
CH-8532 Warth,
Thurgau
*A restored medieval
monastery with 18th-
century monks' cells and a
refectory.*

WILDHAUS

**Zwingli's House
(Zwingli Geburtshaus)**
Lisighaus
CH-9658 Wildhaus
St Gallen
*The birthplace of the
religious reformer Ulrich
Zwingli (1484-1531) is
filled with 15th-century
furnishings.*

THAILAND

BANGKOK

Kamthieng House
Siam Society
131 Asoka Road
Bangkok
*Dating from the 19th
century, this North Thai
house has been preserved
with furnishings of the
period.*

Jim Thompson House
Rama 1 Road
Bangkok
*The house of the
American silk merchant
who, having brought
Thai silk to the West,
disappeared in 1967.
Carefully used Thai
antiques create a
magnificent palace of the
country's art. (See pp.
158-161.)*

TURKEY

ANKARA

Ataturk's House
Cankaya, Ankara
*The house in which the
Turkish patriot Mustafa
Kemal Ataturk (1881-
1938) lived during the
war of independence
(1919-23).*

ISTANBUL

Ataturk Museum
Halaskargazi Caddesi
Istanbul
*The home of the Turkish
patriot (1881-1938) is
filled with items of
personal memorabilia.*

Topkapi Palace
Istanbul
*Built by Muhammed II,
this restored palace
features a perserved
Turkish Harem and a fine
collection of antiques.*

SIVAS

**The Meeting Hall
(Inkilap Museum)**
*The house in which
Commander Ataturk
(1881-1938) stayed while
in charge of the final
Congress on the
Liberation of Turkey in
1919.*

UNITED KINGDOM

ENGLAND

ALCESTER

Coughton Court
Near Alcester
Warwickshire, B49 5JA
Built in 1518, this three-storey gatehouse belonged to the Catholic Throckmorton family between 1409 and 1946. It contains a collection of furniture, porcelain, portraits and family memorabilia.
NATIONAL TRUST.

Ragley Hall
Alcester
Warwickshire
B49 5NJ
A Palladian-style mansion, built in 1680 by Robert Hooke, housing a collection of paintings, furniture and 18th-century porcelain.

ALFORD

The Manor House
Alford and District
   Civic Trust Ltd
West Street
Alford
Lincolnshire
LN13 9DG
Thatched, brick manor house, dating from the 16th century, which documents domestic life in rural Lincolnshire.

ALTON

Jane Austen's House
Chawton
Alton
Hampshire GU34 1SJ
The house in which the author lived from 1809, preserved as it was during her lifetime (1775-1817). Documents, personal possessions and other memorabilia relating to Jane Austen are on view.

Gilbert White Museum
The Wakes
Selbourne
Alton
Hampshire GU34 3JW
The home of Gilbert White (1720-1793), the clergyman and naturalist, features 18th-century interiors, furnishings and memorabilia from his lifetime.

ALTRINCHAM

Dunham Massey
Altrincham
Cheshire WA14 4SJ
An 18th-century mansion, home to the Stamford family until 1976, with collections of furniture, paintings and silver.

AMBLESIDE

Rydal Mount
Ambleside
Cumbria LA22 9LU
Home of William Wordsworth, the Romantic poet, and his wife, Mary, from 1813 until his death in 1850. Now owned by the poet's great-great-grand-daughter, the house still contains his furniture and personal possessions.

AXBRIDGE

King John's Hunting Lodge
The Square
Axbridge
Somerset BS26 2AP
Built around 1500, this timber-framed building, originally a merchant's house, was restored to its 16th-century appearance in 1971.
NATIONAL TRUST.

AYLESBURY

Florence Nightingale Museum
Claydon House
Middle Claydon
Near Aylesbury
Buckinghamshire
MK18 2EY
An 18th-century house with rococo staterooms and carving. Frequently visited by Florence Nightingale, it contains memorabilia and photographs of the celebrated Crimean nurse.
NATIONAL TRUST.

Waddesdon Manor
Waddesdon
Near Aylesbury
Buckinghamshire
This former home of the international banking family, the de Rothschilds, houses works of art by Gainsborough and Reynolds as well as a vast collection of porcelain, French furniture and objets d'art.
NATIONAL TRUST.

AYLSHAM

Blickling Hall
Near Aylsham
Norfolk NR11 6NF
Dating from the 17th century, this red-brick house has a wide collection of furniture and tapestries. Special features include a well-stocked library and an 18th-century orangery.
NATIONAL TRUST.

BAKEWELL

The Old House Museum
Cunningham Place
Bakewell
Derbyshire DE4 1DD
A 16th-century house, divided into tenement dwellings toward the end of the 18th century, and now restored to its original appearance. A 19th-century reproduction kitchen, saddlery and smithy reveal the domestic lifestyle of the period.

BANBURY

Sulgrave Manor
Banbury
Oxfordshire
OX17 2SD
A mid-16th-century house which was occupied by ancestors of George Washington, first President of the United States, for more than a century.

Upton House
Near Banbury
Oxfordshire
OX15 6HT
Built during the 1690s, this local-stone house contains a vast collection of old master paintings, porcelain, tapestries and furniture.
NATIONAL TRUST.

BARNSTAPLE

Arlington Court
Arlington
Barnstaple
Devon EX31 4LP
The 1822 house holds a large collection of 18th- and 19th-century furniture as well as a fascinating assortment of unusual objets d'art, including model ships, sea shells, butterflies and snuff boxes.
NATIONAL TRUST.

BASINGSTOKE

The Vyne
Sherborne St John
Basingstoke
Hampshire
RG26 5DX
Built during the early 16th century but extensively altered in the mid-17th century, The Vyne features a Print Room, a Palladian staircase and a large collection of furniture, family portraits, tapestries and porcelain.
NATIONAL TRUST.

BATH

Herschel House
19 New King Street
Bath
Avon
BA1 2BL
Home of the astronomer Sir William Herschel (1738-1822), this 18th-century house now contains a collection of his apparatus and telescopes.

1 Royal Crescent
Bath
Avon
BA1 2LR
Occupied by the Duke of York in 1776, this impressive building has been carefully redecorated and refurnished to exemplify the style of that period.

BEDFORD

Bunyan Museum
55 Mill Street
Bedford
MK40 3EU
The writer of The Pilgrim's Progress*, John Bunyan, was pastor on this site between 1672 and 1688. Now a church/museum, the building contains some of Bunyan's possessions and a vast collection of translations of* The Pilgrim's Progress*.*

Cecil Higgins Museum
Castle Close
Bedford
MK40 3NY
The home of a local 19th-century brewer now houses an outstanding collection of furniture, ceramics, glass, lace, toys, costumes and English watercolours.

BERKELEY

Jenner Museum
The Chantry
Church Lane
Berkeley
Gloucestershire
GL13 9BD
Edward Jenner, the doctor and naturalist who developed the vaccination against smallpox, treated his patients here during the late 18th century. The Temple of Vaccinia, where – in a notable philanthropic gesture – he vaccinated the poor free of charge, has been restored to its original appearance and forms part of the museum.

BERWICK-UPON-TWEED

Ravensdowne Barracks
The Parade
Berwick-upon-Tweed
Northumberland
TD15 1DF
Built between 1717 and 1721, these barracks are believed to be the earliest in Britain. The buildings include a reconstructed 19th-century schoolroom and an 18th-century barrack room.

BIRMINGHAM

Aston Hall
Aston Park
Trinity Road
Aston
Birmingham
B6 6JD
Dating from the early 17th century, this Jacobean house now forms part of the Birmingham Museum. 30 rooms have been redecorated and refurnished in the style of the 1760s (when the house underwent its most recent alterations).

Blakesley Hall
Blakesley Road
Yardley
Birmingham
B25 8RN
This timber-framed yeoman's house, constructed around 1575, has recently been restored and refurnished in the style of the period. Features include an upper-level gallery and 16th-century wall paintings.

BODMIN

Lanhydrock
Bodmin
Cornwall
PL30 5AD
Dating from 1630, Lanhydrock house was almost totally destroyed by fire during the 19th century, but has since been rebuilt by Richard Coad to its original plan. It contains a splendid fitted 19th-century kitchen with batterie de cuisine, a 116-foot (35-metre) gallery, a large collection of 18th-century furniture and a series of Mortlake tapestries.
NATIONAL TRUST.

Pencarrow House
Bodmin
Cornwall
PL30 3AG
Built during the 18th century, and owned by the Molesworth-St Aubyn family, this house features 18th- and 19th-century furnishings and a magnificent collection of paintings, including works by the portrait painter Joshua Reynolds (1723-1792).

BOLTON

Hall i' th' Wood
Green Way
off Crompton Way
Bolton
Greater Manchester
BL1 8UA
Dating from 1485 and furnished in 18th-century style, this house was home to the Industrial Revolution inventor of the spinning mule, Samuel Crompton (1753-1827).

Smithhills Hall Museum
Smithhills Dean Road
Bolton
Greater Manchester
BL1 7NP
The earliest part of the house dates from the 14th century, although additions were made during the 16th century. The open roof in the Great Hall is of particular interest, as is the wooden panelling in the drawing room.

BOTLEY
Hampshire Farm Museum
Upper Hamble Country Park
Brook Lane
Botley
Hampshire SO3 2ER
Buildings from across Hampshire have been reconstructed on this site to demonstrate the changes that took place in agriculture in the county between 1850 and 1950. A forge, barn, wheelwright's workshop and medieval open hall are among the buildings on display.

BRADFORD
Bradford Industrial Museum
Moorside Mills
Moorside Road
Bradford
West Yorkshire
BD2 3HP
A former mill-owner's residence, Moorside House is furnished in 19th-century style. Nearby, the museum, a converted mill, specializes in the history of the wool-manufacturing industry.

BRENTFORD
Syon Park
Brentford
Middlesex TW8 8JF
A seat of the Duke of Northumberland, Syon House was transformed by Robert Adam in the 18th century.

BRIDGWATER
Admiral Blake Museum
Blake Street
Bridgwater
Somerset TA6 3NB
The birthplace of Admiral Robert Blake (1599-1657), who won the battle of Santa Cruz in 1657, contains his personal possessions and documents.

Coleridge Cottage
35 Lime Street
Nether Stowey
Bridgwater
Somerset TA5 1NQ
The house in which the poet Samuel Taylor Coleridge lived from 1796 to 1799, restored to its appearance in Coleridge's day. NATIONAL TRUST.

BRIGHTON
Preston Manor
Preston Park
Brighton, East Sussex
Built in 1739 and home to the Stanford family for two centuries, Preston Manor features early 20th-century decoration and furnishings as well as collections of paintings and silver.

The Royal Pavilion
Brighton, East Sussex
Designed for George IV by John Nash in 1815, the pavilion exemplifies Regency extravagance.

BRISTOL
Thomas Chatterton's House
Redcliffe Way
Bristol BS1 6NL
The birthplace of the boy-poet Thomas Chatterton (1752-1770) contains memorabilia.

The Georgian House
7 Great George Street
Bristol BS1 5RR
A Georgian town house of the 1790s, restored and refurbished in the style of the period.

The Red Lodge
Park Row
Bristol BS1 5LJ
Furnished in a combination of 17th- and 18th-century styles, this house dates from the early 17th century and is decorated with period panelling and carving.

John Wesley's Chapel
36 The Horsefair
Bristol
Dating from 1739, this is the world's oldest Wesleyan chapel. It looks today as it did at the time of its greatest popularity in the 1760s.

BURNLEY
Queen Street Mill
Harle Syke
Burnley, Lancashire
Working steam mill dating from 1894. The interior of the mill is just as it would have been in its heyday, with all the noise and bustle of the late 19th-century industrial environment.

Weaver's Triangle Vistors' Centre
85 Manchester Road
Burnley
Lancashire BB11 1JZ
19th-century buildings from the highpoint of the industrial era.

BURTON-UPON-TRENT
Hoar Cross Hall
Hoar Cross
Burton-upon-Trent
Staffordshire
A vast neo-Elizabethan mansion built in the late 19th century. Period interiors with William Morris wallpapers and 19th-century furniture.

BURWASH
Bateman's
Burwash
Etchingham
East Sussex TN19 7DR
The home of the writer Rudyard Kipling (1865-1936) from 1902 until his death. A 17th-century mansion with later additions, furnished as it was at the time of Kipling's occupancy.

CADBURY
Fursdon House
Cadbury
Exeter, Devon EX5 5JS
This early 17th-century furnished house contains memorabilia of the Fursdon family.

CAMBRIDGE
Kettle's Yard
Castle Street
Cambridge CB3 9ST
Gallery and home of the 20th-century collector and gallery deviser Jim Eade.

CARNFORTH
Leighton Hall
Carnforth
Lancashire LA5 9ST
The Hall features 17th-, 18th- and 19th-century period interiors and 19th-century furniture.

CARSHALTON
Little Holland House
40 Beeches Avenue
Carshalton
Surrey SM5 3LW
The home of Frank Dickinson, disciple of John Ruskin, is furnished in the late 19th-century Arts and Crafts style.

CHALFONT ST GILES
Milton's Cottage
21 Deanway
Chalfont St Giles
Buckinghamshire
HP8 4JH
The small 16th-century cottage of the poet John Milton (1608-1674), who wrote Paradise Lost, houses his personal possessions and memorabilia.

CHARD
Hornsbury Mill
Chard
Somerset
TA20 3AQ
This 19th-century mill contains its original equipment and tools.

CHELTENHAM
Gustav Holst's Birthplace
4 Clarence Road
Cheltenham
Gloucestershire
GL52 2AY
A Regency house, decorated in the late 19th-century style of Holst's (1874-1934) childhood. Features musical instruments, documents and other personal effects.

CHIPPENHAM
Castle Farm Museum
Marshfield
Near Chippenham
Wiltshire SN14 8PD
A collection of farm buildings on a working farm dating from the 18th century. Period interiors and equipment.

Dyrham Park
Near Chippenham
Wiltshire SN14 8HW
This 1690s mansion was built for the Secretary of War, William Blathwayt, and features interiors that have remained unchanged since the 1700s, at the time of his accupancy. NATIONAL TRUST.

CHUDLEIGH
Ugbrooke House
Chudleigh
Newton Abbot
Devon TQ13 0AD
A Robert Adam house, dating from 1760, built for the Clifford family. Contains 18th-century furniture and paintings.

CLEVEDON
Clevedon Court
Clevedon, Avon
House dating from 1320 with 18th-century interiors and an original 14th-century kitchen. NATIONAL TRUST.

COALVILLE
The Manor House
Donington-le-Heath
Coalville
Leicester
13th-century manor house with 17th-century interiors and furniture.

COLCHESTER
Sir Alfred Munnings Art Museum
Castle House
Dedham
Colchester
Essex CO7 6AZ
Occupied by the painter Sir Alfred Munnings (1878-1959) from 1919 until his death, this museum houses a collection of his equestrian paintings.

CONISTON
Brantwood
Coniston
Cumbria LA21 8AD
The art historian and artist John Ruskin (1819-1900) lived here between 1872 and 1900. Contains many of his personal effects, furniture and paintings.

CORSHAM
Corsham Court
Corsham
Wiltshire SN13 0BZ
In a combination of styles, ranging from the 16th to the 19th century, this house contains pictures and furniture.

CRAVEN ARMS
The White House Museum
Aston Munslow
Near Craven Arms
Shropshire SY7 9ER
A Saxon manor house, home to the Stedman family between 1332 and 1946 and still used as a family home. Outbuildings include dairies, cider house, granary, 16th-century stable block and 13th-century dovecot.

DARLINGTON
Raby Castle
Staindrop
Darlington
Co. Durham
DL2 3AH
Built around a medieval castle, this 19th-century home features collections of porcelain and paintings.

DORCHESTER
Hardy's Cottage
Higher Bockhampton
Dorchester
Dorset
DT2 8QJ
This is the birthplace of the writer Thomas Hardy (1840-1928). It dates from 1800 and is decorated in mid-19th-century style. NATIONAL TRUST.

DORKING
Polesden Lacey
Dorking
Surrey
RH5 6BB
An 1820s house featuring collections of paintings and porcelain. NATIONAL TRUST.

DREWSTEIGNTON
Castle Drogo
Drewsteignton
Exeter
Devon
EX6 6PB
This magnificent castle was built by Edwin Landseer Lutyens in the 1910 and is furnished in baronial style. NATIONAL TRUST.

DROITWICH
Hanbury Hall
Droitwich
Hereford and Worcester
WR9 7EA
Early 1700s house, still in its original condition, with 18th-century furniture and important murals by Sir James Thornhill.

EAST GRINSTEAD
Standen House
East Grinstead
West Sussex
Built by Philip Webb, a friend of William Morris, during the 1890s, Standen House features a collection of original William Morris furniture and wallpaper. NATIONAL TRUST.

EASTWOOD

D.H. Lawrence's Birthplace
8a Victoria Street
Eastwood
Nottingham
NG16 3AW
A miner's cottage of the 1880s, restored to look as it did in D.H. Lawrence's day (1885-1930).

ELLESMERE PORT

The Boat Museum
Dockyard Road
Ellesmere Port
South Wirral L65 4EF
Includes several restored dock workers' cottages of the 19th and early 20th centuries.

ETON

Museum of Eton Life
Eton College
Eton
Windsor
Berkshire SL4 6DB
A re-creation of the study of an Eton schoolboy of the early 20th century.

EYNSFORD

Lullingstone Roman Villa
Eynsford
Kent DA4 0JA
Re-creations of Roman rooms as the villa appeared at the time of the Roman occupation in the 4th century AD.

FARINGDON

Buscot Park
Near Faringdon
Oxfordshire SN7 8BU
Late 18th-century house, filled with collections of furniture and paintings and murals by Burne-Jones. NATIONAL TRUST.

FELLBRIGG

Fellbrigg Hall
Fellbrigg, Norwich
A 17th-century manor house with 18th-century furniture.
NATIONAL TRUST.

GRANTHAM

Belton House
Grantham
Lincolnshire NG32 2LS
A late 17th-century house with 18th-century furnishings and wood carvings by Grinling Gibbons.
NATIONAL TRUST.

GRASMERE

Dove Cottage
Town End
Grasmere
Ambleside
Cumbria LA22 9SH
The house in which the poet William Wordsworth (1770-1850) lived with his sister between 1799 and 1808, restored to its original appearance with personal effects and memorabilia.

GREAT YARMOUTH

Elizabethan House Museum
4 South Quay
Great Yarmouth
Norfolk NR30 2QH
An Elizabethan house of the 1590s with artefacts and everyday items of the period.

HAGLEY

Hagley Hall
Hagley
Near Stourbridge
West Midlands
D49 9LG
Palladian house of the 1750s with fine plasterwork and paintings. Home of the Lyttleton family.

HATCH BEAUCHAMP

Hatch Court
Hatch Beauchamp
Taunton
Somerset TA3 6AA
A Palladian-style house of the 1750s with early 19th-century decoration.

HAWKSHEAD

Hill Top
Sawrey
Hawkshead
Cumbria LA22 0PN
The 17th-century house where the writer Beatrix Potter (1866-1943) lived before she was married and where she wrote many of her stories.

HAWORTH

Brontë Parsonage
Haworth, Keighley
West Yorkshire
The home of the Brontë family of writers, Anne (1820-1849), Charlotte (1816-1855), Emily (1818-1848) and Branwell (1817-1848). Furnished as it appeared in their lifetimes.

HENLEY-ON-THAMES

Fawley Court
D.M. College and Museum
Henley-on-Thames
Oxfordshire
Designed by Sir Christopher Wren (1632-1723) in 1684, this house contains carving by Grinling Gibbons and later decoration by Wyatt.

Stonor Park
Near Henley-on-Thames
Oxfordshire RG9 6HF
Mainly 18th-century house on the site of a 12th-century original, with 18th- and 19th-century decoration. The home of the Stonor family.

HIGH WYCOMBE

Hughenden Manor
High Wycombe
Buckinghamshire
HP14 4LA
House purchased in 1848 by Benjamin Disraeli (1804-1881), the Victorian statesman and prime minister, and furnished as it was in his day. NATIONAL TRUST.

HULL

Wilberforce House
23-25 High Street
Hull HU1 1NE
Birthplace of William Wilberforce (1759-1833), the philanthropist and campaigner for the abolition of slavery.

HUNGERFORD

Littlecote House
Hungerford
Berkshire RG17 0SU
15th-century house with later additions, containing Chinese Regency-style and Chippendale furniture.

IPSWICH

Christchurch Mansion
Christchurch Park
Soane Street
Ipswich
Suffolk IP4 2BE
Dating from the mid-16th century (with some later additions), the mansion features mid-18th-century decoration and contains tapestries and glasswork.

KEIGHLEY

East Riddlesden Hall
Bradford Road
Keighley
West Yorkshire
BD20 5EL
Restored 17th-century house, furnished in period style. NATIONAL TRUST.

KETTERING

Boughton House
Near Kettering
Northamptonshire
NN14 1BJ
Late 17th-century house of the Dukes of Montagu, decorated in 17th- and 18th-century style.

LANCASTER

Cottage Museum
15 Castle Hill
Lancaster LA1 1YS
A simple house of the 1740s, furnished in the style of the 1820s.

LAPWORTH

Packwood House
Lapworth
Solihull
West Midlands
B94 6AT
A 17th-century farmhouse, altered and extended in the 18th and 19th centuries, and furnished as it was in the 1920s. NATIONAL TRUST.

LEDBURY

Hellen's
Much Marcle
Ledbury
Hereford and Worcester
HR8 2LY
13th-century house with later additions and 19th-century interiors.

LEICESTER

Newarke House Museum
The Newarke
Leicester LE2 55N
A house of the 16th, 17th and 19th centuries, with panelled interiors.

LEIGHTON BUZZARD

Ascott
Wing
Leighton Buzzard
Bedfordshire LU7 0PT
The 19th-century country house of a member of the de Rothschild family, filled with paintings, porcelain and furniture.
NATIONAL TRUST.

LEWES

Charleston
Near Lewes
East Sussex
BN8 6LL
The home for 60 years of Vanessa Bell and Duncan Grant, the Bloomsbury artists. Stunning painted decoration of the 1920s. (See pp.80-85.)

Firle Place
Near Lewes
East Sussex
BN8 6LP
The home of the Gage family for 500 years. The house features a 15th-century core with 18th-century alterations and Georgian-style interiors.

Glynde Place
Glynde
Lewes
East Sussex
Elizabethan manor house with later additions of the 17th and 18th centuries. Demonstrates the changing tastes of its owners over the four centuries that they have lived here.

LICHFIELD

Samuel Johnson's Birthplace
Breadmarket Street
Lichfield
Staffordshire
WS13 6LG
Boyhood home of Samuel Johnson (1709-1784), the lexicographer. Contains personal effects and memorabilia.

LIVERPOOL

Croxteth Hall and Country Park
Croxteth Hall Lane
Liverpool
L12 0HB
Ancestral home of the Earls of Sefton. 17th-century house with alterations of the 18th and 20th centuries.

Speke Hall
The Walk
Liverpool
L24 1XD
Late 15th-century, half-timbered manor house with Elizabethan and later decoration and 19th-century furnishings.
NATIONAL TRUST.

LONDON

Apsley House
149 Piccadilly
London W1V 9LA
London house of the first Duke of Wellington (1769-1852), filled with memorabilia of his wars against Napoleon and furnished as in his day.

Carlyle's House
24 Cheyne Row
London SW3 5HL
Home of the historian (1795-1881) with original decoration and furniture.
NATIONAL TRUST.

Dickens's House
48 Doughty Street
London WC1N 2LF
Where Charles Dickens lived 1837-1839 and where he wrote The Pickwick Papers, Nicholas Nickleby *and* Oliver Twist. *Re-created period interiors are filled with memorabilia.*

Fenton House
Hampstead Grove
London NW3 6SP
Late 17th-century house with interiors of the period and collections of furniture, porcelain and musical instruments.
NATIONAL TRUST.

Hogarth's House
Hogarth Lane
Great West Road
London W4 2QN
The country house of the painter William Hogarth (1697-1764) contains copies of his work.

Dr Johnson's House
17 Gough Square
London EC4A 3DE
Samuel Johnson lived in this house for the greater part of his life. Reconstructed period interiors house first editions and memorabilia.

Keats's House
Wentworth Place
Keats Grove,
Hampstead
London NW3 2RL
A Regency house, restored as it was when the poet John Keats (1795-1821) lived there. Keats's furniture and personal effects are on view.

Leighton House Museum
12 Holland Park Road
London W14 8LZ
Built in the 1860s by the painter Lord Leighton (1830-1896). The decoration reflects Leighton's pictorial style in its neoclassical and Arab schemes.

Linley Sambourne House
18 Stafford Terrace
Kensington
London W8 7BH
A typical town house of the 1870s, with carefully preserved original furnishings. Once the home of Edward Linley Sambourne (1844-1910), the artist and cartoonist.

Michael Faraday's Laboratory
The Royal Institution
21 Albemarle Street
London W1X 4BS
Restored laboratory of Faraday (1791-1867), the chemist, with its original 1840s equipment.

Sir John Soane's Museum
13 Lincoln's Inn Fields
London WC2A 3BP
Neoclassical home of the Regency architect and designer of the Bank of England, John Soane (1753-1837). Regency interiors and collections of antiquities and paintings. (See pp.56-63.)

Southside House
3 Woodhayes Road
Wimbledon
London SW19 4RJ
17th-century residence of the Pennington-Mellor family, who have lived here for 300 years. The decoration reflects changing tastes in style throughout their occupation.

John Wesley's House
47-49 City Road
London EC1Y 1AU
The house of the founder of Methodism, John Wesley (1703-1791), next door to his chapel. Original furniture, personal possessions and memorabilia.

MACCLESFIELD
Capesthorne Hall
Macclesfield
Cheshire
Early 18th-century house with mid-19th-century alterations. The rooms house furniture and memorabilia of the Bromley Davenport and Capesthorne families.

MANCHESTER
Wythenshawe Hall
Wythenshawe Park
Northenden
Manchester
M23 0AB
This English country house reflects the changing tastes over the last 400 years and is furnished in the popular style of the early 20th century.

MARGATE
Tudor House Museum
King Street
Margate
Kent
A restored 16th-century house which contains examples of typical period panelling.

MARKET HARBOROUGH
Langton Hall
West Langton
Near Market
   Harborough
Leicestershire
LE16 7TY
An important collection of Chinese furniture is contained in this 18th-century house.

MELBOURNE
Melbourne Hall
Melbourne
Near Derby
DE7 1EN
The home of the British Prime Minister, Lord Melbourne (1779-1848), and his notorious wife, Lady Caroline Lamb (1785-1828), friend of Lord Byron.

MONTACUTE
Montacute House
Montacute
Somerset
TA15 6XP
16th-century house of the Phelps family with original panelling and decoration.
NATIONAL TRUST.

MORPETH
Wallington
Cambo
Morpeth
Northumberland
NE30 3SQ
1688 house with mid-18th-century alterations. Period interiors of the 18th and 19th centuries.
NATIONAL TRUST.

NORTHAMPTON
Castle Ashby House
Castle Ashby
Near Northampton
NN7 1LQ
17th-century house with later interiors and paintings. Home of the Earls of Northampton.

NOTTINGHAM
Thrumpton Hall
Nottingham
A 17th-century house with fine period carvings.

ORPINGTON
Down House
Luxted Road
Down
Orpington
Kent
BRG 7JT
Home of the naturalist Charles Darwin (1809-1892). His study and drawing room have been preserved as in his lifetime.

PENRITH
Dalemain Mansion
Dalemain
Penrith
Cumbria CA11 0HB
A medieval house with an 18th-century neoclassical facade and 18th- and 19th-century interiors.

PENZANCE
St Michael's Mount
Marazion
Near Penzance
Cornwall TR17 0HS
Home of the St Aubyn family since 1660, the 15th-century house boasts furnishings of subsequent eras. NATIONAL TRUST.

PETERBOROUGH
Elton Hall
Elton
Peterborough
Cambridgeshire
PE8 6SQ
A family home since 1660, with an eclectic mixture of furnishings and treasures.

PLYMOUTH
Elizabethan House
32 New Street
Plymouth PL1 2NA
A restored 15th-century house with period interiors.

PORTSMOUTH
Charles Dickens's Birthplace
393 Old Commercial
   Road
Portsmouth
Hampshire PO1 4QL
The house in which the novelist Charles Dickens was born in 1812, restored to its appearance at the time of his birth and housing his memorabilia.

RICHMOND
Ham House
Richmond
Surrey TW10 7RS
The former home of the Earls of Dysart. A restored 17th-century mansion with paintings and a period chapel.
NATIONAL TRUST.

ROTHBURY
Cragside Hall
Cragside
Rothbury
Northumberland
NE65 7PX
Built by Norman Shaw (1831-1912) during the 1860s, this house contains William Morris furnishings and of Pre-Raphaelite paintings.
NATIONAL TRUST.

ROYSTON
Wimpole Hall
Arrington
Near Royston
Hertfordshire
This 17th-century house, with later additions, features 18th-century plasterwork and 18th- and 19th-century furniture.
NATIONAL TRUST.

RYE
Lamb House
West Street
Rye
East Sussex TN31 7ES
The early 18th-century house of the Mayor of Rye in which the novelist Henry James (1843-1916) lived at the turn of the 20th century.
NATIONAL TRUST.

ST IVES
Barbara Hepworth Museum
Trewyn Studio
Barnoon Hill
St Ives
Cornwall TR26 1AD
The house and studio of the sculptor Barbara Hepworth (1903-1975), restored to its appearance during her lifetime.

SHEFFIELD
Bishop's House
Meersbrook Park
Norton Lees Lane
Sheffield S8 9BE
Dating from the 16th and 17th centuries, the house has 17th-century interiors.

SHERBORNE
Sandford Orcas Manor House
Sandford Orcas
Sherborne
Dorset DT9 4SA
A 16th-century manor house, as it was at the time of its construction. The interiors are decorated in 17th- to 19th-century styles.

SHILDON
Timothy Hackworth Museum
Soho Cottages
Shildon
Co. Durham DL4 1PG
The home of Timothy Hackworth (1786-1850), the railway engine designer, features period furnishings and displays of his designs.

SHREWSBURY
Attingham Park
Atcham
Near Shrewsbury
Shropshire SY4 4TP
This 18th-century house was altered by John Nash at the beginning of the 19th century and is furnished in the style of the 19th century.
NATIONAL TRUST.

SOUTHEND-ON-SEA
Southchurch Hall
Southchurch Hall
   Gardens
Southend-on-Sea
Essex
Authentic medieval furnishings in a moated manor house of the 13th century.

STAFFORD
Shugborough
Milford
Stafford ST17 0XA
Built by the Anson family in the late 17th century and enlarged in the 19th century, the house holds a large collection of paintings and 19th-century furniture, together with Anson memorabilia.
NATIONAL TRUST.

STOCKPORT
Bramhall Hall
Bramhall Park
Bramhall
Stockport
Cheshire SK7 3NX
Built during the 15th and 16th centuries, the half-timbered Hall was home to the Davenport family for 500 years. Special features include a set of wall-paintings in the chapel and a 20-ft(6-metre)-high heraldic tapestry from the 16th century.

Lyme Park
Disley
Stockport, Cheshire
Home to the Leigh family, this 16th-century house was altered during the 18th century. The interiors are filled with family memorabilia, furniture and tapestries.
NATIONAL TRUST.

STOURTON
Stourhead
Stourton
Warminster
Wiltshire BA12 6HQ
The house, which developed gradually between 1724 and 1839, is home to the Hoare family and contains furniture and porcelain.
NATIONAL TRUST.

STRATFIELD SAYE
Stratfield Saye House
Stratfield Saye
Reading
Berkshire RG7 2BZ
Presented to the Duke of Wellington as a reward for having defeated Napoleon at Waterloo. The early 19th-century interior features memorabilia relating to the Iron Duke.

STRATFORD-UPON-AVON

Mary Arden's House
Station Road
Wilmcote
Stratford-upon-Avon
Warwickshire
CV37 9UN
Shakespeare's mother's house, preserved as it was in her lifetime with 16th-century decoration and furnishings.

Anne Hathaway's Cottage
Cottage Lane
Shottery
Stratford-upon-Avon
Warwickshire
CV37 9HH
The home of Anne Hathaway before her marriage to William Shakespeare has 16th- and 17th-century interiors.

Hall's Croft
Old Town
Stratford-upon-Avon
Warwickshire
CV37 6BG
Owned by Shakespeare's son-in-law, this 16th-century house features 16th-century furnishings.

Shakespeare's Birthplace
Henley Street
Stratford-upon-Avon
Warwickshire
CV37 6QW
The house in which William Shakespeare (1564-1616) was born, now restored to its 16th-century appearance.

STYAL

Quarry Bank Mill
Styal
Cheshire
An 18th-century cotton mill with period interiors. NATIONAL TRUST.

SUDBURY

Melford Hall
Long Melford
Sudbury
Suffolk
CO10 9AA
Dating from the 16th century, and home to the Parker family, Melford Hall is filled with paintings, porcelain and memorabilia relating to Beatrix Potter, a family friend. NATIONAL TRUST.

TAUNTON

Poundisford Park
Poundisford
Taunton
Somerset TA3 7AF
A country house from the 16th and 18th centuries.

TENTERDEN

Ellen Terry Museum
Small Hythe Place
Small Hythe
Tenterden
Kent
Home of the music hall artiste Ellen Terry (1848-1928) from 1899 to 1928, featuring early 20th-century interiors and memorabilia. NATIONAL TRUST.

THIRSK

Sion Hill Hall
Kirby Wiske
Near Thirsk
North Yorkshire
YO7 4EU
An early 20th-century house, with 18th- and 19th-century furniture and decorative arts.

THULSTON

Elvaston Castle
Borrowash Lane
Elvaston
Thulston
Derby DE7 3EP
Life in a country house at the turn of the 20th century is recreated in this castle. The Elvaston Working Estate Museum features a smithy, carpenter's, saddler's, cobbler's shop and a dairy.

TORPOINT

Antony House
Torpoint
Cornwall PL11 2QA
Ancestral house of the Carew-Pole family with 16th- to 19th-century furnishings. NATIONAL TRUST.

WALSALL

Jerome K. Jerome's Birthplace
Belsize House
Bradford Street
Walsall WS1 1PN
West Midlands
The birthplace of Jerome K. Jerome (1859-1927), author of Three Men in a Boat. *Mid-19th-century furnishings and memorabilia.*

WAREHAM

Clouds Hill
Wareham
Dorset BH20 7NQ
The home of Lawrence of Arabia (1888-1935) from 1929. The interiors have been preserved as they were during his lifetime, with 1920s furniture and memorabilia. NATIONAL TRUST.

WELWYN

Shaw's Corner
Ayot St Lawrence
Welwyn
Hertfordshire
AL6 9BX
Built in 1902, this former rectory was occupied by the playwright George Bernard Shaw from 1906 until his death in 1950. The ground-floor rooms have been preserved intact since his death. NATIONAL TRUST.

WESTERHAM

Chartwell
Westerham
Kent
The home of Sir Winston Churchill (1874-1965) from 1924 to his death. The interiors are as they were during his lifetime. NATIONAL TRUST.

Quebec House
Westerham
Kent
The family home of general James Wolfe (1727-1759), the victor of Quebec. Memorabilia of Wolfe's career. NATIONAL TRUST.

WEST WYCOMBE

West Wycombe Park
West Wycombe
Buckinghamshire
HP14 3AJ
The early 18th-century house of Sir Francis Dashwood contains 18th-century interiors and furniture. NATIONAL TRUST.

WEYMOUTH

Tudor House
3 Trinity Street
Weymouth
Dorset DT4 8TW
The house of a 17th-century sea captain, restored with 17th-century interiors.

WOLVERHAMPTON

Wightwick Manor
Wightwick
Wolverhampton
West Midlands
WV6 8HF
The Arts and Crafts mansion of Samuel Mander, with William Morris furnishings and Pre-Raphaelite paintings. (See pp.74-79.) NATIONAL TRUST.

WORCESTER

Elgar's Birthplace
Crown East Lane
Lower Broadheath
Worcester
House in which the composer Sir Edward Elgar (1857-1934) was born, preserved as it was during his lifetime.

YORK

Beningbrough Hall
Shipton-by-Benington
York
YO6 1DD
Early 18th-century house of the Bourchier family. The period interiors illustrate the different lifestyles upstairs and downstairs in the 18th and 19th centuries. NATIONAL TRUST.

Shandy Hall
Coxwold
Near York
YO6 4AD
The novelist Laurence Sterne (1713-1768) lived in this house, where he wrote Tristram Shandy *and* A Sentimental Journey. *The interiors have been restored as they were during Sterne's lifetime.*

Sutton Park
Sutton-on-the-Forest
York
Early 18th-century house with 18th- and 19th-century furnishings and collections of porcelain.

CHANNEL ISLANDS

ST PETER PORT

Hauteville House
28 rue de Hauteville
St Peter Port, Guernsey
The home of the French novelist Victor Hugo (1802-1885) while in exile, 1856-1870. Hugo's own decorative schemes and memorabilia.

ISLE OF MAN

CASTLETOWN

Nautical Museum
Bridge Street
Castletown
A sailor's cabin of Nelson's time and a sailmaker's loft from the 19th century.

RAMSEY

The Grove
Andreas Road, Ramsey
A middle-class house of the mid-19th-century with furnishings and artefacts.

NORTHERN IRELAND

ANNAGHMORE

Ardress House and Farmyard
64 Ardress Road
Annaghmore
Portadown
Co. Armagh BT12 1SQ
Once owned by the designer George Ensor, who redesigned part of the 17th-century farmhouse in the 18th century. Early agricultural machinery is on display in the 19th-century farmyard. NATIONAL TRUST.

BALLYGAWLEY

President Grant's Ancestral Home
Dergenagh
Ballygawley
Co. Tyrone
The home of the ancestors of the US president and Civil War general, with 19th-century interiors.

STRANGFORD

Castle Ward
Strangford, Co. Down
Late 18th-century house in neoclassical and Gothic styles. NATIONAL TRUST.

SCOTLAND

ALFORD

Craigievar Castle
Alford
Aberdeenshire
AB3 4RS
An outstanding example of Scottish baronial architecture, noted for its ornate Renaissance plasterwork ceilings. The castle has been privately owned by the Forbes-Semphill family since the early 17th century.

ALLOWAY

Burns Cottage
Alloway
Ayrshire
KA7 48Y
Birthplace of Robert Burns (1759-96), the Scottish poet, restored to its appearance at the time of his birth and furnished in period style using many items that belonged to the Burns family.

ANSTRUTHER

Scottish Fisheries Museum
St Ayles
Harbourhead
Anstruther
Fife
KY10 3AB
Housed in a variety of buildings from the 16th century onward, the museum features a reproduction of the interior of a fisherman's home in 1900.

ARNOL

Blackhouse
Arnol
Bragar
Isle of Lewis
PA86 9DB
A typical example of a Lewis thatched farmhouse, furnished in the traditional style, and outbuildings.

AYR

Tam O'Shanter Museum
High Street
Ayr
A thatched building that has retained the atmosphere of a 19th-century public house, with a wide variety of Robert Burns memorabilia.

BANCHORY
Crathes Castle
Banchory
Kincardineshire
AB3 3QJ
*Built during the 16th
century, this turreted
castle forms part of the
estate that King Robert
the Bruce gave to the
Burnetts family in 1323.
It contains an interesting
collection of tapestries and
needlework. NATIONAL
TRUST FOR SCOTLAND.*

BIGGAR
**Greenhill Covenanters'
House**
Biggar Museum Trust
Moat Park, Biggar
Ayrshire ML12 6DT
*An old farmhouse, rebuilt
in the 1970s, with many
refurnished rooms in the
style of the 17th and 18th
centuries. A miniature
costume collection is
housed upstairs.*

BISHOPBRIGGS
Thomas Muir Museum
Huntershill Recreation
    Centre
Crowhill Road
Bishopbriggs
Near Glasgow
Lanarkshire G66 1RW
*Home of the Scottish
radical and reformer
Thomas Muir.*

BLAIR ATHOLL
Blair Castle
Blair Atholl
Perthshire PH18 5TH
*Dating from 1268, the
castle has a collection of
furniture, armour, lace,
porcelain and children's
games. The current
owners have recreated the
atmosphere and lifestyle of
the 16th to 20th centuries.*

BLANTYRE
**David Livingstone
Centre**
Station Road
Blantyre
Lanarkshire G72 9BT
*The missionary and
explorer was born in this
single-roomed dwelling,
which forms part of a
tenement house. The
entire building has now
been redecorated and
refurnished as it was
during Livingstone's
boyhood.*

COMRIE
**Scottish Tartans
Museum**
Drummond Street
Comrie, Fife
*A typical weaver's croft of
the 19th century with all
the equipment used in the
production of tartans.*

CROMARTY
Hugh Miller's Cottage
Church Street
Cromarty
IV11 8XA
*The house in which the
geologist Hugh Miller
(1802-1856) was born.*

CUPAR
Hill of Tarvit
Cupar, Fife
*An early 20th-century
Scottish baronial house by
Sir Robert Lorimer, with
English furniture and
Dutch paintings.
NATIONAL TRUST FOR
SCOTLAND.*

DUMFRIES
Burns House
Burns Street
Dumfries DG1 2PS
*The home of the poet
Robert Burns (1759-
1796) from 1793 to his
death. Features late 18th-
century interiors in the
Scottish vernacular style.*

DUNBEATH
Laidhay Croft Museum
Dunbeath
Caithness KW6 6EH
*A restoration of a 19th-
century Highland croft.*

DUNFERMLINE
**Andrew Carnegie's
Birthplace**
Moodie Street
Dunfermline, Fife
*House in which the
philanthropist Andrew
Carnegie (1835-1918)
was born, restored to its
appearance at the time of
his childhood.*

ECCLEFECHAN
Carlyle's Birthplace
The Arched House
Ecclefechan
Dumfriesshire
*Birthplace of the historian
Thomas Carlyle (1795-
1881), built by his father
and restored to its
appearance at the time of
Carlyle's birth.*

EDINBURGH
The Georgian House
7 Charlotte Square
Edinburgh EH2 4DR
*A restored Georgian town
house of the 1770s,
decorated in the style of
the early Regency period.
(See pp.64-69.) NATIONAL
TRUST FOR SCOTLAND.*

Lauriston Castle
Cramond Road South
Edinburgh
*A 16th-century tower
house with later neo-
Jacobean additions of the
1820s. Furnished as it was
when lived in at the turn
of the 20th century.*

EOCHAR
Eochar Croft Museum
Bualadubh
Eochar
South Uist PA81 5RQ
*A Western Isles croft with
agricultural and weaving
equipment and
memorabilia of the
crofting way of life.*

FALKLAND
**The Royal Palace of
Falkland**
Falkland
Fife
*The core of the palace is
16th century, but it was
extensively altered during
the 1880s by the Marquis
of Bute. Features some
spectacular furniture,
including the deathbed of
James V of Scotland.
NATIONAL TRUST FOR
SCOTLAND.*

GLASGOW
Hunterian Art Gallery
University of Glasgow
82 Hillhead Street
Glasgow
*Contains the Mackintosh
House, a re-creation of
the Glasgow residence of
the celebrated Scottish
architect and designer
Charles Rennie
Mackintosh (1868-1928).*

Pollok House
2060 Pollokshaws Road
Glasgow G43 1AT
*Built in the 1750s, the
house was altered during
the early 20th century and
contains collections of
silver and paintings,
particularly works by
Spanish masters.*

Provand's Lordship
3 Castle Street
Glasgow G4 0RB
*Dating from the 15th
century, this is the city's
oldest house. It has been
converted into a museum
and contains a
reconstruction of a 16th-
century room.*

The Tenement House
145 Buccleuch Street
Garnethill
Glasgow G3 6QN
*Dating from the 1890s,
this Glasgow tenement
house is furnished in the
style of the period. (See
pp.70-73.) NATIONAL
TRUST FOR SCOTLAND.*

GORDON
(ABERDEENSHIRE)
Haddo House
Gordon
Aberdeenshire
*House by William Adam
in the Palladian style with
interiors decorated in the
late 19th-century style of
luxurious excess.
NATIONAL TRUST FOR
SCOTLAND.*

GORDON
(BERWICKSHIRE)
Mellerstain House
Mellerstain
Gordon
Berwickshire
*House by Robert Adam
with notable plasterwork
and original painted
decoration.*

HADDINGTON
**Jane Welsh Carlyle
Museum**
Lodge Street
Haddington
East Lothian
EH41 3DX
*The family home of Jane
Welsh Carlyle, wife of the
historian Thomas Carlyle,
presented as it would
have appeared in the early
19th century, showing the
lifestyle of a typical
middle-class household.*

Lennoxlove House
Haddington
East Lothian
EH41 4NZ
*The seat of the Dukes of
Hamilton, this Scottish
tower house contains a
collection of memorabilia
and paintings.*

HELENSBURGH
The Hill House
Upper Colquhoun
    Street
Helensburgh
Dunbartonshire
*Hill House was built by
Charles Rennie
Mackintosh in 1902 for
the publisher Walter
Blackie. NATIONAL TRUST
FOR SCOTLAND.*

HUNTLY
Leith Hall
Kennethmont
Huntly
Aberdeenshire
AB54 4NQ
*1650 house with additions
of the 18th, 19th and 20th
centuries. Memorabilia of
the Leith family.
NATIONAL TRUST FOR
SCOTLAND.*

INNERLEITHEN
Traquair
Innerleithen
Peeblesshire
EH44 6PU
*Tower-house castle filled
with memorabilia of the
Maxwell-Stewart family.
The main gates have
remained closed since the
fall of the house of Stuart.*

INVERNESS
**Abriachan Croft
Museum**
Old Schoolhouse
Abriachan
Near Inverness
Inverness-shire IV3 6LB
*Restored croft houses and
outbuildings, furnished
with a wide collection of
crofting tools, photographs
and household equipment.*

INVERURIE
Castle Fraser
Sauchen
Inverurie
Aberdeenshire
AB51 7LD
*16th-century castle with
later furnishings and
17th-century architectural
additions. Fraser family
memorabilia.*

JEDBURGH
Jedburgh Castle Jail
Castle Gate
Jedburgh
Roxburghshire
*A 19th-century jail,
preserved as it looked in
the 1830s.*

KILBARCHAN
Weaver's Cottage
The Cross
Kilbarchan
Renfrewshire
PA10 2JG
*A weaver's cottage of the
early 18th century,
restored to its original
appearance with 19th-
century furnishings.
NATIONAL TRUST FOR
SCOTLAND.*

KILMUIR
**Skye Museum of
Island Life**
Kilmuir
Isle of Skye
*Several thatched crofters'
cottages, furnished in late
19th-century style.*

KIRRIEMUIR
Barrie's Birthplace
9 Brechin Road
Kirriemuir
Angus DD8 4BX
*The birthplace of the
author of Peter Pan,
J.M. Barrie (1860-1937),
contains original
furnishings and the
author's personal effects.
NATIONAL TRUST FOR
SCOTLAND.*

LANARK
**New Lanark
Conservation Village**
The Counting House
New Lanark
Lanark
*A complete village of the
late 18th century, restored
to its appearance at the
height of the local cotton
spinning industry.*

LERWICK
**The Shetland Croft
House Museum**
Voe
Dunrossness
*A 19th-century crofter's
house of the post-
clearances period, when
fishing became the staple
livelihood of the
Highlands.*

LEUCHARS
Earlshall Castle
Leuchars
St Andrews
Fife
*A late 19th-century
adaptation of a 16th-
century tower house by
the architect Sir Robert
Lorimer (1864-1929).*

LIVINGSTON
Livingston Mill Farm
Millfield
Kirkton
Livingston
West Lothian
EH54 7AR
*18th-century farm
buildings with working
equipment and period
19th-century tools.*

MELROSE
Abbotsford House
Melrose
Roxburghshire
*The home of the writer
Sir Walter Scott (1771-
1832), preserved as it was
in his time. Neo-Gothic
interiors with Scott
memorabilia and curios.*

SOUTH QUEENSFERRY
Dalmeny House
South Queensferry
West Lothian
EH30 9TQ
*Early 19th-century house
in neo-Gothic style.
Period interiors with
18th-century furnishings
and Napoleonic
memorabilia.*

Hopetoun House
South Queensferry
West Lothian
EH30 9SL
*Early 18th-century house,
enlarged by William and
John Adam, with original
18th-century furnishings
and decoration. Fine
paintings.*

TARBOLTON
Bachelors' Club
Tarbolton
Ayrshire
*The house in which
Robert Burns formed his
debating society, the
Bachelors' Club, in 1780.
NATIONAL TRUST FOR
SCOTLAND.*

TURRIFF
Session Cottage
Castlehill
Turriff
Aberdeenshire
AB53 7BD
*A small Scottish cottage of
the 18th century.*

WALES

BEAUMARIS
Beaumaris Gaol
Steeple Lane
Beaumaris
Gwynedd
*Built in 1829, the prison
has remained unchanged
since its closure in 1878.*

CONWY
Plas Mawr
The Royal Cambrian
Academy of Art
High Street
Conwy
Gwynedd LL32 8DE
*Dating from 1580, this
house features 19th-
century interiors and
furniture.*

HAVERFORDWEST
Penrhos Cottage
Llanycefn
Maenclochog
Haverfordwest
Pembrokeshire
Dyfed
*A squatter's cottage,
simply furnished and
maintained as it would
have looked in the 19th
century.*

LLANFAIRPWLL
Plas Newydd
Llanfairpwll
Anglesey
Gwynedd LL61 6QD
*Built by James Wyatt, the
house features a Gothic
hall and mural decoration
by Rex Whistler (1905-
1944). NATIONAL TRUST.*

MERTHYR TYDFIL
**Joseph Parry's
Birthplace**
4 Chapel Row
Merthyr Tydfil
Mid Glamorgan
CF48 1BN
*House in which the
composer Joseph Parry
(1841-1903) was born,
preserved in the style of
the early 19th century.
Personal possessions and
memorabilia.*

WREXHAM
Erddig Park
Wrexham
Clwyd LL13 0YT
*An early 18th-century
house with its original
decoration and
furnishings.
NATIONAL TRUST.*

UNITED STATES

ABILENE
**Dwight D. Eisenhower
Center**
S. E. Fourth and
Buckeye Streets
Abilene, KS 67410
*The boyhood home of the
World War II general
and the nation's 34th
president, preserved as it
was in 1946.*

ADRIAN
**Governor Croswell's
House**
228 North Broad Street
Adrian, MI 49221
*Dating from the 1840s,
this house retains its
original decoration and
furnishings.*

AKRON
Stan Hywet Hall
714 North Porye Path
Akron, OH 44303
*Built for Frank A.
Seiberling (the founder of
the Goodyear tyre
company) in 1911, this
house contains 16th- and
17th-century furniture.*

ALBANY (NY)
Historic Cherry Hill
South Pearl Street
Albany, NY 12202
*This colonial house dates
from 1768 and features
original furniture,
antiques and paintings.*

Schuyler Mansion
Clinton and Catherine
Streets
Albany, NY 12202
*1762 mansion with
original furniture and
pictures. The English
general Sir John
Burgoyne was held here
by General Shuyler after
the battle of Saratoga.*

ALBANY (TX)
Ledbetter Pickett House
1010 Railroad Street
Albany, TX 76430
*An 1870s house with
decoration and
furnishings of the period.*

ALEXANDRIA
Carlyle House
121 North Fairfax Street
Alexandria, VA 22314
*This colonial house dates
from the 1750s and retains
its original decoration.*

**Robert E. Lees Boyhood
House**
607 Oronoco Street
Alexandria, VA 22314
*A colonial house, where
the Confederate general
Robert Lee was brought
up, with original
decoration and
memorabilia of the
soldier's life.*

Wood Lawn
9000 Richmond
Highway
Route 1
Alexandria, VA 22309
*A late-colonial house,
given to the Lewis family
by George Washington in
1805, with Federal period
furnishings.*

AMESBURY
**John Greenleaf
Whittier's House**
86 Friend Street
Amesbury, MA 01913
*This 1820s home is filled
with 19th-century
furnishings.*

AMSTERDAM
Guy Park House
366 West Main Street
Amsterdam, NY 12010
*1760s house featuring
18th-century decoration.*

ANNAPOLIS
Chase-Lloyd House
22 Maryland Avenue
Annapolis, MD 21401
*Samuel Chase, one of the
original signatories of the
Declaration of
Independence, lived in
this 1760s house with
18th-century decoration.*

Historic Annapolis
18 Pinkney Street
Annapolis, MD 21400
*Three houses furnished in
period style: Paca House
(1765), Hancock's
Resolution (1670) and
Slicer Shipley's House
(1723).*

ARLINGTON
**Arlington House
(Robert E. Lee
Memorial)**
Arlington National
Cemetery
Arlington, VA 22211
*Early 19th-century house,
preserved as it was in
1861 at the outbreak of
the Civil War.*

ARROW ROCK
Arrow Rock Tavern
Route 41
Arrow Rock, MO 65320
*A restored wayfarers' inn
of the 1840s – all that's
missing is the smoke and
the barmaids.*

**George Caleb Bingham
House**
Arrow Rock State Park
Arrow Rock, MO 65320
*The house of the mid-
19th-century artist,
furnished in the style of
the period and filled with
his work.*

Dr Matthew Hall House
Arrow Rock State Park
Arrow Rock, MO 65320
*The 1840s house of the
local doctor.*

ASHEVILLE
Bittmore House
Asheville
NC 28803
*Built during the 1890s,
this 250-room mansion is
filled with collections of
pictures, antique furniture
and porcelain.*

ASHLAND
Scotchtown
107 Stebbins Street
Ashland, VA 23005
*Home of the statesman
Patrick Henry (1736-
1799), who became a
lawyer in 1760 and was
instrumental in arousing
the American people to
revolution.*

AUBURN
Seward House
33 South Street
Auburn, NY 13021
*The house of the
politician W. H. Samuel,
who purchased Alaska in
1867, gives an insight into
the lifestyle of a typical
prosperous household
during the late 19th
century.*

AUGUSTA (GA)
Meadow Garden
1320 Nelson Street
Augusta, GA 30904
*George Walker, the
American patriot who
signed the Declaration of
Independence, lived in
this house, which is filled
with furniture and
pictures of the 1770s.*

AUGUSTA (ME)
Blaine House
State Street
Augusta
ME 04330
*The residence of the
Governor of Maine
during the 1830s is fitted
out in the style of the era.*

AUSTIN
O Henry Museum
409 East 5th Street
Austin, TX 78701
*The writer William
Sydney Porter (1860-
1910), who wrote short
stories under the pen
name of O Henry, lived
here during the 1880s.*

AU TRAIN
Paulon House
U.S. Forest Service
Road 2278
Au Train, MI 49806
*Dating from the early
1800s, this pioneer's log
cabin is filled with simple
19th-century furniture.*

BALTIMORE
Evergreen House
4545 North Charles
Street
Baltimore, MD 21210
*The house where the U.S.
ambassador John W.
Garrett lived in the 1850s
is furnished in the style of
his lifetime.*

Homewood House
3400N Charles Street
Baltimore, MD 21218
*Federal-style home of
Charles Carroll Junior
with turn-of-the-19th
century furnishings.
(See pp.10-17.)*

Edgar Allan Poe House
203 North Amity Street
Baltimore, MD 21233
*The home of the master of
the horror story during the
1830s is decorated in the
style of the period, with
Poe memorabilia.*

BARDSTOWN
**My Old Kentucky
Home State Park**
U.S. Highway 150
Bardstown, KY 4004
*House of the Rowan
family where, in 1852,
the songwriter Stephen
Foster conceived "My Old
Kentucky Home". 1850s
furnishings.*

BATH (NC)
Bonner House
Bath, NC 27808
An 1825 house with its original decoration, furnished with 19th-century antiques.

Palmer-Marsh House
Bath, NC 27808
Dating from 1744, this house features original decoration and 18th-century furnishings.

BATH (OH)
Hale Farm and Wester Reserve Village
2686 Oak Hill Road
Bath, OH 44210
A recreated pioneer village with six houses dating from the 1800s, all with original decoration and period furniture.

BEACON
Madame Brett Homestead
50 Van Nydeck Avenue
Beacon, NY 12508
This 1700s house has been restored to its original splendour, with contemporary furnishings.

BEAUFORT
Joseph Bell House
Turner Street
Beaufort, NC 28516
The 1760s home of a local plantation owner, painstakingly restored to recreate the lavish interior of the period.

John Mark Verdier House
(Lafayette House)
801 Bay Street
Beaufort, NC 29902
A 1790s house with original decoration and furnishings.

BENTONSPORT
Mason House
Bentonsport
Keosauqua, IA 52565
Luxurious 1846 steamboat hotel with original furnishings, including the bar.

BEVERLY
John Balch House
448 Cabot Street
Beverly, MA 01915
An early 17th-century house, filled with furniture of a later era.

Rev. John Hale House
39 Hale Street
Beverly, MA 01915
The 1690s house of the local minister, John Hale, with later furnishings.

BILOXI
Jefferson Davis Shrine
West Beach
Biloxi, MS 39531
The 1840s home of the Confederate president, who entered congress for Mississippi in 1845.

BIRMINGHAM
Arlington House and Gardens
331 Cotton Avenue
Birmingham, AL 35211
This ante-bellum plantation, set in the heart of the Deep South, recalls "Gone with the Wind".

BLACKSBURG
St James' Cottage
1300 Charles Street
Blacksburg, VA 24060
A 1770s house with 18th-century furnishings and memorabilia.

BLOOMINGTON
David Davis Mansion
Davis Street and
Monroe Drive
Bloomington
IL 61701
Dating from the 1870s, this mansion features typical decoration and furnishings of the era.

BLUE HILL
Parson Fisher House
Blue Hill, ME 04614
The 1800s house of the local preacher and artisan Rev. Jonathan Fisher, with colonial-style furniture made by him.

BLUE MOUNDS
Little Norway
U.S. 18-151
Blue Mounds,
WI 53517
An 1856 farm with log cabins, barns and outbuildings built by one of the first Norwegian families to settle in the area. The replica of a 12th-century stave church houses a wide variety of Norwegian antiques, including chests, rocking chairs and embroidered wall-hangings.

BLUE MOUNTAIN LAKE
Adirondack Museum
Routes 28 North and 30
Blue Mountain Lake
NY 12812
Pioneer-style log cabins featuring rough-hewn rustic furniture, exposed wooden ceilings, peeling log beams and stone fireplaces.

BOALSBURG
Boal Mansion
Route 322
Boalsburg, PA 16827
A 1780s house with, attached, a 16th-century chapel that was brought from Spain in 1919.

BODIE
Bodie SHP
Box 515
Bridgeport, CA 93517
100 buildings, preserved and furnished in the style of the 1860s at the height of the gold rush.

BOSTON
Adams National Historic Site
135 Adams Street
Quineys
Boston, MA 02100
The mansion of the Adams family which included two presidents of the USA – John (1735-1826) and John Quincy (1767-1848) – decorated in mid-19th-century style.

Mooer Pierce-Hichborn House
29 North Square
Boston, MA 02100
A 1700s dwelling, complete with 18th-century furnishings and colonial memorabilia.

Otis House
141 Cambridge Street
Boston, MA 02199
Otis House was designed by Charles Bulfinch between 1795 and 1808 for Harrison Gray Otis, a local dignitary.

Paul Revere House
19 North Square
Boston, MA 02133
Built in 1680, this house was occupied by the patriot who alerted his countrymen to the British troops during the Revolution.

BRAINERD
Lunbertown
Brainerd, MN 56401
1870s village comprising 30 furnished buildings, including a sugar plant, sawmill, ice-cream parlour, saloon and undertakers.

BRIDGEPORT
Captain Brook's House
199 Pembroke Street
Bridgeport, CT 06608
1780s house with original decoration, furniture and memorabilia of the Revolutionary era.

CALDWELL
Grover Cleveland's Birthplace
207 Bloomfield Avenue
Caldwell, NJ 07006
A three-storey frame house, dating from 1837. Grover Cleveland was the only native of New Jersey to be elected president.

CANTERBURY
Shaker Village
Canterbury, NH 03224
1790s Shaker community with restored buildings including schoolhouse, meeting house and carriage house.

CATALDO
Coeur d'Arlene Mission of the Sacred Heart
Cataldo, IA 83810
This 1850s mission was instrumental in the conversion of local Native-American tribes to Christianity. It has been preserved intact as Idaho's oldest building.

CHARLESTOWN
Old Fort Number 4
Charlestown, NH 03603
Built during the 1740s, this log fort was defended in 1749 against the French. It includes a reconstructed great hall, stockade and barns.

CHARLOTTESVILLE
Monticello
Charlottesville,
VA 22902
Imposing mansion, designed by President Thomas Jefferson between 1769 and 1826 and furnished as it would have been during his lifetime.

CHEROKEE
Oconaluftee Indian Village
Cherokee, NC 28719
The village recreates Native-American life as it was 200 years ago. Cherokees in traditional dress carry out skills such as woodcarving, beadwork and arrow-making.

COLUMBUS
Waverley
West Point
Nr Columbus, MS 39773
Built in 1852, this Ante-Bellum plantation house features an unusual octagonal-shaped cupola. (See pp.18-23.)

CONCORD
Ralph Waldo Emerson House
Concord, MA 01742
Constructed in 1820, this white brick house contains memorabilia relating to the poet and essayist Ralph Waldo.

Orchard House
Concord, MA 01742
The house where Louisa May Alcott began writing Little Women, furnished in traditional Victorian style.

CRIPPLE CREEK
Cripple Creek
Cripple Creek
CO 80813
Restored gold town, with recreated saloon, dance halls and gambling houses.

DEADWOOD
735 Main Street
Deadwood, SD 57732
Features include several original furnished buildings from the gold-mining days and Boot Hill Cemetery, the burial site of "Wild Bill" and "Calamity Jane".

DECORAH
Vesterheim
502 W. Water Street
Decorah, IA 52101
A collection of nine buildings which trace the history of the Norwegian immigrants. Includes a three-room house, an operating smithy, a pioneer cabin and a mill.

DEERFIELD
Old Deerfield Village
Deerfield, MA 01342
Restored houses dating from colonial times to the 19th century, including Frary House which is associated with the revolutionary general Benedict Arnold.

DEER LODGE
Grant Kohrs Ranch
Deer Lodge, MT 59722
One of the largest 19th-century ranches in the United States. Dating from 1862, the two-storey building has been preserved intact, with its Victorian furniture.

DEFIANCE
Au Glaize Village
Krouse Road
New Defiance
OH 43512
This late 1800s rural community features a restored cider mill, a doctor's surgery and a railway station.

DES MOINES
Living History Farms
2600 N.W. 111th Street
Des Moines, IA 50322
500-acre farm comprising an 1840 pioneer farm with log cabin and outbuildings, an 1879 mansion and a 1900s horse farm.

DEVILS LAKE
Fort Totten
Route 57
Devils Lake, ND 58301
Preserved fort of the Plains Indians Wars. Dating from 1867, the fort's 16 buildings have been restored to their original condition.

EDENTON
Edenton Town
NC 27932
A complete town of 50 houses dating from the 1720s onward, restored and refurbished.

FALLSINGTON
Historic Fallsington
4 Yardley Avenue
Fallsington, PA 19054
William Penn's Quaker settlement of the 1690s with restored 17th- and 19th-century buildings.

FAYETTE
Fayette Garden
Fayettte, MI 49835
Dating from the late 19th century, the restored buildings that make up the town include a doctor's office, an opera house and a hotel.

FLAT ROCK
Carl Sandburg Home
Box 395
Flat Rock, NC 28731
Mountain farm where the novelist Carl Sandburg spent the last 22 years of his life. The restored farmhouse dates from 1838.

FOND DU LAC
Galloway House
336 Old Pioneer Road
Fond du Lac, WI 54935
A 30-room mansion in the ornate American Victorian style, filled with many original furnishings and antiques.

FORT ATKINSON
Fort Atkinson
IA 52144
A pioneer fort of the 1840s. Among the buildings are barracks, blockhouses and a powder magazine.

FORT LARAMIE
Route 26
Fort Laramie
WY 82212
Originally founded as a fur-trading post, this restored 1830s fort was at the heart of some of the bloodiest fighting in the Mid-West.

FORT RILEY
Fort Riley
KS 66442
This 1853 fort was once the headquarters of Lt. Col. George Armstrong Custer (1839-1876), who was active in the Civil and Indian Wars.

FOUNTAIN CITY
Levi Coffin House
Fountain City
IN 47341
From here between 1826 and 1846, the Quaker abolitionist Levi Coffin and his wife, Catherine, helped 2,000 slaves escape to freedom in Canada.

FRANKLIN VILLAGE
Franklin Village
32325 Franklin Road
Franklin, MI 48025
A complete farming village of the 1820s, consisting of 25 restored buildings with period furnishings.

FREDERICKSBURG
Mary Washington House
Fredericksburg
VA 22404
The colonial mansion was bought in 1772 by the first President of the United States, George Washington, for his mother.

GANADO
Hubbell Trading Post NHS
Box 150
Ganado, AZ 86505
An 1870s trading post, filled with a collection of 19th-century furnishings.

GENTRYVILLE
Lincoln Boyhood House
Route 162
Gentryville, IN 47552
Abraham Lincoln (1809-1865) grew up on this farm between 1816 and 1830.

GRAND ISLAND
Stuhr Museum of the Prairie Pioneer
Junction of Routes 34 and 281
Grand Island, NE 68801
A prairie town of 55 buildings, including a bank, barbershop, stores, houses and barns.

GREEN BAY
Hazlewood
Green Bay, WI 54305
The 1830s house of Morgan L. Martin, a local pioneer lawyer, is filled with 19th-century antiques and lavish furnishings.

GREENVILLE
Andrew Johnson House
Depot Street
Greenville, TN 37743
The 17th President of the United States, Andrew Johnson, lived here until his death in 1875. Original furnishings and memorabilia.

HANNIBAL
Mark Twain Boyhood Home
206-208 Hill Street
Hannibal, MO 63401
It was here that the novelist Samuel Clemens (Mark Twain) experienced the childhood he was to immortalize in Tom Sawyer.

HARRODSBURG
Shakertown at Pleasant Hill
Lexington Road
Harrodsburg, KY 40330
A restored 19th-century Shaker village, featuring dwelling houses, communal buildings, stores and a mill.

HARVARD
Fruitlands Museums
Prospect Hill
Harvard, MA 01451
The 18th-century farmhouse where the educationalist Amos Bronson Alcott (1799-1888) founded his transcendentalist community.

HERMITAGE
Historic Hermitage
4580 Rachel's Lane
Hermitage, TN 37076
The estate of Andrew Jackson, seventh President of the United States. The Greek-revival-style house dates from 1819 and contains many of Jackson's possessions.

HILLSBORO
Franklin Pierce Homestead
Hillsboro, NH 03244
Dating from 1804, this Federal-style house was home to the 14th President of the United States during the first 30 years of his life.

HODGENVILLE
Abraham Lincoln Birthplace
Route 1
Hodgenville, KY 42748
A one-room log cabin of Sinking Spring farm, where the 16th President of the United States was born in 1809 to a pioneer family. Now a memorial with 19th-century furnishings.

HYDE PARK
Franklin D. Roosevelt's Home
Hyde Park, NY 12538
The birthplace of the 32nd President and where he spent his summers between 1933 and 1945. Also where he and his wife Eleanor are buried.

Vanderbilt Mansion
Hyde Park, NY 12538
A 54-room mansion, built between 1896 and 1898 for the financier Frederick W. Vanderbilt, includes a fine art collection and lavish furnishings.

JENNER
Fort Ross
Route 1
Jenner, CA 95460
A restored stockaded pioneer fort and trading post of 1812 with stores and barracks.

JOHNSON CITY
Lyndon B. Johnson
Johnson City, TX 78636
The house where the 36th president of the United States, Lyndon B. Johnson (1908-1973), spent his boyhood, restored to its 1920s appearance at the time of his childhood.

KEY WEST
Audubon House
Key West, FL 33040
The naturalist painter John James Audubon worked in this house in 1832. It features 19th-century furnishings, memorabilia and pictures.

Ernest Hemingway's House
Key West, FL 33040
The house in which the writer lived and worked in the 1950s. Rooms are still furnished as they were when he lived there and contain personal items of memorabilia.

KNOXVILLE
Marble Springs Farm
Knoxville, TN 37901
A two-storey log house, together with barn, loom house, kitchen and smokehouse, built as a trading post and later used as a refuge for settlers.

LARNED
Fort Larned
Route 3
Larned, KS 67550
An important military post on the Santa Fe Trail, abandoned in 1878. Nine of the fort's original buildings, including the barracks, storehouses and workshops, have been restored to their 19th-century condition.

LA JUNTA
Bent's Old Fort
35110 Highway
194 East
La Junta, CO 811050
An 1833 fort, restored to its original appearance.

MADISON
Prairie Village
Route 34
Madison, SD 57042
Dating from the 1870s onward, these 50 buildings recreate the atmosphere of a typical pioneer village.

MANDAN
Fort Abraham Lincoln
Route 1806
Mandan, ND 58554
The fort from where Lt. Col. Custer led his men to their last stand at the Little Bighorn in 1876.

MARBLEHEAD
Jeremiah Lee Mansion
Marblehead, MA 01945
Restored 18th-century house with antiques and Revolutionary memorabilia.

MARION
Harding Home and Museum
380 Mount Vernon Avenue
Marion, OH 43302
The house of the 29th President of the United States, Warren Harding, features original furnishings, and decoration.

MEMPHIS
Victorian Village
4140 Chanwill Avenue
Memphis, TN 38117
Nine 19th-century houses, notably Fontaine House (with colonial and late-Victorian furniture) and Mallory-Neely House (a turreted Victorian home).

MENDOTA
Mendota
MN 55050
Dating from the 1820s, this is the oldest settlement in Minnesota and includes Henry H. Sibley House, a restored and refurbished 1835 limestone house.

MENTOR
Lawnfield
8095 Mentor Avenue
Mentor, OH 44060
The Victorian mansion of James A. Garfield, 29th President of the United States, contains family belongings, furnishings and a memorial library.

MITCHELL
Spring Mill Village
Route 60
Mitchell, IN 47446
A restored frontier village of the mid-1800s, with dwelling house, stores, barns and jail.

MONTEREY
Monterey Old Town
210 Olivier Street
Monterey, CA 93940
Restored buildings of the 1840s, including an old custom house and California's first theatre.

MONTGOMERY
First White House of the Confederacy
644 Washington Street
Montgomery, AL 36130
The home of the Confederate president Jefferson Davis in 1835 contains 19th-century furnishings and memorabilia.

MOUNT VERNON
Mount Vernon
VA 22121
*This colonial mansion was built in 1735 and restored to its former glory under its owner, first President George Washington.
(See pp.48-53.)*

Pope-Leighey House
Woodlawn Plantation,
Mount Vernon, VA 22121
*Built in 1940 from cypress, brick and glass, this was one of Frank Lloyd Wright's early Usonian designs.
(See pp.36-41.)*

NANTUCKET
Jethro Coffin House
Nantucket, MA 01945
Dating from 1686, this is the island's oldest house and features early 18th-century interiors and whaling memorabilia.

NEW BERN
Tryon Palace Restoration Complex
610 Pollock Street
New Bern, NC 28560
Early buildings, including the 18th-century governor's palace and the state's first capitol.

NEW PALTZ
New Paltz Town
NY 12561
Founded by the exiled French Huguenots in 1692, this town includes stone houses.

NEW PHILADELPHIA
Schoenbrunn Village
U.S. 250
New Philadelphia
OH 44663
A reconstructed 1770s Moravian village comprising 60 log cabins, school and church.

NEWPORT
Hunter House
Newport, RI 02840
1740s house with period Newport furniture.

NORFOLK
Adam Thoroughgood House
Norfolk, VA 23501
Built in 1650, this is thought to be one of the nation's oldest brick houses.

NORRIS
Museum of Appalachia
Norris, TN 37828
Dozens of authentic log cabins recreate the lifestyle of an Appalachian village.

OLD BETHPAGE
Old Bethpage Village Restoration
Round Swamp Road
Old Bethpage,
NY 11804
Typical rural 19th-century village with many buildings, including an inn, a church, stores and houses.

OREGON CITY
Dr John McLoughlin House
713 Center Street
Oregon City, OR 97045
An 1840s colonial-style building, filled with 19th-century furnishings.

OYSTER BAY
Sagamore Hill
Oyster Bay, NY 11771
The keen huntsman and President of the United States, Theodore Roosevelt, spent his summers in this 22-room cottage which features memorabilia, hunting trophies and animal skins.

PASADENA
The Gamble House
4 Westmorland Place
Pasadena CA 91103
Built between 1908 and 1909 by Charles and Henry Greene, this is a masterpiece of the American Arts-and-Crafts style. (See pp.42-47.)

PAWTUCKET
Slater Mill
Pawtucket, RI 02862
A restored early 19th-century cotton mill with machinery and tools.

PHILADELPHIA
Hill-Keith-Physick House
Philadelphia, PA 19102
1759 house of "the father of American surgery", Dr Philip Physick, with 18th-century furnishings and memorabilia of the doctor and his work.

PHOENIX
Pioneer Arizona
Box 1677
Black Canyon Stage
Phoenix, AZ 85029
A complete 500-acre village. The buildings include stores, a saloon, a miner's camp and a school house.

PINEVILLE
James K. Polk Birthplace
U.S. 521
Pineville, NC 28134
The boyhood home of the 11th President of the United States. Alongside, a reconstructed log cabin and farm buildings.

PITTSFIELD
Hancock Shaker Village
Pittsfield, MA 01202
The third of 18 Shaker communities to be established in the United States, with Meeting House, Round-Stone Barn and Dwelling House. (See pp.30-35.)

J.F. Kennedy House
83 Beals Street
Brookline, MA 02146
The birthplace of J. F. Kennedy, 35th President, was restored by his mother in 1917.

PLYMOUTH NOTCH
Calvin Coolidge Homestead
Plymouth Notch,
VT 05056
Boyhood home of the 30th President of the United States. A simple white frame farmhouse with many original furnishings.

PORTLAND
Victoria Mansion
109 Danforth Street
Portland, ME 04101
Ruggles Sylvester Morse's brownstone Italian villa townhouse, built in 1958-1962 under architect Henry Austin, is a tribute to French, Italian and Oriental styles. (See pp.24-29.)

PORTSMOUTH
Portsmouth Old Town
Portsmouth, NH 03801
A coastal town with sea-faring associations dating from the 1690s to the 19th century.

QUINCY
Adams
135 Adams Street
Quincy, MA 02169
The 1731 home of the Adams family, whose scions included John Quincy Adams, the sixth President.

SAN ANGELO
Fort Concho
213 E. Avenue
San Angelo, TX 76903
Native-American war fort, used as the headquarters of the "Buffalo Soldiers". Features 16 original and 4 reconstructed buildings.

SAN ANTONIO
The Alamo
San Antonio, TX 78298
A memorial to the 187 Texans who were killed here in the 13-day siege by the Mexicans of 1836, including Davy Crockett and Jim Bowie.

SAN DIEGO
Old Town
San Diego, CA 92101
A village from the Mexican period of the town. Three large family mansions, a school, stable, newspaper office and mission house.

ST JOSEPH
Pony Express Museum
914 Penn Street
St Joseph, MO 64503
A collection of 1860s buildings which were the easternmost starting point of the Pony Express that carried the mail to the Wild West.

ST PAUL
Fort Snelling
St Paul, MN 55111
This 1824 stone fort is comprised of 15 original or reconstructed buildings, including the Round Tower which is thought to be the oldest building in Minnesota.

TARRYTOWN
Lyndhurst
635 South Broadway
Tarrytown, NY 10591
Lavish Gothic revival mansion which belonged to the military tycoon Jay Gould. Contains original furnishings, paintings, stained-glass windows, carved woodwork and marble fireplaces.

TOMBSTONE
Tombstone NHL
Tombstone, AZ 85638
A complete town of restored 1880s buildings of the gun-fighting era.

VICKSBURG
Shirley House
3201 Clay Street
Vicksburg, MS 39180
The only surviving Civil War house in the town, which suffered notoriously after being besieged for 42 days in 1863.

VINCENNES
Grouseland
Vincennes, IN 47591
The Georgian-style mansion of William Henry Harrison, the territorial governor, graces Indiana's oldest town. The interiors are furnished in the style of the 1840s with family portraits and antiques.

WARM SPRINGS
Little White House
Warm Springs
GA 31830
Franklin D. Roosevelt's holiday cottage between 1932 and 1945, maintained as it was on the day the 32nd President of the United States died.

WASHINGTON D.C.
Frederick Douglass Home
1411 West Street, S.E.
Washington, DC 20020
The home of the author and orator on slavery features 21 rooms that are furnished in Victorian style and filled with anti-slavery memorabilia.

WEST BRANCH
Herbert Hoover House
Box 607
West Branch, IA 52358
The 31st President of the United States, Herbert Hoover (1874-1964), was born in this 1870s cottage which has been restored and refurbished in the style of his lifetime.

WESTMINSTER
Carroll County Farm Museum
Westminster, MD 21157
A restored 1850s farm with furnished farmhouse, barn and outbuildings containing early tools and implements.

WEST ORANGE
Edison House
Main Street and
Lakeside Avenue
West Orange, NJ 07052
Where the scientist Thomas Edison (1847-1931) invented the phonograph. Also on display are his workshop, laboratories and a selection of his numerous inventions.

WICHITA
Historic Wichita Cowtown
Wichita
KS 67203
17 acres of restored buildings, dating from the 1870s, including Wyatt Earp's jail, a church and houses filled with 19th-century furnishings and memorabilia.

WILLIAMSBURG
Williamsburg
VA 23187
The restored colonial capital of Virginia boasts over 100 period buildings that date from the mid-1700s onward.

WINSTON-SALEM
Old Salem
Winston-Salem
NC 27108
Dating from the 18th century, these buildings belonged to an 18th-century Moravian community.

WOODVILLE (MS)
Rosemount Plantation
Woodville
MS 39669
The largely unchanged boyhood home of the Confederate president Jefferson Davis, established here by his father in 1810.

WOODVILLE (TX)
Heritage Garden Village
Woodville, TX 75979
30 pioneer buildings, including a log cabin, apothecary and smithy complete with original late 19th-century equipment.

YORK
York Historic Village
York, ME 03909
An entire village of typical colonial houses and a church dating from the 1740s onward.

ZOAR
Zoar Village
Route 212
Zoar, OH 44697
Village home of the 1800s German pietist community, now restored to its original appearance with period furnishings.

ACKNOWLEDGMENTS

The author, photographer and publishers would like to thank the following house-museums, individuals and institutions for their co-operation:

Carl Larsson-gården, Sundborn; Casa de Pilatos and Fundación Casa Ducal de Medinaceli; Charleston Farmhouse, Christopher Naylor and The Charleston Trust; Frank Lloyd Wright's Pope-Leighey House and the National Trust for Historic Preservation; The Gamble House, the University of Southern California and the City of Pasadena; The Georgian House, Sheila Kennedy and The National Trust for Scotland; Goethe's Houses and Stiftung Weimarer Klassik; Hancock Shaker Village, Pittsfield, Massachusetts; Homewood House and John Hopkins University; Hvitträsk, Luoma, Bobäck; Jim Thompson's House on the Klong, The James H.W. Thompson Foundation and the Jim Thompson Thai Silk Company; La Maison de Tante Léonie, Madame Borrel and Association Marcel Proust; Mount Vernon and The Mount Vernon Ladies' Association; Musée Gustave Moreau, Paris; Musée Horta, Bruxelles; Musée Nissim de Camondo, Paris; Palazzo Davanzati and Soprintendenza per i Beni Artistici e Storici delle Provincie di Firenze e Pistoia; Rose Seidler House, Dr James Broadbent and the Historic Houses Trust of New South Wales; Rouse Hill House, Dr James Broadbent and the Historic Houses Trust of New South Wales; Schloss Charlottenhof, Potsdam; Sir John Soane's Museum, London; The Tenement House and The National Trust for Scotland; Victoria Mansion and the Victoria Society of Maine; Villa Barbaro at Maser and Mr and Mrs Vittorio Dalle Ore; Waverley Plantation and Robert Snow; Wightwick Manor and The National Trust; the staff of the London Library and the staff of the National Art Library.

Mitchell Beazley would like to thank Cathy Rubinstein, Chris Wood and Kirsty Seymour-Ure for additional editorial assistance, and Leigh Priest for compiling the index.